SEAN OF THE CONGO

A CIP catalogue record is available for this
book from the British Library

Hardback IBSN 978-0-9532724-3-3
Paperback IBSN 978-0-9532724-2-6
Ebook IBSN 978-0-9532724-4-0

Printed and bound in The United Kingdom by
TJ International Ltd, Padstow

www.seanofthecongo.co.uk

For my long-suffering mum and late, great dad.

The author today

CONTENTS

INTRODUCTION

In 1989 the World Wide Web was invented. It was also the year of Tiananmen Square, the Hillsborough disaster, the fall of the Berlin Wall, and the end of the Cold War. In the meantime, over in Africa, a further episode entered the annals of history when two young men became the first documented foreigners to attempt to paddle a native dugout down the Congo's longest navigable stretch. The tale would become the stuff of Congolese legend.

What follows is the account of that unique voyage. Beginning with one man's desire for adventure, it encompasses a perilous trip that led him and a friend into the equatorial rainforests of Africa and, finally, on to the forbidding Congo. It starts 4,000 miles, one continent and two seas from Africa's core, in England.

It is my story.

FOREWORD by Chengdu Panda Ambassador, Wildlife Legend Nigel Marven

Who were the first Europeans to paddle a native 'dugout' canoe down the mighty Congo River? There was a rumour in Zaire (now the Democratic Republic of Congo) that two Belgians were doing just that when they were eaten by cannibals in 1989. But the voyage was, in fact, made by a couple of Englishmen — and they did not end up on a cannibal menu!

One of them, Sean McCarthy, has written a rip-roaring narrative of their journey. *Sean of the Congo* is a travel book I relished reading. Before their adventure, Sean and his buddy Shaggy hadn't set foot in Africa, let alone handled a dugout. With zero preparation and little planning, in the spirit that epitomises the English eccentric, they attempted an outrageously ambitious and unique voyage down the immense Congo.

This entertaining warts-and-all account vividly describes the diseases, deprivations and hardships. I laughed out loud at Sean's description of the effects of dysentery, and winced with a shared pain as wicked-sharp thorns ripped through his flesh. Just getting to the position of dropping their dugout into the water was no mean feat. It involved a hair-raising flight from London to Moscow, on to Nairobi in Kenya, then to Kigali in Rwanda, for an overland trek to Kisangani in Zaire.

As with all good travelogues, Sean transports the reader to the humid tropics of Central Africa, sprinkling his story with top facts about the geography and history of this troubled region. On the way there are plenty of colourful characters, among them: Bad Max, a suicidal taxi driver; Goldfinga, a pygmy gold prospector; Cheesy, a shocking visa official; Mathew, a master of profanity; Halitosis, a dugout seller with dubious breath.

In the river at last and of course things don't go to plan. On the banks of the Congo, the watching crowd erupt in gales of laughter as two hapless Englishmen, with no idea of how to manoeuvre a dugout, spin the craft in circles, getting nowhere fast. I hope you enjoy finding out what happened to Sean and Shaggy on the Congo as much as I did. And the end is as surprising as it is tasty!

FOREWORD by Olympic Champions
Etienne Stott MBE & Tim Baillie MBE

When we read this inspirational book, we were struck by numerous parallels and similarities between our journey to the Olympic Gold Medal at London 2012 and the adventure Sean undertook with his friend Shaggy on the Congo. For us, these parallels are important, as we were inspired by the stories of other athletes in our sport, athletes in other sports and by any number of people whose undertakings could be put into the 'extraordinary' category. These parallels give a person the notion that maybe they are not that different from these so-called heroes or superstars, these adventurers and daredevils. If you can understand one of these heroes and see where they are coming from, then who is to say that you could not decide to try to do something extraordinary yourself, in a domain that excites and interests you?

We knew each other from a young age, and grew up together in the sport of canoe slalom, sharing many adventures and experiences. We attended the same university and lived in the same house for many years; we had some big highs and some tough lows. It strikes us that a good yarn is helped by a good sidekick. While the Congo mission was Sean's vision, the adventure is his and Shaggy's. It is hard to imagine this story with only one of the lead characters.

We also share the idea of a journey and a destination, as well as the blurring of the lines between them. Many would think that sports are all about the destination, that is winning. Many would think that adventures are all about the summit, the objective, the claim. We would contend that the journey never ends and that these targets are just places on the way. The Congo was Sean's dream, and our dream was winning the Olympics in canoe slalom, but looking back, even the shortest shortcut would have taken something away from the satisfaction of the route. It may have been said before, but sometimes the journey *is* the destination, and sometimes reaching it just begs more journeying.

Finally, like Sean and Shaggy, we have been fortunate to meet many brilliant people along the way (although it's fair to say, perhaps we haven't encountered some of the 'darker' characters that they came across). The people we met have sometimes affected us directly and immediately by their actions, but sometimes they have left us with something else of great value: an idea or a thought that reveals its true significance further down the line. It is always interesting to meet new people, however and wherever you meet them. These encounters add something to the journey and to the tales that come afterwards.

It would be nice to think and hope that people reading this book might find something that pushes them to make a choice, be that in nature, sport, art, science, love, or anything else. That one choice might propel them in a direction that takes them somewhere that was up to that point inconceivable. Potential adventures are all around. You just need the inspiration to take the first step. That's why we think you'll enjoy reading *Sean of the Congo*, it is an adventure that tempts the imagination to get up, stretch its legs and hit the road!

PROLOGUE

Tick tock. Tick tock. Tick tock. Tick tock. Ninety inches, eighty inches, seventy inches, sixty inches — little by little the tiny island's eroding bank continued to edge towards us, as against it the explosive waters beat out an incessant war cry, the gales whipping the river into such a furore that any attempt to reach the mainland remained suicidal folly. Caught between the devil and the deep blue sea, into the mix the embattled dugout rocked ever more ominously, its violent jerks threatening to uproot the already storm-weakened tree to which we had tethered it. Yet, with the rains still drenching us to the bone, through every nail-biting sway and pounding wave all we could do was watch silently, as living off borrowed time we figuratively crossed our fingers, hoping against hope that the island would outlast the blitz. But as the seconds and minutes ticked agonisingly by, tragedy seemed to spiral inexorably closer, and slowly but surely I began to understand what it was like to await the hangman's noose, as the knot in my stomach tightened progressively, the moment of doom looming ever larger. And through it all there was absolutely nothing we could do except pray for a miracle, while every now and then a glint of sunlight poked teasingly through the blackened sky. It gave us hope, but unfortunately it was false, for just as suddenly the light was gone, and once more a disastrous end came calling. Tick tock. Tick tock. Tick tock. Tick tock.

Mercifully, there was a let-up in the storm — a bona fide one this time. Whether this meant it was dying out altogether or merely tempting us to presume so, we didn't know. What we did know was that, although it was some distance away, this was our chance to make the mainland. Any doubt as to whether we should attempt it was quelled by the thought that the island might literally soon be gone. So we pressed on, and as Shaggy went to untie us I hoisted myself into the dugout and readied my paddle. In an act of defiance I then turned to look at the calmer but still menacing swirls of the ocean-like obstacle we were about to face, and with my most spirited glare beckoned the river to 'bring it on'. If I was going to exit this world, it wasn't without putting up one hell of a fight. A second later I felt the dugout angle as Shaggy embarked behind me, a movement that corresponded with something else: a disquieting noise that forced me to swiftly revolve. It was then that I saw a most remarkable sight — half of the island had vanished.

"Whoa!"

Hesitation reigned. It was like that moment when, in his mind's eye, a cricket umpire replays what may or may not have been an LBW. That split second when all around ceases to exist whilst the brain puts things into perspective. Was it my imagination, or had half an island just been wiped out? If so, what a brilliant piece of timing on our part. Especially since the now-defunct half was that on which we had sat. All the same, minds can play tricks. I did a quick assessment: There was a raging torrent? Check. The island was subsiding? Check. There were previously more trees and bushes? Check. Half the island is now missing? Yes! Check! Good Lord, and how lucky that Shaggy, who only a second earlier had stood in the exact same spot that now held nothing but water, had managed to get into the dug... managed to get into... into the... the... Shaggy? Where the hell was Shaggy? Surely not overboard. As choppy as the waters were, the storm's lull had ensured they weren't *that* turbulent. 'Wait a minute, Sean – think,' I told myself. 'Did he even get into the dugout? The tilting you assumed was Shaggy's weight had happened at the same time the island had collapsed. Oh my word, it was the island that had caused the lift, not Shaggy! So that means...'

I replayed the scene in which I had last seen him. Yes, he had been standing on this side of the island. But had he been swallowed by the abyss? Yet it was only too obvious – my sole companion was now a victim of the Congo.

ACKNOWLEDGEMENTS

Once upon a time someone said that getting a book into print is not so much a sprint, but a marathon. I'll endorse that, although in my case I guess it's been more of an ultra-ultra-marathon. For those who might be querying why it has taken me the best part of three decades, the truth of the matter is that the first seven chapters were written within a few months of my return. Thereafter followed many years of inserting it between pressing matters, not so pressing matters and, just as JK Rowling was, being ignored by myriad publishers. Fortunately for my desire to accomplish, I'm not the kind to throw in the towel, so here you go. Of course few writers ever complete a journey without at least one helping hand, and luckily for me the occasional dispiriting voice has been easily drowned out by those offering practical assistance, inspiration, or simply encouragement. I would therefore like to give heartfelt thanks to:

David Martyn Davies, Robert Ashcroft, Pat Matthews, Tom Crowdy, Professor Christopher Cramer, Grayson Schaffer, Charlotte Ecroyd, Christina Dodwell FRGS, Dr Reuben Loffman, Ivan Lawler MBE, Etienne Stott MBE, Samantha Davis, Sarah Wooding, Vicky Allum, Tim Baillie MBE, Brigit Sullivan, Nadeem Sajjad, Deborah Atkinson, Nigel Marven, Jacqui Stewart, Lesley Walker Timms, Wayne Walker, Geoff Thompson, Steve Kellar, Kevin Green MD, Zulf Choudhary, Perry 'The Original Stig' McCarthy, John Harris Hussar, Shaun Kelly, Sir Ben Ainslie, Anthony Davis, Ian Visser, Carol Lee, Nigel Mitchell, Ben Shephard, Owen Burnham, Dave Benmore, Joe Ball, Russ Aspin, Ben Fogle FRGS, Sean O'Toole, Andy Reid, Lee Crew, Neville Yates, James Cracknell OBE, Martin Astin, Ben Smallwood, Kristen Ellison, Steve Backshall, Andrea Holt, Tony Follett, Mary Grey, Alan Samson, Benedict Allen FRGS, Tom Kennedy, Colin Benmore, Stephen Ball, Sir Ranulph Fiennes, Alan Chadwick, Ste Drayton, Lynda Sedgwick, Alistair Brownlee MBE, David Klein, Teresa Wright, Dennis Linskey, Jonathan Brownlee, James Harris, Sue O'Mara, Richard Vickerstaff, Louise Minchin, Trav Lawrence, Gary Davenport, Hannah Vaughan Richard Madeley, Harish Deepak, Karen Donohue, Derrick Binning, Judy Finnigan, Mark Taylor, Nicola Spiby, Kelsie Shute, Janet Brown, Professor Noel Fitzpatrick, Russell Jarmesty, Guy Parkinson, Arran & Ryan, Gill & Dave Ward, Sue & Allan Davis, Suzan & Zeynel Aydin, Sir David Attenborough, Ann Fyles, Co McIntosh, Gary Brown, Jo & Jim Arnold, abfire-prevention.co.uk, siteeng.co.uk, sweetdeceits.com.

Chapter 1

A LEAP INTO THE UNKNOWN

I had been intending to travel to the heart of Africa for some time. For years I'd been fascinated by the thought of fortune and glory, quests and exploration, danger and risk, and every other element of the concept of derring-do. Ever since I was a child, reading superhero comics and Enid Blyton tales, I had dreamed of leading a life away from the everyday drudgery that's so easy to fall into. I was going to be different. I was going to boldly go. Surgeon, jockey, astronaut – most people have aspirations that somehow get discarded upon adulthood, but not me. I was so positive I would fulfil my every objective, and especially exploring Africa, specifically its interior, probably the easiest to achieve of my many goals. Unless becoming an Olympic champion and winning Academy Awards is simpler (I had big dreams).

Why deepest Africa? I recall that, at that childhood phase when I was discovering adventure could be had in distant lands, I would turn time after time to Africa in an atlas. With its immense deserts, mighty rivers and steamy jungles, the whole place seemed so far away from the norm. Any part of it would have offered the experience of a life-time, but my eyes were always drawn to what had been its last bastion of uncharted territory: the once-unconquerable, ominous core. Here, along the equator, it was shaded a rich green, representing lush and dense rainforest. And through the green came a vivid blue line that arced its way across the middle. I don't know how many times I read the enchanting, yet equally menacing, word that went with that green shading and blue line, but I was hooked... "Congo." Now combine this with the imagery of the *Tarzan* TV series I was watching at the time, and my desire for exotic adventure became a concrete ambition. One that over the years kept tempting me, luring me, nagging me, goading me: "I dare you to man up. I dare you to go to the tropics. I dare you to brave darkened forests — I dare you to face the Congo."

Then, one day, I received a letter from an old training partner I'd roomed with at an athletics camp some five years earlier. His name was Lee Walker, though we all called him Shaggy.

The letter Shaggy sent was the game changer: dumped the job; left England; living in Germany; injured again, etc. It was the 'etc' bit that caught my attention. Forced to take a breather from intense training sessions, he could still walk, so had made the decision to hitchhike around Europe. Did I fancy going with him? My "Let's go to Africa instead!" was not the answer he had been expecting. To someone like Shaggy, however, it was very inspirational. After all, when your screen hero is Indiana Jones and you harbour the impulse to go trailblazing, how could you not be stirred by such a prospect? No doubt the blood surged through his body, and excited by my having similar escapist aims he quickly headed back to England.

On his arrival at my house, Shaggy actually tried persuading me to accompany him to whichever city it was in South America (he'd read of a bejewelled hidden antiquity and fancied uncovering it, *à la* his screen hero), but I'd had my heart set on African travel far too long to be discouraged at this stage of the game. So I set about reshaping his thinking. Yes, by definition a quest is classically associated with the search of a prized trinket of some kind, the en route adventure more of a by-product. And yes, of course I would like to go jewel hunting in South America. But I had already made plans.

"Keep talking," said Shaggy.

So I did, telling him how instead of an actual item we would make adventure itself our task. We would go to the legendary Congo river "...and paddle down it in a native dugout."

"You're out of your tree."

"Completely. But that's only half of it."

"What's the other half?"

"Getting there. Our starting point is smack in the middle of Africa. That means we'll have to first cross at least three countries and then hundreds of miles of jungle."

"You're definitely out of your tree."

"Says the guy who thinks we can find lost treasure that none of the experts have. You've been watching too much Indiana Jones."

"Says Tarzan."

"Just so you know," I added, "from what I can gather there's no registered or even anecdotal evidence of anyone ever paddling a dug-out from where we'll be starting. We'd be the first."

Whether it was "the first", "the Congo" or, more likely, a combination of the two, Shaggy's imagination had clearly been ignited as he gazed into the distance at nothing in particular.

"Congo?" he whispered, his thoughts now so alive with visions of African jungles and tribes and wild animals, and the limitless chance of adventure, that his infatuation for Latin booty soon diminished. "Tell you what," he said, rubbing his hands enthusiastically, "perhaps we can go to South America next year."

"Sure — if we get back."

And so it was set. We were going to Africa.

A newspaper photoshoot before the off. Shaggy is on the left.

Over the upcoming weeks we endured the necessary typhoid, cholera and yellow fever injections, procured the relevant kit and ordered our malaria tablets. We also had to organise insurance, tickets, and capital for the journey ahead — and figure out how on earth we were going to subsidize all of this. There's little more sobering than rejoicing the decision to go venturing in far-off lands, only in the next instant to remember you don't actually have any money. In my case, with a dire credit rating I had to borrow from my father, whilst Shaggy managed to secure a bank loan. The biggest challenge came when picking up his cash. Time constraints meant I was forced to step in for him and, despite our both having blue eyes, there was no way my two years of theatre study could overcome our clear differences. Shaggy, so-called because of a fleeting resemblance to Scooby Doo's sidekick, was a gangly six-feet-two and had fair hair and a small ponytail, whereas I was nearly three inches shorter and had trim, Brylcreemed dark hair. Fortunately no physical ID was required, and with funding now in hand we swiftly obtained everything else needed. The scheduled day of departure would be Friday, 9th June, 1989. I therefore had time to celebrate my twenty-third birthday and Shaggy his twenty-fifth, as we looked forward to the day of reckoning.

When it came to it, that day almost never happened. With Shaggy living halfway between my home in the north and our flight in the south, the strategy was to travel by rail to his nearest station and then, to save money, hitchhike the remaining six miles. Everything ran like clockwork until I took the platform guard's advice to "Change trains at Crewe". Only after I'd debarked and watched it head off did I learn that "Crewe" should have been "Birmingham". (Don't guards always do that to you?) Even more disastrous, the next connection wasn't due until the following day.

I couldn't believe it. I hadn't yet reached the middle of England, let alone Africa, and already my blueprint was falling apart. Salvaging things, I worked out another practicable route, ultimately arriving a full five hours after my intended midnight target. This meant having to abandon my original hitchhiking policy, so I jumped straight into a taxi, which for me was breaking with type. Although I deem myself a charitable person, spending money needlessly has always been a big no-no, and definitely at this juncture, as I was very much trying to conserve what little I had for Africa – before the taxi, the same as Shaggy, £690 (which equates to about £1,500 today). This may seem a decent sum to the stony broke, but considering that we were planning to travel through several countries, over a period of many weeks, you can perhaps appreciate why I was resolved to stay as frugal as possible. Hence it irritated me even more that the taxi – driven by a man who weirdly found it necessary to inform me he'd recently had one testicle removed – appeared rather overpriced. His 'man down' was probably lost to a disgruntled customer's boot.

Once finally at Shaggy's, we scoffed half of his parents' food, as you do, then grabbed our luggage – one full-to-the-brim rucksack and one bursting holdall each – and from the nearest terminal took two buses, via London, to Heathrow Airport. Our flight, a one-year open return, included a plane change at Moscow and was set to land at Kenya's capital Nairobi, towards the east coast of central Africa. Thereafter we would make our way inland to our Congo start-point.

Before any of this happened we had to first leave England, yet, typical of my luck so far, long after the scheduled time of departure we remained confined to the waiting room. Looking out of the window I noticed the familiar shape of Concorde and couldn't help but day-dream that that was our plane. I had a substantial fear of flying and assumed the then 'wonder of the skies' was radically safer than our budget booking (oh, for hindsight). Being within audible range of a pair of merchants of doom didn't help either, bearing in mind they were swapping tales of cataclysmic aviation mishaps, such as: "And then the air traffic controller said 'Climb like your life depends on it. ...Because it does'."

In due course the many fed-up passengers were eventually allowed to board — only to receive more bad news. A collective groan went up as we were told the plane had now been refused permission to take off. Apparently, some blockhead had put an extra suitcase in the hold and the officials could neither match it with the passenger directory, nor account for it in any other way.

Another hour passed.

Then another.

By this time we were all becoming quite tetchy, so when everyone was asked to vacate the plane and check their baggage, now strewn by the side of the jet, tempers began to flare — not least one Scotsman, who had obviously had too much alcohol during the wait and started to raucously blaspheme. As the expletives persisted, an official warned Mr Irate about his language, insisting that any more obscenities and he would be ejected from the plane (no, not in full flight). Despite being cautioned, the Caledonian's language remained markedly blunt and loud, and so he was escorted, still swearing, off the aircraft.

More time passed, and to counter any belief that things couldn't possibly get more wearisome, we were instructed to check our luggage a second time. Worse still was the rumour that the anonymous bag belonged to a terrorist and contained a bomb, which didn't exactly boost my already very low confidence in heavy objects staying airborne — my overactive imagination repeatedly telling me: 'You're on a plane that's about to explode. Get off! Get off!'

After *five more* mind-numbingly boring hours, the pilot was given the green light and at long last the aeroplane's engines were fired and we took off. Destination: the capital of the Union of Soviet Socialist Republics. The next 210 minutes, the time it took to make Moscow, were the most nerve-racking and terrifying I had ever experienced.

As if the possibility of sitting on a live bomb wasn't bad enough, the decidedly old-looking plane (called a balsa wood model by Shaggy and 'Death Machine' by me) then coped so badly with the turbulence that any macho demeanour I may have coveted was now but a fading memory.

'Why did I reserve something that was advertised as Low Budget, No Frills?' my self-questioning continued, as I looked across at the wing, merrily flapping away as though it were meant to be doing that. A few more judders and jerks and I could no longer curb my fears.

"That wing's going to come off," I proclaimed.

At times the archetypal sloth, my absurdly calm colleague simply shrugged and carried on reading one of the boxing magazines I had brought. Even when the pilot — whom I named Captain Kamikaze — chose to play 'let's bounce Death Machine off every air pocket under the sun', Shaggy remained as cool and as impassive as ever. Not me — I was a total wreck. With the plane now uncontrollably jolting, my pulse was already stuck in overdrive when Kamikaze hit the biggest air pocket yet, and we lost altitude dramatically: goodbye to agnosticism, hello heartfelt prayer. If this 'nosedive' wasn't sufficiently petrifying, a red warning light began flashing. And just in case anyone hadn't yet messed themselves, this happened in tandem with a horrible 'death to all' siren. Well, I went straight into labour — my tepid "That wing's going to come off" now substituted by an involuntary and loudly screamed "Fuck!" Thankfully, my embarrassing expletive was drowned out by a chorus of like-minded passengers, and just as I was toying with the idea of finding a parachute, or something from which to fashion one, the flight attendant, who was being thrown all over the place by the violent surges and seeming loop-the-loops, somehow managed to make her way to the intercom.

"Do not panic! No need to panic!" she said a touch belatedly, and with an evident tremble in her voice added, "Fasten your seatbelts!"

Do not panic? Fasten your seatbelts? "Fuuuuuuuck!"

Seeking empathy, I again turned to my pal. With Death Machine's rapid descent, I had by this time expected to see a fellow quivering wimp. But no, for the listless Shaggy was apparently unaware of our impending doom and just continued reading the magazine.

"Bloody hell, Shaggy... Aren't you... Why aren't you... How come... Why...?" I was stammering, unable to get the words out, trying desperately to co-ordinate speech whilst my legs were doing a better *bossa nova* than any finalists ever seen on *Strictly Come Dancing*.

Shaggy looked up, albeit briefly, from the mag: "What's wrong?"

"WHAT'S WRONG?" My eyeballs nearly popped out of their sockets.

"I'm having bloody twins here!" I spluttered.

"Congratulations. Picked out any names yet?"

Customarily I would have found Shaggy's wisecrack amusing and offered a riposte, but since I was about to leave this world, I dispensed with the joking and pointed out that he needed to put on his seatbelt.

"If you're going to go, you're going to go," he remarked coolly, and returned to the magazine.

'Sod that,' I thought, and checked, double-checked, then triple-checked the clasp of my own seatbelt, at the same time half-expecting Captain Kamikaze to say, "If you look through the window to the left you will note the fast approaching sea. To the right is a dinghy. That is where I am speaking to you from." And yet, whether an almighty being intervened, or the air pockets vanished, or Kamikaze's piloting improved, Death Machine somehow managed to keep its nose above the waterline and the passengers of Flight 445 survived.

Once on the ground, my toes clutching for all their might at *terra firma*, I mentally denounced anyone who ever ridiculed the Pope's floor-kissing ritual.

In Moscow we should have had to wait a few hours before our next flight, but since the initial one had already been delayed, we were all rushed through the system faster than a fifth pint of best lager. Once onboard, the comprehension that we were getting closer to Kenya hit home, as it was full of Africans. I also noticed that, although Death Machine II was much smaller than Death Machine I, it was still very balsa wood, and I instantly made for the seat next to the sign marked 'Emergency Exit'. In the event, though, the air pockets weren't nearly as brutal, and even if they were, once we were in full flight I largely forgot about crashing because we soon found ourselves in deep talks with a handful of the other travellers – predominantly a young Arab, Ali, who studied at the University of Warwick in England but was now heading back to his adopted home, Rwanda. Other talkative passengers included two brothers from New Zealand, who over the course of the next seventy-two hours we bumped into every day; an Australian woman, Meredith, and also Dean, a big bruiser of a fellow Aussie who regaled us with a host of stories, such as how in Hollywood he'd auditioned for the part of boxing great Jack Dempsey (who he avowed was a distant relative) and also many exciting tales of his travels around the globe. His last epic venture was a motorbike trip that took him all the way from North Africa, right across the Sahara, then down to Ghana in South-West Africa. Ah yes, the plane was filled with go-getters, who had decided to see our magnificent planet first-hand and not just from watching television.

Before we arrived in Kenya we had to make two refuelling stops, at Cyprus and South Yemen. Neither lasted more than an hour, but it was the latter which offered an inkling of what might be in store for us — at some point the airport had obviously come under terrorist attack, as the windows were riddled with bullet holes. To fortify this reality check, the officials chipped in by confiscating one tourist's camcorder. Still, what measure of stupidity would you need to start filming in an official building in that region of the world without first obtaining permission?

A full twenty-six hours after boarding the plane in England, we finally landed in Africa. Here, our journey proper would begin. One that would bring many moments of not only enjoyment, camaraderie, heroism and swashbuckling adventure, but also danger, hardship, desolation and, if I'm frank, total horror. Even death. More personally, it would achieve the first of my many ambitions, whilst fulfilling our mutual craving for an unforgettable leap into the unknown.

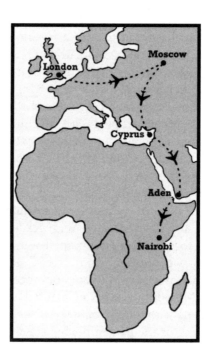

Chapter 2

TRESPASSERS WILL BE POISONED

There was a very valid reason why Shaggy and I chose Kenya to begin our African passage. With a shoreline steeped in Indian Ocean sunshine, its diversity of landscapes, national parks like Maasai Mara, and an endless array of wildlife and top-drawer safaris, Kenya had for many years received a copious quantity of holidaymakers. As such, we saw it the perfect place in which to ease ourselves into our adventure, especially since we had sidestepped the rainy season. That its capital, Nairobi, sat a mile above sea level also meant its temperature wasn't as sweltering as its lower plateaus — June was very similar to a British July, hot but not oppressively so. Into the bargain, after sixty-eight years of British colonial rule, Kenya's first language was English. In contrast, the motherland of the Congo river, then called Zaire, was a French-speaking nation. And since our French was as creaky as the Addams Family's front door, we figured it pretty dumb to fly straight into the jungle and then start asking, "Which way to the Congo, old bean?" No, our best bet was to first dip our tootsies in the pool that was Africa, hence our reason for beginning in Kenya. Well, that and the fact that it was by far the cheapest flight.

When we at long last arrived at Nairobi airport, Shaggy spent so much time claiming he'd had his camera stolen (only to find it in the exact same place in his bag where he had left it) that by the time we had filled in money declaration forms, had had our bags inspected and changed some currency, everyone had disappeared. Everyone, that is, except a recognisable face we spotted leaving an airport payphone. It was Ali, the young Arab we had met on the plane. Apparently his travel plans had gone awry — his father, who was initially supposed to be picking him up, was still at their home in Rwanda, and the cousin who lived in Kenya and would now house him wasn't answering his calls. To add to his woes, he was as luckless when ringing around for a hotel room. So we stepped in to save the day. Would he care to share a taxi to the centre? If so, until he could get hold of his cousin would he also consider staying with us in Shaggy's tent? Ali thanked us for our generous offer, agreed to split a taxi, but was confident he could find a hotel somewhere.

"Won't that be expensive?" I enquired. "You're quite welcome to share the tent."

"Don't worry, we won't charge you," quipped Shaggy.

9

Despite our gesture, Ali remained adamant he'd find a hotel, but for our kindness insisted we let him show us the sights and sounds of Nairobi. We spent the best part of the next ten days with Ali — the son, it transpired, of the richest man in Rwanda.

Ali Hassan was a very mature twenty year-old who reminded me a little of the Hollywood actor Omar Sharif, though this was probably less to do with their respective features and more so the blend of a comparable charm and Arabic looks. His choice of attire, like the majority of all men we saw in Africa, was Western. In Ali's case this usually meant a black leather bomber jacket, buttoned shirt, jeans, and the latest Nikes, which combined in an appearance of cleanliness. That may seem a needless thing to comment on, but in Africa many a person presented a grimy exterior (like Shaggy and me, over time). Originally from the Sultanate of Oman, half of Ali's relatives had relocated to Rwanda because his father thought he could make more money there. And make it he did: he was a multi-millionaire. More-over, it turned out that Ali owned ten per cent of his father's assets — and we'd asked him if he would like to save money by squashing into an ancient and microscopic tent. A born businessman, Ali's greatest love in life was being precisely that. He loved doing business the way another man might love a woman, or so it seemed in the brief space of time that I came to know him and call him a friend. Always busy concluding some type of deal, the line "I'm sorry, I have to go, I have some calls to make" came from him so often, I wondered if it really was business he loved, or just the telephone. He had something of an intellect too, and could hold a conversation on many subjects, most notably world affairs and finance. These had been part of the degree he'd undertaken in England, where he drove around in his BMW; in Rwanda he settled for a Mercedes. One thing was for sure, he rarely walked anywhere. Beyond that, Ali, always prudent with his money, treated everyone as though they had a station in life. Peasants were peasants and the rich were rich, although he did appreciate people as individuals, whoever they were. At heart he was a caring man whom I liked and admired, even if his outward philosophy could be summed up by quoting him: "Money can buy you anything."

Our first night in Africa — and our only night in the tent — was an uncomfortable event. Not only were we charged what we perceived to be an exorbitant price for the use of a bit of ground, but also neither of us slept well. At first we were too cold, then, as daylight broke, we were too hot, and the rock hard ground was ineffably lumpy. So when we were invited to spend the following night with Ali at his hotel, we jumped at the chance faster than my deplane at Moscow.

After we had sneaked our bags into Ali's room, he escorted us on a mini-tour of Nairobi, a city which I quickly liked and felt at ease in. Whether this was due to the locals' friendliness or the large throng of other 'familiar' Brits, the answer probably lay in a mixture of both. But it wasn't all moonlight and roses. Before leaving England I had read a couple of travelogues hoping to gain an insight into what I was letting myself in for. These had described 1989 Nairobi as an 'ultra-modern' and 'strikingly modern' city, which didn't account for the occasional dilapidated building, the odd waft of latrine, and the many vehicles that looked as though they had come straight from a scrap yard. Particularly the taxis, none of which had a meter, and while now and again one can barter over a fare in Britain, in Kenya it was always haggle, haggle, haggle.

More unforgettable than the taxis were their drivers, the biggest danger to the heart since the emergence of the deep-fried chocolate bar. Akin to many parts of the world with a British colonial history, Kenya has left-hand traffic, but so many Nairobian taxi drivers habitually used whichever side took their fancy, it wasn't easy to tell. Time and again we would have to leap from the path of an oncoming cab, even when we weren't on the road. That didn't matter. You could be on the road, on the pavement, or even on the moon – the Nairobian cabbie would still find you. To endorse this, our lift from the airport had been an experience, or at least that's what we had thought, until we employed our second taxi, which proved to be almost as terrifying as our flight to Moscow. It all began when we got into the exhaust-stinking Death Machine III thing in the first place, and the driver – 'Bad Max' – turned around and asked us where we wanted to go. Strewth, talk about devilish-looking. One look from him would have turned Medusa to stone. He had the ideal horror-flick mug: intense creepy eyes and jagged teeth. If he had stuck his tongue out, I swear it would have been forked.

From there it got worse, as Bad Max started to play 'chicken' with the other psychotic demolition derby drivers, all of whom continued, in some sort of bizarre suicide ritual, to cherry-pick which side of the street to drive on. When that failed to generate a fatality, our driver turned his expertise to mowing down unwary pedestrians. This began when he spun on to a new road and detected a group of young men innocently crossing in the distance. Salivating at the idea of wiping out the lot, Bad Max hit the gas – hard. No doubt the young men had deemed our cab too far away to reach them (the fools), especially as they were virtually on the kerb by now. But our determined driver refused to be denied. Foot to the floor, he swung Death Machine III towards them, the crazed glee upon his face a palpable contrast to the blind panic of the youths, who dived in all directions. Unfortunately one of them didn't have the necessary reflexes. But instead of trying to miss him, which would have been only too simple, Bad Max caught the poor lad slap on the rump, spinning him through the air until he landed, in agony, on the pavement. That he was still alive incensed Bad Max, who waved his arms in anger, shouted a few obscenities and drove off, his outburst coming to a finish only when he turned, still driving, to face Shaggy and me with what was now a feverish chuckle; his raised eyebrows giving the signal that he wished for us to convey our approval. Afraid of the consequences, we duly appeased him by enacting our own fevered chortles.

Several heart-stopping minutes later, Bad Max thankfully released us. No haggling from me; I hastily paid him his fare, and off he shot to his next victim. I didn't even get the chance to ask him when he might be off duty, so we could walk the streets without having to wear a rabbit's foot or full body armour.

At some point during Day Two in Africa, Sayeed at last materialised. A year older than Ali, the combination of Arabian features, a similar build and choice of attire, all added up to the cousin he had been waiting for. The genealogy was further cemented when, humorously to Shaggy and me, within a minute of their greeting each other they were robustly quibbling over the incumbent black market rate.

Widespread in Africa, the black market was used both by local people and clued-up travellers because, with no charges to pay, the rate of exchange was always better. The trick was to get a balance. Too much at the bank and you were out of pocket, but too much on the street and upon leaving the country sceptical customs officers may detain you. Hence the only way to use the black market intelligently was to not disclose your entire wherewithal on the entry declaration form. Guess which two lame-brained novices had done so? Lesson learned.

The cousins took us on another short tour of Nairobi, then for a spot of boating, and on to Snake Park, a reptile zoo that among other scaly things was home to some imposing ten-foot black mambas: the world's fastest and Africa's longest venomous serpent. The signs on the enclosures were equally memorable, each offering an entertaining witticism, such as the black mambas' *'Trespassers will be poisoned'* and one crocodile's *'Visitors throwing litter into this pit will be required to retrieve it'*.

Come teatime, Sayeed had to leave. Hungry but not yet up to savouring the indigenous fare (typically roasted goat and *ugali*, a starchy
cornmeal), Ali took us to the Wimpy, where we each tucked into that
awfully British of ice cream sundaes, a Knickerbocker Glory. We also
came across an old pal of Ali's, whom he immediately invited to join
us for a chat later that evening at the hotel.

Larry X — and yes, that was the handle he went by, undoubtedly
nicked from the rather more famous Malcolm — was an eloquent,
ebony-hued, slim, poker-faced young Kenyan, my age to be accurate,
who smelled of tobacco and detested political correctness. He also
took every opportunity to boast about being, "The coolest dude in
Nairobi." The son of a wealthy doctor, he'd had by Kenyan standards
an extremely privileged upbringing, but appeared to care little for that
in comparison with his apparent main concern in life — looking cool.
And for the most part, I suppose I would have to say that he wasn't
wrong: the turned-up chinos and in-vogue long-sleeved cotton shirt
with its unbuttoned collar may not instantly say 'cool' to you, but I
wouldn't have been surprised to find some local dictionary carrying a
picture of him next to the term. Moreover, while Shaggy and I, and
Ali for that matter, disliked smoking, we had to admit that Larry's execution of it looked more like an art form than a bad habit, as though
he had been watching Bogart films his entire life. To top it all, he
underlined his coolness by walking with a bounce in his step, *à la*
John Travolta's character Tony Manero of *Saturday Night Fever*, which
he claimed was, "A natural gift, bestowed on me from birth." He was
every bit as forthright about his darker side, too. Released recently
from six months in prison — "I provoked the wrong person" — Larry
alleged the authorities involved were crooked enough to have allowed
his father to have paid a bribe for his freedom, but his old man wasn't
too pleased with his colourful image and let him stew.

"My country has its corruption," said Larry, "but we still have a lot
more class than the non-English speaking nations of Africa. That is
because Britain brought true culture to us. I cherish that."

"Careful, it's not all sweetness and light. They've just sent us here,"
I joked.

Whether or not Larry was trying to ingratiate himself with us, who
knows? Regardless of his take on culture, a man with his knowledge
would have known full-well that any positive British influence had
come at a price. The pith-helmeted gatecrashers had, for one, deceit-
fully displaced many of his farming forefathers (shepherded to sub-
standard regions, they were caused to return subsequently to their
own farmland, but this time as mere labourers). Still, being no expert

I was happy to take him at face value and listened attentively as he continued to cast opinions on all manner of topics, including African traditions, philosophy, politics, and in particular politics in sport. His ambition was to become the minister for sport, and I found it an audacious mix when he combined sport, cool, and his abhorrence of political correctness, by describing the Frank Bruno vs Mike Tyson heavyweight world title boxing bout earlier that year as, "A fight to see who were the coolest – the British niggers or the American niggers."

"If ever you realise your dream," said Shaggy, "your time in office will be interesting."

Monday was all go. To quell any possible 'three for the price of one' suspicion we left the hotel separately, then reunited at the Wimpy. After stocking up on another Knickerbocker Glory each, we set about ruminating on Shaggy's and my travel options. Our objective was to head to the home of the Congo river, Zaire (it's now called Democratic Republic of the Congo – not to be confused with neighbouring Congo), and then on to a place called Kisangani, which was situated alongside the river, deep in the jungle. Here, we planned to obtain a native 'dugout' canoe, which the Congolese call a *pirogue*, and then paddle it to Kinshasa, not far from the mouth. It was also the capital, so would be the ideal place from which to make our return. How we achieved all this depended upon our first getting to Zaire, and the overland option was to travel around the enormous Lake Victoria. To the north meant passing through Uganda; to the south, Tanzania, and on through Rwanda or Burundi. From any of these three nations we could then make our way into Zaire.

North or south? However we looked at it, either way seemed time-consuming and my impatience soon triggered an alternative from Ali, who had by this time arranged to fly out to Rwanda the following day.

"Why not come with me? The plane will be landing at Kigali, the capital. This is where I live. From there it is very simple to get to the border, one bus ride. If you come, I can show you Kigali and also how to get to Zaire."

"To be honest, we've ruled out flying," I responded.

"Yeah, flights cost too much," said my ever-thrifty sidekick.

"The flight to Rwanda is actually rather cheap. In my estimation you would spend twice as much money in the two weeks it would take travelling around Lake Victoria."

Suddenly Ali's solution sounded just the ticket. If we could chop a few days off the journey to our definitive Congo goal, and in doing so save money that we may later need, then so much the better. Not as bothered about time constraints, the thought of saving money none-theless sold it for Shaggy, although he did express our reservations about Rwanda's stability, above all its history of warfare.

"There has been much violence in many African countries — Zaire especially," wasn't the answer we had been hoping for from Ali. All the same, he did go on to assure us that we would be fine in Rwanda, as long as we were with him. "My father is a very powerful man. The only person more powerful is Juvénal Habyarimana, the president. I used to play football with one of his sons when I was younger. We are still friends. The Hassan name is very big in Rwanda, very powerful."

Up until now Shaggy and I had been aware that Ali's father was a successful businessman, but with this latest revelation and then more dialogue came the full impact of just how far-reaching that success was. With offices in a number of countries, Hassan Senior not only controlled a thriving import-export business, but he also owned the franchise to produce and supply Pepsi-Cola to the whole of Rwanda. He was a very rich and influential man, and the more Ali talked, the more awestruck we became by his family's patent clout, to the point that Shaggy felt compelled to ask, "What if, say, we are with you and we got into a fight with someone and they died. What would happen then? Not that we're intending to get into any trouble."

"Of course not. You are speaking hypothetically. Shall we say that, if you know me, they will not punish you, but you will be told to go home."

"Seriously?"

"Yes."

"Looks like we may be coming with you," I added, as increasingly the flight started to seem too good to miss. Not because we could get away with murder, but because we would now have the omnipotent Ali as both guide and protector.

Despite the benefits, there were still two snags with Ali's proposal. Firstly, the idea of boarding another plane didn't appeal to me — had Shaggy and I been cats, our nine lives would already have been cut to seven, courtesy of Captain Kamikaze and Bad Max. The more rational second predicament was one that couldn't be ignored: the plane was leaving the following day, and to enter Rwanda we would need a visa. Acquiring one of those apparently took no less than two days.

"Bloody typical," said Shaggy, utilising one of his pet maxims.

He needn't have fretted, as once more the heroic Ali leapt to our rescue and led us to his father's Nairobi office, whereupon he intro-duced us to his Mr Fix-it, Albert, a forty-something Kenyan donning a 1970s-style jacket and jeans combo.

Although determined to talk of nothing beyond how God-fearing he was (and consequently being very boring, a trait amplified by the charismatic company we had kept of late in the form of Ali, Sayeed and Larry X) 'Albert the Bore' knew the bribery ropes well enough to get anybody anything they wanted – a visa, a driving licence, even a passport – for a small donation, that is. And so he promised to get our visas sorted out that very day. The required amount corresponded to thirteen pounds, plus two more for whichever office staff member would be accepting the backhander, half of which doubtless found its way into Albert's pocket.

Everything went smoothly.

The visas sorted, Ali next directed Mr Fix-it to take us to the travel agency to purchase our air tickets, where we again found problems, and again they were twofold. The first was that we had to spend more time with Albert the Bore, who still couldn't be drawn on any topic of conversation other than to bellyache about how he would be struck down and consigned to hell if he ever did anyone a wrong. Given he had just broken the law of the land, not only did he have a terrible memory, and an odd sense of being a Christian, but so repetitive was his drone, one could also be forgiven for hoping the striking down would happen sooner rather than later. The second part of the problem, however, was more worrying. Once at the travel agency, disaster struck. We were refused service on the basis that we hadn't brought any receipts for the money we had changed previously at the bank. Another lesson learned – hang on to all relevant receipts. What the assistant really wanted was for us to pay with US dollars (the accepted international currency), but alas, we were still rather green about all these money matters. Even so, I was damned if I was going to buy a ticket with anything except Kenya's own currency, and I blew a fuse.

"What you are trying to say is that we're allowed to enter Kenya, but we're not allowed to leave!"

The assistant shrugged, but there was no way I was dropping the subject and declined to give her any quarter, carrying on my protest until the manager came out and agreed to complete the transaction, receipts or no receipts. Catastrophe averted.

That night Ali had arranged to stay with Sayeed, but rather than have Shaggy and me kip in the tent again, he asked Albert the Bore to take us to a no-frills doss-house called The New Kenya Lodge. Here, we were handed the key to a very basic – two beds and a wooden chair only – moth-eaten and musty room, which may seem unsavoury (and sure, you wouldn't choose it for your honeymoon) but it was nothing less than we were expecting within our budget. Besides, not only was it more comfortable and safer than camping, and only half the price, but it also gave us the ability to come and go without our baggage.

Once settled, we locked the door and followed Ali's directions to our given rendezvous, a little café a couple of miles out of town. Soon we were being presented to some of his Arab connections, a similarly gracious and philosophical lot whose discourses also revolved around world affairs and commerce. Ordinarily I wouldn't have believed this too problematic, but compared to Ali and his friends' more extensive insight, I have to say I did feel something of a thicko. Especially since, whenever I was about to chip in with anything that seemed vaguely fitting, Shaggy kept beating me to the punch with much the same idea – at one stage I swear my entire input amounted to, "Lovely weather here, isn't it?"

Halfway into the evening all the business talk reminded Ali that he had contracts to clinch and, with an itchy dialling finger, he soon left everyone with his usual, "I have to go, I have some calls to make." An hour later his friends decided they too had people to ring, so Shaggy and I shook their hands and wandered back to the centre, where we unexpectedly ran into the coolest dude in Nairobi, and his girlfriend Suzette.

A charmer, Larry took advantage of our not yet having eaten and in no time we were treating them at a Greek-owned, sort of African-Chinese restaurant. Here, he opened the chitchat with his favourite subject – himself – before moving on to debate politics in sport, and ultimately our forthcoming voyage.

"So your Congo journey commences at Kisangani. I've heard this is the centre of Africa."

"Geographically speaking, that's right," I answered. "It's the same distance from Cairo as is it to Cape Town, and also the same east and west, from the Atlantic and the Indian Ocean."

"This is why you have chosen Kisangani, not further upriver?"

"No, no. We have no choice. Waterfalls make it impossible to navigate prior to Kisangani. If there is a way of getting past or down them, we wouldn't have a clue."

"Besides," said Shaggy, "neither of us has ever been in any kind of canoe before, let alone a paddle a pirogue."

"Never?"

"No, never. Or done any survival training."

"You're both crazy."

"Pretty much."

"And you say you're going to paddle to Kinshasa. How far is this?"

My "a thousand miles" raised Mr Cool's eyebrows.

"Impressive. Even ten miles would be good."

"Don't forget," I added, "once we get into Zaire there's still several hundred miles of jungle to get through before we reach Kisangani. And that's bound to create a tale or two."

"You should write a book," was somewhat prophetic from Larry.

"Oh, Sean of the Congo's going to do everything," jibed Shaggy, "write best-sellers, play James Bond, win the Olympics, win..."

"Yeah, nothing major," I cut in, wishing to play down my usually mocked, expansive ambitions.

But Shaggy knew how to press the right buttons.

"Fiver against you doing any of them."

"Done!"

We shook hands, while a smiling Larry kindly refrained from any ribbing and redirected the discussion to our travels, and with a bump.

"You do know there are cannibals along the Congo, don't you?"

Shaggy and I were indeed aware of Congolese cannibalism, which, in the stories we'd read, appeared to involve only their own kind, so we weren't too concerned and answered accordingly (if we'd had the ability to see into the future, to read the books I since have, where myriad Johnny Foreigners seem to have kicked the bucket in this foul way, we might not have been so blasé).

"As long as you are conscious of this, then fine," continued Larry. "Take some advice, though. Never travel at night, anywhere in Africa. Africa can be an amazing place to be during the day, but at night — beware."

"Don't worry, we're both very cautious people," I replied, trying but failing to sound as cool as our esteemed dinner guest.

"Anything else, Larry?" asked Shaggy.

"Just one thing. I would like to pass some words of wisdom on to you for your journey."

Without warning Larry became very mellow. He'd spoken a great deal during our time with him and I could tell that whatever he was about to say had deep meaning. When Larry X talked people listened, and in an effort to ensure no one else could hear, he leaned forward, summoning us closer as he did so. When next he spoke it was to state one line only, which he delivered with hushed reverence.

"The ox is slow, but the earth is patient."

He then gradually eased rearward, until his back once more rested against the chair, his right leg again crossing his left so that his ankle lay upon his knee, as what seemed usual for Larry.

Pondering his words, I glanced at Mr X's partner, then at Shaggy, then back at guru Larry.

"Hang on," I said, "you've been watching that movie High Road to China. That's where that line comes from!"

Everyone suddenly stared at Larry, who froze for a moment, then burst into the broadest of smiles.

"Good line, though," he replied, beaming.

We all laughed at Larry's stab at looking even more sagacious than usual.

After the meal, during which I was cajoled into trying a revolting yoghurt-type drink I vowed I would never touch again, Larry and his girlfriend bade us farewell.

It was the last time I ever saw Larry X.

When Shaggy and I arrived back the lodge, our cynical side told us to thoroughly check our belongings. Since we always carried our cash, passports, cameras and malaria tablets, our luggage should still have contained each of the following: a waterbottle; matches; compass; first aid kit; diary; pens; towel; mosquito netting; penknife; bedding; wet-wipes; water-purifying pills; vitamins; clothes; razors; extra camera films and batteries; talc and a toilet roll. There should also have been: Shaggy's torch, insulation tape and tent (which, like nearly all of his gear, was borrowed), and my contact lenses' kit, map, hammock, rope, some magazines and books, a French-English dictionary, some spare trainers, and, dare I say, Brylcreem. Happily all was in place, and we contently turned in at the end of our second full day in Africa.

The next morning we were up bright and breezy and ready for action. Bags packed, we were standing outside The New Kenya Lodge, await-ing Ali, who said he'd pick us up at 10am. The flight was scheduled at noon. Passengers had to be there no later than 11am.

10am came and went.

No Ali.

As relaxed as when we were 'nose-diving' on the plane to Moscow, Shaggy sat patiently by the road, but true to form I couldn't stay com-posed and paced up and down nervously.

"Tell you what, I'll bet he's still making some calls," said Shaggy, hoping frivolity would help ease the frustration.

"More likely he's gone straight to the airport and asked Albert the Bore to pick us up, only God's chosen today to have him struck down and consigned to hell."

Shaggy emitted what was a routine giggle whenever we employed banter, even if half-hearted — or naff — but my frustration was still pent up. Feeling I had to do something, I walked to the nearest shop, purchased a carton of milk, guzzled it down, and was vainly looking for a bin when an inquisitive local approached me.

"It is fine," said the Nairobian, holding out his hand, "give me the rubbish."

Thanking Mr Kind for the offer, I voluntarily handed it over and, intrigued as to where the bin was, watched as he screwed the carton into a ball. He then stepped towards the side of the pavement — and tossed it into the road.

"There we are," he said, gave a polite bow to me and walked off.

10:40am, and still no Ali. The airport was nine miles away but a taxi was out of the question, as the milk had spoken for the last of our Kenyan currency. With no lift or cash for a taxi it was now panic stations, and at long last Shaggy cracked.

"What shall we do?" he asked, the sharp tone of his voice betraying any calm façade he may have wished to present.

"If only you'd brought your ruby slippers, you could have tapped your heels three times and transported us to the airport."

"Knowing our luck we'd end up in Kansas."

As usual we had endeavoured to calm ourselves with humour, and think more rationally, but once again it didn't work — we still had no answer. The plane departed at noon, we were miles away, we had no shillings, and even if we did manage to get there, we would still have to find time to check in, pay the twenty dollars airport tax, have our currency papers checked, our baggage checked, ourselves checked, our passports checked, our tickets checked, and goodness knows what else checked.

We were right in it.

By chance, a ray of hope fell our way when the lodge's sympathetic receptionist offered a partial remedy. Apparently, a colleague needed to run an errand and, if we liked, he could drop us off at the Nairobi Airport freeway, which would enable us to at least try to gain a hitch. Having abandoned all hope of Ali arriving, we gratefully accepted, and before long we were by the main route, our thumbs wagging for all they were worth.

11:15am. In spite of our best efforts we were still standing by the freeway. With no other option, we decided the only way out of our quandary would be to offer a cabbie some dollars and hope he would take the deal. Of course that was what he would have preferred in the first place, but we were still being educated on that score.

Soon we were back to shitting bricks while at the mercy of another suicidal driver, finally skidding to our arrival at check-in forty minutes beyond its cut-off time, to face a bewildered Ali.

"What happened to you two?"

"You mean what happened to *you*?" I replied.

I was right. Ali had sent Albert the Bore to meet us, only "I can't do anybody any wrong" Albert hadn't turned up.

"I'll talk to him when I'm back," said Ali. "At least you're here."

"Like Batman and Robin, we always arrive in the nick of time."

"And there's your exes saying you usually come too prematurely," joked Shaggy.

Although we had tried to pass off our relief in the usual light-hearted way, "in the nick of time" was a perfect phrase because the plane had to be postponed for us (and one other straggler, and how lucky for them that the influential Ali Hassan had asked for that delay) while we passed through what seemed like the most complex airport system in the world. Worse still, because I had paid the taxi driver in dollars and he didn't have an official stamp to say he had received it, my currency declaration form didn't match my money. I needn't have worried, though, for the officer in charge couldn't (so obviously) count, and despite his checking my cash against the form, he therefore had no idea that the totals were erroneous. That said, he still tried to pretend there was something wrong with my papers and hinted transparently that if I paid a bribe he 'may' let me through. Told this was a common practice in many parts of Africa, since Mr Can't-Count had assumed my documentation correct, I called his bluff and hinted back to him that I was far too stupid to understand what he was talking about. It worked, and moments later I was about to jeopardize one of my remaining seven cat lives by boarding my first African aeroplane, which, if you have just been on Captain Kamikaze's Death Machine, wasn't the most appealing thing to look forward to.

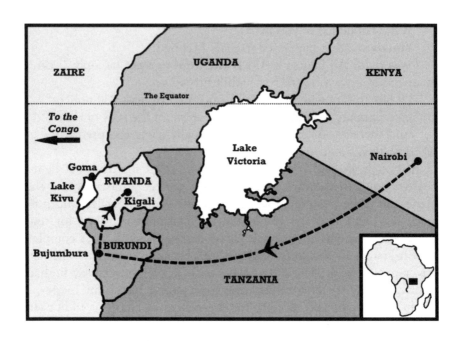

Chapter 3

THE KILLING ZONE

Lying near the heart of Africa, the tiny landmass of Rwanda (the 'land of a thousand hills') has, for all the wrong reasons, featured in many a news article since its 1962 independence, the headlines of which can usually be condensed into one word – war.

A thousand years ago the predominant people of this area were The Twa (pygmy), but a slow process of infiltration by two migrant tribes over the next few centuries saw them systematically displaced. Today they account for only one per cent of the population. The rest is shared between the Tutsis and Hutus, who throughout the ensuing years have vied for control. The bloodiest clashes occurred after, and are generally attributed to, German, then Belgian, occupation. Where once Tutsi and Hutu had enjoyed a reasonably flexible relationship, regularly intermarrying, colonialism helped encourage a 'them and us' ethos, particularly under Belgian rule. A 1934 census, for example, arbitrarily classified anyone owning more than ten cows as a Tutsi, and so all 'rich' Hutus and poor Tutsis suddenly found themselves reshuffled. It led to a rich–poor divide, one that was aggravated by the manner in which enforced labour was metered out – to Hutus only, whilst Tutsis were installed as their superintendents. Bloodshed was inevitable.

Historically significant post-independence episodes include mass butchery of the Tutsi in 1963 and 1973, the latter as a repercussion of the 1972 slaughter of thousands of Hutus in neighbouring Burundi. Since then not much had changed, with the worst chapter beginning one year after our presence, and escalating each year until 1994 and the appalling genocide that wiped out almost a million people, many by machete.

In terms of our arrival, if we wind back slightly, again in next-door Burundi, thousands of Hutus had been slain by the Tutsi authorities, with the knock-on effect that thousands more fled to Rwanda – and now had an axe to grind. And this was only ten months prior to our setting foot in Africa. Be that as it may, in 1989 Rwanda was at peace with itself, even if history has taught us that tribal violence was always just around the corner. Yet here we were, entering the killing zone.

Ethnic cleansing aside, Rwanda is as renowned for something else. Located in the west and clothed by imposing forests, the massif above

Lake Kivu is home to that legendary creature, the mountain gorilla. And with the ape-spotting industry boosted by the success of the film *Gorillas in the Mist*, by the time we hit Africa tourists were flocking to catch a glimpse of them in their natural habitat. As such, the cost of seeing the largest of all anthropoids was regrettably too high for our humble pocket.

This tourism was evident the second I stepped on to the plane — foreign sightseers everywhere — and with its being full to capacity and my being late, I couldn't make out where a spare seat was, so I paused at the end of the gangway. As I scanned the cabin a voice came from behind.

"Is this the flight for Rwanda?"

It was the straggler who had arrived at the airport even later than we had.

My reply sustained my own doubts: "I certainly hope so."

To anyone who has never travelled in this part of the world, this question and answer might sound daft, but the truth of the matter was that there were two identical aircraft standing side by side and no staff to tell you which one was yours. You just had to take your pick and pray you'd guessed correctly. Even Ali, it transpired, had initially boarded the wrong plane.

Two hours and one transitory stopover at Bujumbura (the capital of Burundi) later, we were at Kigali airport being greeted by a smartly suited middle-aged gentleman of obvious Arabian heritage, and an entourage of personnel. Possessing similar features to Ali's, his father looked sharp of mind and carried an air of confidence about him, although his guarded body language gave away an expected suspicion towards us. I put this down to his being a busy man; the last thing he needed was a couple of wannabes clouding his son's arrival. Even so, upon introduction his firm handshake and amiable manners were appreciatively accepted, and at Ali's request he was genial enough to have us transported to Pepsi-Cola headquarters, where we were given a tour and handed a business card. It read: '*Pepsi Sobolirwa. Société de boissons de limonades au Rwanda. Hamud Hassan. Administrator. B. P. 653 Kigali*'. Remembering Ali owned ten per cent of all his father's interests, Shaggy and I gazed at the plant, and then at each other with an expression that said: 'Jammy sod.'

Next on the agenda was the problem of our accommodation, and while Ali had offered to let us stay with him at his father's residence (by all accounts, an exceptionally palatial stately home), he would first need permission. Although luck was on our side in this matter, what with Ali being a smooth, persuasive talker, I metaphorically crossed my fingers. With all thoughts of the Congo now taking a back seat, I indulged my mind with a scenario of powerful millionaire Hassan Senior throwing himself at our feet and begging us to stay with them indefinitely, thereafter whisking us off to his Taj Mahal-esque palace in an awaiting helicopter. Here, we would divide our time between Jacuzzi sessions, banqueting with dignitaries, hobnobbing with celebs, and being waited upon hand and foot by beautiful dancing girls. The hottest of them would take me to one side and...

It was at this moment that my daydream was interrupted, by Ali wandering over.

"My father is too busy for guests."

Oh well, it had been a nice fantasy while it lasted.

But, hold on, what was this? No sooner had we received the Sod's Law news when, in the same breath, a reprieve was granted.

"He has, however, instructed one of his drivers to take you to the Meridien."

"The Meridien?" I queried.

"Yes, it is the finest hotel in Rwanda."

I was about to say "You seem to be forgetting our limited budget", but Ali was two steps ahead of me.

"Do not worry, you will not have to pay for anything."

Silly me. Coming from a working-class upbringing, I hadn't stopped to think that people such as this would have a pre-paid hotel suite all kitted out for visiting guests. Way to go, Ali and his dad!

"Because," continued Ali, "I have heard you can pitch your tent in the field next door for free. Just ask at reception. I will be along soon to make sure you are okay. Enjoy your camping. Bye."

Shaggy and I tried not to look too deflated as we waved goodbye from our departing lift — the only banger in a fleet that included at least one top-of-the-range Mercedes.

When we arrived at the Meridien, another of Sod's Laws was to follow — no, we couldn't pitch our shitty tent in their field, and even when Ali arrived and put a good word in for us, the duty manager was adamant we peasants should keep as far away from their hallowed soil as humanly possible.

Back to square one.

With the field out of the question, Hassan Junior again leapt to our rescue, offering an alternative which turned out to be a far better proposal than the Meridien, and we were chauffeured to his family's import-export office, in the centre of Kigali.

While travelling I visually assessed a city that would prove to be our home for the next seven, noticeably hotter, days, much of which was pleasing to the eye, as enormous palm plantations and leafy forest lined very clean, garbage-free roads. The impression of greenery was enhanced by the fact that Kigali straddled several hills, the outline of which remained clearly visible due to the bulk of the capital's homes being so small and plain. Gabled or flat-roofed rectangles, they were erected so closely together across the shallow slopes that it looked as though someone might have tipped a big box of Monopoly houses in a pile, and then smoothed them to a single layer.

We soon arrived at the Nyarugenge borough and pulled to a stop across the road from a half-erected building, which was memorable because the scaffolding was partly made from whittled logs which were far from straight. Still, they appeared to do the job. On our side was the Hassans' import-export workplace, a prefab-looking concrete construction that was painted an orangey beige, its two tiers consisting of one small room each. The groundfloor office, occupied by their secretary, Felicité, was a sparse room containing a desk, chair, phone and large but near-empty shelving unit. To get to the second-floor main office, a matching room with the exception of the added mod con of a filing cabinet, you had to ascend a set of stairs on the outside of the building. These offices overlooked the adjoining compound, which apparently included three rooms and a toilet, all utilised by two caretakers. More crucially, it was also owned by the Hassans.

Prior to being shown around, we had been greeted by another of Ali's relatives, an uncle, Sajid, who ran this particular office, and after a brief discussion he ordered the head caretaker to give us the keys to one of the rooms. With just an old table and some chairs decorating its bare concrete floor, save for a lick of green paint, it may not have been Hassan Senior's imperial abode, but who were we to complain? A free roof over our heads right in the heart of Kigali — we peasants were more than happy to accept the invitation.

Now that he was back with his ever-busy father, Ali had business to attend to and, after arranging to meet up afterwards, left with his standard, "I have to go, I have some calls to make."

In his late thirties, Ali's uncle was a clever, sturdily built, buoyant man who bucked the family trend by wearing a *thobe* — an Arabian ankle-length tunic — although this was where any diversity started and finished: like Ali and his dad, Sajid was a born businessman forever on the go. This didn't stop him from exuding kindness, however, and he assisted Shaggy and me whenever asked, such as by exchanging cash for us on the black market. He was also rather prophetic. Having explained that Rwanda was Africa's most densely populated country, he proceeded to predict the advent of more conflict.

"There are six million people living on ten thousand square miles of land, and the average Rwandan mother has eight or nine children. And I guarantee there will be ten million people in twenty years. This is why the government has asked parents to stop at four children. But it isn't enough. Far more than religion or politics, it is overcrowding that sets off wars. And one will happen again. You will see."

He was proved to be right on all counts.

Sajid liked to philosophise too, chiefly on what seemed to be the 'in' themes: commerce and world politics. Due to visit other nations where their company had interests, he talked candidly about political tensions, especially in the Asian countries with which their family had connections, such as Lebanon. One day he confessed to knowing "for a fact" that the famed Englishmen Terry Waite and John McCarthy, along with Irishman Brian Keenan and Americans Terry Anderson, Tom Sutherland and Frank Reed – just six of many foreigners taken hostage by the Islamic Jihad Organisation – were alive. This was an eye-opener, because no one in the UK appeared to have a clue about their welfare. Moreover, while I might not have known Sajid well, I had every confidence that his information was accurate, to the point that I made a mental note to inform the authorities of this news upon my return home (in the event, I wrote to the government and various media, all without reply). As history has shown, these men were not only alive but within three years were also all released.

Unable to obtain a Zairian visa due to the immigration office being closed, Shaggy and I unpacked our belongings, locked the room, and with time to waste made for some tree-covered hills in the distance. To accomplish this we had to first pass through Kigali's main market, which basically was no different from those in England: a large square full of rows of stalls that showcased clothing, bric-a-brac, food, etc.

Clucking chickens, bleating goats and a chatty parrot competed for attention against a backdrop of many barterers, the sights and sounds of which highlighted the most prominent difference between Nairobi and Kigali, as here there were significantly fewer foreigners. Another disparity was that the Kenyans spoke English, and whilst Kinyarwanda was the indigenous tongue in Rwanda, because their co-official language was French many of the Kigalians spoke both. One such vendor asked Shaggy to buy a chicken, which prompted a curt reply, although on this occasion not because of my friend's limited French (five years of *Français* at school had rendered neither of us a linguist). Like me, Shaggy had a soft spot for animals and couldn't understand why the man felt it necessary to display his live birds by hanging them upside down. And so on we wandered – directly into another abrupt Shaggy response. The boldest of a set of children had asked my compatriot for one of the badges he kept on his cap, but received short shrift because Shaggy was hoping to trade them should the necessity arise. At least that's what he reasoned – my penny-pinching was decidedly small-time compared to Shaggy's. If at death's door he was offered life-saving pills that cost next to nothing, I wouldn't have bet against him turning them down if he knew they were cheaper elsewhere.

Once past the market, differences within Kigali itself materialised. The houses became progressively smaller, and far more rudimentary, until they eventually turned into what I would describe as clay cabins. Similarly, although the men continued to wear Western garb, albeit more raggedy, women now favoured traditional clothing in the form of brightly coloured sarongs, shawls and wraps. The biggest trans-formation, however, occurred once we reached the suburbs, as here there were no Johnny Foreigners at all. And it showed. Where once we had been asked to purchase chickens and hand over badges, the Kigalians now stared, laughed and pointed at us. Others would pass us and, preoccupied, not notice until the last moment, when they would drop their jaw, then holler "Umuzungu! Umuzungu!" ("White man! White man!"). And children would at first back away, then, realising we were friendly, tag along, their flock now so voluminous it was as if they were joining some great carnival procession.

In time we arrived at the bottom of the nearest faraway hill, upon which I asked a teenager if it was possible to make the crest. Having suddenly witnessed a large group fronted by two *umuzungus* bearing down on him, it was no bombshell to find the teen's face a fusion of shock and puzzlement, but the look soon altered to that of a gigantic beam and he motioned us to follow him up a well-trodden pathway. So follow we did, the ever-growing procession of children cheerfully pursuing, while men and women, wondering what all the commotion was about, emerged from what were now mud huts, many of them greeting us with handshakes, good luck wishes, pats on the back and cries of excitement – to such an extent that we felt like pop stars.

"I feel like the Pied Piper of Hamlin," I afforded, musing over our newfound 'stardom'.

"They're most probably thinking – Wow, the blond one is Indiana Jones," said Shaggy.

"Nah – The dark-haired one is James Bond."

"More like Frankenstein's monster."

"Says Quasimodo."

Shaggy giggled, and we carried on up the faraway hill.

The incline steepened. So much so that it was impossible for any more huts to have been erected here, and our resident guide stopped the procession and beckoned us to keep on up the little track and into the woods ...alone. With many cheers ringing in our ears (and youthful optimism dismissing the possibility that what we assumed to be "Goodbye and good luck!" was actually "Abandon hope all ye who enter there!") we followed the guide's advice and made our way up the hillside, which was now inhabited by such an intoxicating kaleidoscope of trees that it wasn't until we were deep into the forest that we realised something rather telling — there was no longer a pathway. All the same we maintained our trek, but after thirty minutes we still couldn't see the summit. With daylight starting to fade, we decided to take some snapshots before the shadows became too long.

"Hold still. Say chee..."

I didn't get the chance to finish my sentence. Through the viewfinder, behind Shaggy, I had seen something move. Something big. Hurriedly, I retracted my camera, but only trees adorned the scene before me. Whatever had been there had now vanished into the bush. Or, rather, was now watching us from within the bush, undoubtedly waiting to pounce. When I informed him of this worry, an instantly less cool Shaggy spun on his heels. Heartbeat rising, his eyes hungrily scanned the vegetation on which mine were already fastened, but only shadows and forest remained. A moment turned into ten before my apprehensive friend spoke.

"There's nothing there."

"I'm sure I saw something."

We continued to stare at the surrounding landscape.

"Hang on! I think I saw something too."

We strained our eyes again.

Nothing.

"Maybe I was wrong. Tell you what, Sean, if there is anything there, it's definitely in hiding."

"Yeah, still waiting to pounce."

Shaggy fired me a 'thanks for reminding me of that' glare, but my mind was already on other things — like why no one had pursued us once we had reached the periphery of the woods. Given our angst, I felt it appropriate to mention the fact.

"Well," said a faux-brave voice, "it's too dark to go on now anyway. Reckon we'd better head back."

"I think you are right," replied the other faux-brave voice. "But only because it's too dark to see."

"Of course."

Shaggy took out his torch and we descended as best (and as fast!) as we could.

Our little adventure for the day was over.

On the way back to the compound Shaggy tried to persuade some children to be photographed but found he had to hand over a badge for the privilege. As they were lining up, a young man came by and asked if he too could be in the shot. The more the merrier as Shaggy saw it. Just as he was about to take the picture, however, half of the children ran away (with his badge) but after much toing and froing he finally managed to extract some kind of photo — as confirmed by the front cover of this book.

Shaggy thanked the children who had stayed, but when he turned to show gratitude to the young man he was met with a bit more than he bargained for.

"J'ai besoin vingt francs."

"Sorry, I don't speak much French," said Shaggy, determined not to give a penny to anyone he didn't want to.

"Give me twenty francs!"

Let it be known now that right through our entire duration in French-speaking Africa, the majority of English sentences uttered in our direction seemed to start with: "Give me..."

Fearing an acceleration of wills, I made ready to move off sharpish and signalled Shaggy, who liked a good spat and was now pointlessly laying down the law, to follow. When eventually he had rid himself of his antagonist, we again found ourselves 'sitting targets', this time to a large group of children, who had surely been in search of two foreign-looking blokes to trail and shrill at. At least that's how it appeared, judging by the ear-splitting effort they put into their piercingly high-pitched voice projection. After a while this fervour became a tad too raw for us (picture thirty children repeatedly scraping their fingernails down a blackboard). With our eardrums now frayed, Shaggy echoed my own thoughts when he said he felt like "strangling the little shits". Not that we would have, although we might well have yelled back at them had there not been a surfeit of machine-gun-toting army guys kicking about. So we just put up with it.

Aching of limbs, and eardrums, we at last escaped the children and reached the compound. Not long after, Ali stopped by for half an hour, bringing two offerings in the process. The first was a welcoming bowl of fruit. The second, a personal present for me — a nice chunky blanket similar to Shaggy's. In spite of the towering heat of the day, it wasn't lost on Ali that, come night time, our 'bed' — the compound's concrete floor — was far from warm, and in particular for idiot here, who had brought only a sliver of a sheet.

After Ali had left, Shaggy and I decided to turn in. In my case this meant having a wash, taking out my contact lenses, re-assessing our travel itinerary, jotting down notes, and then settling down with my new blanket. Contacts aside, Shaggy's evening always concluded much the same, although this night had closed a bit differently following a toilet incident.

"I was in mid-flow when a giant cockroach came out of nowhere and charged at me!" he wheezed. "I wasn't expecting it and nearly hit the roof. I ended up having to drown it."

"Since cockroaches can supposedly survive nuclear war," I replied, "please refrain from having a piss anywhere near me."

The compound's chief caretaker, a willowy thirty-three year-old with turned up trousers and an attitude, was a snobbish so-and-so. Boasting that he was a university graduate, fortunately he didn't look down his snout in our direction whenever we spoke. It was a shame, then, that he didn't extend the same gentility to his sole underling – Claver – a young local whose job was to keep the place clean, discourage intruders, and generally kiss everybody's backside, or so it seemed. The nineteen year-old lived in a pint-sized room next to ours, and always sported two things: an apparently second-hand blue imitation Adidas tracksuit, and also a big smile, which disappeared whenever 'Snooty' showed up. I deduced this to be a result of being persistently bossed about by him, especially when it appeared to be completely meaningless – on several occasions Snooty summoned Claver in our presence and commanded the put-upon teen to do something trivial, before flashing us a 'check out how important I am' smirk.

Every sundown Claver would cook Snooty the most beautiful of meals, with ingredients purchased at the market for what amounted to forty pence. Shaggy, his mouth watering, asked Claver if he would cook for us also; we would provide money enough for all three of us, as long as he did the shopping. Even if he hadn't been promised a free dinner Claver would have been happy to help, and that evening he laid on the most gorgeous, fulfilling and authentic meal you could ever hope to buy for a few pence. It consisted of a range of vegetables, including yams, sweet potatoes and, the core ingredient, plantain, all of which Claver placed into a small kiln-like stove and then smoked beneath a mound of earth. Not *au fait* with some of the local fare, I have to confess that I had presumed the plantain was a large unripe banana – that I was wrong now explains why, when dimwit here later tried to bake a banana, it didn't taste anything like potato the way plantain had.

Once he had started to cook for us, we requested Claver also eat with us at the table. But Snooty flatly forbade it, as it meant Claver would be dining in the same room as he, so he made him sit outside.

Throughout the world, prejudice comes in many forms.

After three days of tolerating Snooty's behaviour, Shaggy and I, and certainly Claver, were chuffed to see the back of him. The reason for his departure, once we had learnt it, staggered us. Apparently he wasn't the head caretaker at all (he was away visiting relatives), but merely a friend who had stopped over for a few days. And there was Claver, not only slaving after him day and night, but also being made to sit outside whenever he dined.

"If I'd have known this beforehand," said Shaggy, who had spent some time teaching Claver his limited French, "I'd have made *him* sit outside whenever Claver ate."

Looking back, in our ignorance I'm pretty sure there was a degree of Tutsi-Hutu rivalry, as opposed to a solitary 'I've been to university' mind-set. It would be logical that Snooty had a chip on his shoulder if the ethnic group to which Claver belonged had at some point in the past been at loggerheads with his. Still, at the time we felt that an injustice had been done, and I found myself handing some francs to Claver, who immediately misread the gesture and began to head back to the market for more food. I stopped him and signalled that it was his to keep. He was ecstatic — seemingly, this was an enormous tip. I was later told it was also something of an honour. I had given him the equivalent of seventy pence.

When I confessed my act to Shaggy, rather than scoff at my having 'wasted' money, he instead started to chuckle.

"What's so funny?"

"I gave him the same tip earlier this morning!"

"Ha, I'll laugh if he's scamming us."

"I bloody won't."

Shaggy's riposte notwithstanding, it was good to see him displaying a principled and caring side that was every bit as prevalent as, if often masked by, his frugality and black-and-white thinking. As for Claver being a scammer, he was anything but. And from that day forwards we insisted he eat with us, at the table, every day.

Chapter 4

DEATH KNELL

Friday, 16th June. "Come back for them this afternoon" didn't fill me with any great expectation of acquiring our Zaire permits on arrival. The statement had been offered to us by the bureaucrat in charge of doling out visas, but that was first thing this morning. Now it was the afternoon and we were back at the agency. Had the documents we'd filled and handed in been inspected as promised? No, apparently they hadn't.

"Come back on Monday. You can have your visas then."

Talk about déjà vu.

"Bloody typical," muttered Shaggy on the way out.

Keen to move the journey closer to our goal, we had called at the Zairian consulate every day since arriving here, and today, our fourth in Kigali, was the first time it was open. And now this, the worry that we may have to wait another God knows how many days for our visas – no doubt processed much faster if accompanied by a 'tip', a strategy we witnessed working for someone else. Not that miser Shaggy was about to copy it, especially as he was still smarting over the extra cash we'd tipped Albert the Bore for the Rwandan passes. I could scarcely disagree, since the three-month Zairian visa we had been hoping to procure was priced at a monstrous £130. To add insult to injury, had we had the foresight, we could have got one in Kenya for a fraction of the price. It seemed clear to us that someone was intent on creating a second income, but what could we do? As we understood it, corrupt authorities were commonplace, and now, following Albert's crooked visa deal and Mr Can't-Count's attempt at bribery, we supposed we'd had another taste of it. Licking our wounds, we decided the best bet would be to buy a one-month visa, and then have it extended later in the journey, although this still cost us a whopping £45 each.

The frustrating aspect of the visa-wait wasn't just the inability to move our odyssey forward to the Congo, but also the tedium of the delay. With Ali busy making calls, for the most part we'd had to find our own entertainment. And since, oddly, there were no museums or the like in Kigali, unless you were off on a gorilla search or had funds for nights outs, once you'd had some rambles and visited the market a few times, that was your lot. That's why, except for a couple of trips to the local restaurant, and a meal at the Meridian the preceding evening (not the brightest of decisions, given the expense – and the manager's

'Aren't you those peasants with the shitty tent?' frown), our time here had proved no more exciting than a rainy Sunday. To compensate, we had toyed with the idea of roaming up into the gorilla mountains without a guide and having a peek, but the odds of being shot as a poacher or mauled by a protective silverback didn't exactly match our plans, so we walked randomly around Kigali, taking photographs and sunning ourselves; the latter invaluable to your average holidaymaker, especially with the immense heat and zero cloud cover, but quite the reverse to two livewires with thoughts of the Congo on their mind.

'we walked randomly around Kigali, taking photographs'. Below, Shaggy.

The following morning I had barely finished writing some postcards when a character wearing pressed charcoal trousers and a black cotton formal shirt appeared before me. Nothing abnormal about a mid-twenties black man in these parts, but upon introducing himself, a first-impression gut feeling told me Mbonyunkiza was as false as they come. However, since he was there in the compound, sporting pricey togs and polished shoes, he was obviously an associate of the Hassans, so I kept my intuitions on standby. Anyway, he said that he had been a university student and would welcome the opportunity to converse in English, and for a spell Shaggy and I found this use of our native tongue a refreshing relief — until, that is, he tried pocketing my pen. Even if he hadn't, that minute or two we spent answering personal questions, whilst he doggedly evaded ours, seemed to verify my initial suspicions.

After Mbonyunkiza had disappeared, Shaggy and I moaned at Ali's choice of colleagues and prayed he wouldn't return. Our wishes were surprisingly granted ...for a while.

"Hello, Shaggy. Hello, Sean."

Now that he was here our latest crony at least made himself useful. Although you could purchase chips in Kigali, the flavour and texture was different. So, having overheard Shaggy pining for "proper" British chips, 'Limpet', as we later nicknamed him, pledged that a local place had similar files, and offered to take us there. The thought of spending more time with Limpet didn't swing it for me, but Shaggy's chips yearning erased all barriers and in no time they were out of the door.

When shortly they returned, I was in the process of taking a photo of Claver and Magolitte, the maid from next door. Seeing this, Limpet suddenly exited stage left, re-emerging five minutes later with some films, and asking if I'd care to exchange them for twenty dollars. We shook hands on a radically lower figure. After I'd paid him, though, I noticed something peculiar. Whilst attempting to covertly slip the proceeds into his wallet, turning his back as he did so, from my angle it was impossible to miss its bulging cluster of notes. Of course this affluence was no shock, his being a friend of the Hassans, but herein lay the conundrum. During Limpet's exodus, Shaggy had whined not just about the "comparable, my arse" chips, but that he'd also had to buy a portion for his new buddy, who had claimed to have no hard cash on him. Admittedly, Limpet could have obtained his stash when he went for the films, but his actions left a nagging doubt.

Whatever the truth, we would have to watch this one, especially when within seconds he was caught rummaging through our belongings, a sickly sweet 'I'm not a thief, just nosy' smile his defence. Yes, very dodgy, although our qualms about Limpet's honesty were soon moderated when Ali rolled up and, after greeting Shaggy and me with a "Hi", gave Mbonyunkiza a respectful 'business acquaintance' nod. Ali wanted us Johnny Foreigners to help him promote Pepsi by downing gallons of it at a variety of bars — his viewpoint was that if we were seen drinking Pepsi then the locals might follow suit. And so off we trotted, any remaining misgivings about Limpet's legitimacy expunged when Ali asked him to join us.

In due course our Arabian friend ran out of time, which was a blessing, as our bellies were painfully bloated by the Pepsi, and with a parting "I have to go, I have some calls to make" he dropped us back at the compound. Stuffed or not, with its being teatime, Limpet, still firmly attached to us, talked us into giving Claver a miss in favour of the neighbouring restaurant. We didn't really want to go, what with the extra expense, but after all that Ali had done for us we felt obliged to humour anyone in his circle. Making the decision a bit easier was the fact that Sajid had informed us previously that this restaurant was the only local place he knew to promote a delicacy both Shaggy and I worshipped. Once inside we were thrilled to learn that it did indeed serve our *raison d'être* — ice cream, its exalted appeal now magnified by the combined lack of home comforts and Kigali's immense heat.

Having been spoiled in Nairobi by the Knickerbocker Glories, we were hoping for more of the same, so were suitably devastated when the dessert turned out to be 'only' sorbet — not that that stopped us ordering one each, to be eaten after our chicken and chips main meal. As if the ice cream let down wasn't frustrating enough, the restaurant was typical of most of the eateries we visited in Africa. By this I mean that, as we would later discover, if you were the only two people in the place and had ordered merely a glass of milk each, they would still take longer than an hour to fetch them.

We were pleased when the bill for the eventual meal finally came. Throughout our Pepsi-guzzling time with Ali, Limpet had said little, opting to abstain from the bulk of our conversations while he loaded up on drinks, and although he hadn't proffered one "thank you" or shown any form of gratitude for the freebies afforded him, he didn't seem as much the thorn in our sides as he had earlier. Not so at the restaurant, however, where any topic we did try to discuss was met by his telling us to stick a sock in it. That, or he'd verbally shut up shop, preferring instead to slurp his food nauseatingly and beam his all too regular 'honestly, I'm not a scallywag' smile. We were totally baffled as to why Ali chose to be linked with him, as the only things he seemed interested in were freeloading and provocation. This became all the more clear when, without warning, despite having half of his own fare in front of him, he stuck his fork into my chips!

"Where I'm from, that would be deemed rather bad-mannered," I reprimanded, which would perhaps have been more effective had the scene not caused Shaggy to erupt into a writhing spasm of laughter.

Without apology, the troublesome one just popped my chips into his mouth and flashed another sugary sweet smile.

Aghast at Limpet's rudeness, I was even more flabbergasted when his fork again headed towards my platter. This time, however, I was ready for action and clasped his wrist, squeezing it a little harder than necessary before letting go.

"Sorry about that," I offered, with limited sincerity.

Limpet, though, didn't flinch. He just gave me another irritating smirk — then tried his luck for a third time.

If it was war he wanted, no problem — I thwarted him again, and with my fork hand snaffled some of *his* chips. Ha!

The outcome? His treacly grin turned at once to a look of sheer contempt, the cheeky sod.

By this time Shaggy was doubled over howling, and I was truthfully torn between wanting to join him and doing my nemesis some grave mischief — never before, ever, had I wanted so badly to get hold of someone's head and then pound their face, over and over, into a plateful of food, if not the table beneath. But I resisted the urge, and to appease my growing rage instead decided on a mode of retribution that probably shouldn't be disclosed here, but what the hell.

From the moment we had walked into the restaurant I had been struggling with the consequence of the Pepsi, the result being that I was desperate to release what my old dictionary described as 'a small explosion between the buttocks'. Any doubt about whether I should employ my choice of revenge was extinguished when, after Shaggy had managed to stifle his hooting, the sound of Limpet's slurping attained a new level of repulsiveness. 'Two can play at being uncouth, Bucko,' I thought to myself, whilst in his direction I let fly with a classic silent assassin. To my utter horror, however, rather than the noiseless waft I had intended, the now-quiet restaurant was treated to a considerably thunderous '*faaaaaaaart*'! Oh, the humiliation. Especially since everyone stopped eating and stared (most notably the lady to our right, who gave me a 'do excuse yourself to the bathroom' frosty glare). Everyone, that is, except two people. One was Shaggy, who was now hanging off the table with further tears of laughter streaming down his face. The other was Limpet, who, stone me, didn't bat an eyelid — he just shot me another sugary smile, and then continued slurping. Still, at least I managed to get to the end of my meal without his cutlery finding its way in there again.

It wasn't until he saw the bill being brought over that our insolent guest disappeared, so no surprise there. Or that he had again offered no parting thanks. We did, however, agree to meet him at two o'clock the following day. Lost our minds? Not likely, for what Limpet didn't know was that Ali had agreed to take Shaggy and me out all afternoon, so we wouldn't be anywhere in sight at two o'clock.

When Ali arrived the next day he told us to watch out for Limpet.

"We've already gathered that much!" I griped. "But since you've mentioned it, why do *you* bother with him?"

"Me? I don't know him."

"Huh? He isn't an associate of yours?"

"No, I've never even seen him before."

Confused? Welcome to the club! Either way nobody knew who the hell Limpet was, though it dawned on me that he must simply have walked in off the street as bold as brass, inducing us to guess he knew Ali. Of course this still left an unanswered question.

"So why did you ask him to join us?"

"You were talking to him, I thought you'd made a friend and had invited him back. I was being hospitable."

"Well can you go back to being a dour, unfriendly git," I joked.

Whoever mystery man Limpet was, at least he wouldn't be vexing us again, especially since we had left without him: to guzzle more gut-popping Pepsi. This time our bellies ached so much that by teatime the only food substance worth trying to swallow would be the sorbet. So we left Ali at one of the hotels (making calls) and headed back to the restaurant, hoping we would be able to walk off the gas — more than ever after my last performance.

On the way we passed a few men holding hands. This was nothing new to us, since it was the first 'other worldly' thing we had noticed here in Rwanda. It had no sexual overtones, but in their culture was a universal expression of friendship. *Que sera, sera,* as far as Shaggy and I were concerned, but having grown up in a town where you had to chew granite, not hold hands, to be accepted, it was still an odd thing to witness, even after five days. And I wasn't the only granite-chewer.

"I've got a confession to make," said Shaggy, staring at two gents walking past hand-in-hand.

"No need, mate," I cut in. "I've got your drift. Go on then, I'll give you five minutes. But if they don't fancy you, don't come running to me for relief."

"Very funny. Anyway, I didn't know whether to mention this or not, because I know you'll take the piss, but when we went for some chips yesterday, that Limpet kept trying to hold my hand."

An age later and I was still squirming with mirth at the thought of man's man Shaggy having to fight off Limpet, while at the same time hastily trying to think up a great comeback, but succeeded only with, "And did you?"

"Did I bollocks! Tell you what an' all, if that slimy toe-rag pops up and comes anywhere near my hand, he's going to get it."

"Marriage?"

By now we were both laughing.

"It'll be funny if we get to the restaurant and he's sat at the same table," I added.

"You'll definitely know he's at the table behind us, because a fork will zip past your shoulder and into your chips."

"He'd better not try sticking anything into my chips again, or I'll let him have it."

"All three inches?"

Our giggles had hardly come to a close when by chance we caught sight of Claver. Feeling generous, and using makeshift sign language as we had whenever we'd wanted to 'speak' with him, when we learnt he was on a break we volunteered to treat the put-upon teen to some sorbet, which he'd probably never had before.

Five minutes later and but forty paces from the restaurant...

"Holy shit."

Our tranquil walk was disturbed by the recognition of something unappealing before us. Alas, that certain something also saw us.

"Trust him to be late," replied Shaggy.

"Hide your hands," I joshed.

Limpet skipped over to us, so I promptly explained that we were going to the restaurant and couldn't stop to talk.

"If you want real ice cream, I know somewhere," he professed.

Although exceedingly dubious, given yesterday's 'comparable fries' twaddle and the ensuing proceedings, goaded by the only thing in the world that would have made us bother with him, we ice cream fanatics reluctantly followed the shady one for what seemed like miles, until we arrived at a place that made your typical greasy spoon look like the Savoy. I wasn't best pleased and, convinced they didn't serve ice cream, shot Shaggy a look that said 'someone is going to get hurt'.

Sure enough, once we were inside the shack, it came as no surprise to discover it didn't sell ice cream, or sorbet.

Even so, we were here now.

"Thanks for leading us here, Mbonyunkiza," I said, unsure of how to go about politely telling him he was less welcome than a stray dog at a game of skittles, so offered a plain, "We will see you later, bye."

"It is okay, I have some free time. I shall come sit with you."

Groan.

Unable to rid ourselves of Limpet (short of the increasingly tempting solution of smacking him one), we relented, and parked ourselves at the closest table and scrutinised the menu. We chose the only food they appeared to have beyond bushmeat and palm grubs.

"You speak the local language, Mbonyunkiza, so please order me some chips and gravy. Shaggy wants chips, gravy and rice, and order Claver the same, but I haven't much money, so if you want something you will have to buy it yourself. You understand that? You'll have to pay for your own meal."

Limpet nodded, and went ahead and ordered the food.

When it arrived, true to form there was a fourth plate, consisting of chips, rice and gravy, the latter of which was served in separate bowls, so that each person could pour at his own discretion. In the twinkling of an eye, Limpet emptied every last drop of his gravy on to his chips, and then, in what was almost the same movement, picked mine up and made ready to drink it.

'On your bike,' I thought (okay, perhaps something a bit stronger), swiftly reacquiring my bowl with an accompanying, "I think you will find that that's *my* gravy."

Plainly unmoved, Limpet just gave me that same sickly sweet smile he'd used the day before — then tried snatching it back. Luckily I was one step ahead of him and blocked his grabbing mitt.

"I—told—you—that—was—my—gravy," I said, through clenched teeth.

"I thought it was mine," came the lying reply.

"You've—just—poured—yours."

Limpet again beamed that stupid grin, but heeded the reprimand and went back to eating his own food — but I couldn't let it drop. Not only had the guy been a total ball-ache from the second we had met him, but once again he started making the most awful slurping noises (with food that he would no doubt try to wriggle out of paying for). No, I couldn't let it drop, and a few squelches later my fury rose, to the point that Shaggy sensed something was about to go down and began to chuckle.

"You are going to pay for your own meal, aren't you?" I enquired.

Limpet shook his head — ! — and then carried on slurping.

"So you're expecting me to pay for it? Even though I said I can't."

This time Limpet had the nerve to say he hadn't brought any cash (now where had I heard that before?), while again flashing that infuriating smirk. One that no doubt was supposed to say 'Oh well, no hard feelings' but actually registered as 'Tough shit'.

Oh really?

"If I'm paying for that meal," I resumed, "*I'm* bloody well going to eat it!" and I quickly snatched his plate: an action that caused Shaggy to burst out into his usual bout of wild hysterics, while non-English-speaking Claver just looked on stunned. But Limpet refused to learn his lesson and tried to retrieve what had been his plate.

"Get your hands off, it's mine!" I asserted, gripping the dish like mad with both hands.

So he made a big grab at *my* plate instead.

"Touch any single thing on this bloody table again," I snapped, my arms and hunched body now frantically trying to shield everything against Limpet's incessant grabbing hands, "and I'll damned well pull your balls out through your bloody gob!"

Shaggy was nigh-on dying with fits of laughter by this time, while a perplexed Claver felt compelled to ask Limpet what was going on.

"He wants me to ask why you did that?" said Limpet.

"YOU SERIOUSLY CAN'T ANSWER THAT YOURSELF? TELL HIM IT'S BECAUSE YOU'RE A FUCKING WANKER!!!" I exploded.

By now Shaggy's bellowing had gone into overdrive, but when Limpet yet again tried to take hold of my plate, he had to send in the reserves and desperately gulped for air. Finally realising I wasn't in the mood for games and categorically wouldn't be handing anything back, Limpet brusquely ended Shaggy's guffawing – by sticking his fork straight into *his* chips. Of course that was his death knell – touching Shaggy's chips was tantamount to strolling through a pride of hungry lions having first basted yourself.

I offered a 'he who laughs last' wave as a frogmarched Limpet went sailing out of the door and, thankfully, into posterity.

Tuesday, 20th June. After a lazy week in Kigali, it was time to depart. Our game plan was to catch a bus to Gisenyi, near the border, then walk over to the adjacent town in Zaire, Goma. From here we would be able to make our way to Kisangani, our Congo start-point. To do any of this we had first to collect our visas, so yesterday we had gone back to the consulate, as directed. Worried that the official in charge of transactions would make up some lame excuse and hold on to our passports unless we paid a bribe, to our surprise and relief, no further payment was asked for – possibly because the sweetener was included in the titanic fee.

With our passes now granted, all we needed to do was get to the relevant bus stop. It wasn't far and would have been only too easy to walk to, but Ali insisted he drive us there. He wanted to say goodbye.

"Keep these if you like," he said, producing a stockpile of Pepsi-sloganed T-shirts.

Being kind or merely helping to promote his business, I suspected a mixture of both. But hey – these were items we may need, for free, so I wasn't complaining.

A couple of profound handshakes later and Shaggy and I were off, in an African 'matatu' minibus. And whilst it was predictable that the driver fancied using up one of our surviving seven cat lives, given his Kenyan cousins, the stakes were also off in terms of the *matatu* getting a puncture – since the tyres hadn't a fragment of tread left on them – which is precisely what happened. At least they had a spare, although that was just as bald.

One way or another we reached Gisenyi, debussed, then walked to the border. Here, bureaucracy remained subjective – the duty officer wanted some additional money. However, we were starting to get the lie of the land by now and were certainly not in the mood to hand out unnecessary bribes, and with the line "we are good friends of the Hassans" ringing in his ears, the official eventually gave up and let us through. Moments later and we were across the border, our friend Ali and Rwanda now behind us, and all before us the country formally known as the Kingdom of Kongo.

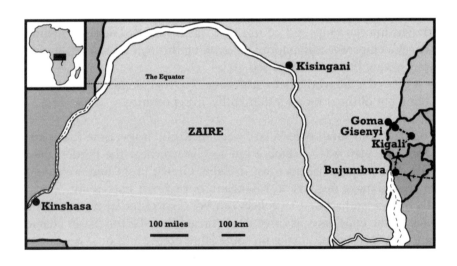

Chapter 5

KINGDOM OF KONGO

When the Portuguese first visited tropical Africa in the 15th century, they came across an assortment of tribes. Of these, the Kongo was by far the most widespread and dominant, and had set up a ruling state primarily named: The Kingdom of Kongo. Governed by their king, 'the Manikongo', economic muscle was achieved by dealing in ivory, hides and slaves — a rife domestic affair long before colonial involvement made things very much worse. Seizing the chance to increase wealth, trade was established between the two, and the next century saw The Kongo's empire grow and prosper. But a crisis loomed. With the need for slave labour outweighing The Kongo's capacity to supply, the Portuguese had long since started on their own method of raid-acquisition-extraction, a move that destabilized not only The Kongo's economy but also their authority. They were not happy bunnies. War was declared, but the evolved weaponry of the Portuguese was far superior, and The Kingdom of Kongo went into rapid decline.

During later years, Kongo territory was colonised and expanded; it was also renamed several times, even after its 1960 independence. We were there during its 'Republic of Zaire' phase, as termed by infamous dictator Joseph Mobutu. Who else would alter their name to *Mobutu Sésé Seko kuku Ngbendu Wa Za Banga*, which loosely translated means 'Mobutu, the all-powerful warrior who, because of his stamina and inflexible will to win, will go from conquest to conquest, leaving fire in his wake'? His plundering of the kingdom's finances accentuated Mobutu's despotism. A realm rich in resources, Zaire's people should have been far wealthier, but Mobutu had stolen almost their entire fortune, leaving the nation dirt-poor. Oddly, it could be said that this poverty is what helped sustain Zaire as an explorer's dream. Instead of half of the rainforest being destroyed by well-to-do citizens wanting to build monumental estates and endless infrastructures, it remained the mysterious domain whose remotest stretches were still essentially uncharted. The sultry climate, steamy jungles, huge mountains and prolific wildlife ensured that only those of Livingstone and Stanley's ilk would ever dare to tread its dangerous, and definitely deadly, path.

Enter those two nuggets Walker and McCarthy.

Goma could have been described as one of those old time Wild West settlements. That is to say it had the dust-covered roads and veranda-fronted buildings one would link with a Spaghetti Western. Another apt description would be 'somewhere you don't want to be', although that would depend upon your level of acceptance, the vibes you felt when entering the area, and also whether or not you thought you had been ripped off.

We did.

Of course I could have been wrong — some travellers I later spoke to idolized the place — but from the moment we arrived in Goma, I didn't like it. I couldn't explain why, I just sensed an evil atmosphere, and even the more laid back Shaggy voiced similar disquiet, which spoke volumes. It was also somewhat prophetic, as within a few short years Goma would provide the home for a mass Rwandan migration, which triggered an outbreak of cholera, closely followed by the start of the First and Second Congo Wars. Assuming we weren't psychic, the only tangible thing we could come up with was that while the people seemed courteous enough, they also had an unsafe aspect about them; many looked as though they would just as happily beat you as greet you. Whatever the reasons for our consternation, they were very real. Now add this unease to our worry regarding the police, rumoured to be the meanest sidewinders this side of the OK Corral, and no, we weren't cock-a-hoop. Accordingly, we decided to stay no longer than absolutely necessary, and the first person to do us what we considered a disservice was, of all people, a relation of Ali.

Prior to leaving Rwanda, Ali had told us of a relative living here, and wrote a note saying that Shaggy and I were friends and needed to exchange money with him, on the black market. Ali reckoned this would be the best way to avoid being conned. Oh yeah? Upon finding the address, we must have spent all of two minutes with his relative, who didn't do a very good job of concealing that he couldn't get rid of us fast enough, and gave us some right tatty old bills, the amount being rather less than Ali had suggested. To underscore our naivety, instead of asking someone else for directions to a pleasant but cheap place for the night, we stuck with the relative, who hurriedly pointed us towards what was most likely the first place of any kind that caught his eye, the nearby hotel Mount Goma.

Although suspicious, unaccustomed to the cost of living in Zaire we went with his recommendation and ended up with a room that transpired to be neither pleasant nor inexpensive, although the lizard nestling in the corner had no complaints — unlike a certain friend of mine.

"Cheap place, my arse. If you have to stay in a cesspit, you should at least be expected to pay cesspit prices," he moaned.

To qualify Shaggy's position, neither the lizard nor the state of the dwelling troubled us: we had of course anticipated more than modest accommodation in this region of Africa. Moreover, when it came to sleeping rough neither of us were spoiled brats — we had just done seven evenings on a concrete floor and been grateful for it. Likewise, fields and toilets, even an industrial bin once; I'd slept rough many a night. What did concern us was whether acquired services/products reflected the price, and for a handsome ten pounds (for this locale, a substantial sum) we had expected something with a little more, albeit rustic, charm. I guess the proprietor must have misinterpreted "with toilet, please" as "with lizard, please". To rub salt in the wound, when we ventured out that night, although not for long, we soon discovered that our scepticism was warranted — there were far better places for less than half the price. Thank you, Ali's relative.

Far in advance of our Goma arrival, we had already decided to hitch-hike the several hundred miles to our Congo starting point. But there was an alternative. A doorway to and from Rwanda, Goma was also flanked by two tourist attractions, the active volcano Nyiragongo and the colossal Lake Kivu. The combination made it a town of particular significance, in that it had an airport and we could therefore catch a flight to Kisangani. Now that's a good idea, I reckoned, so put it to Shaggy, stressing we would have plenty of time for thrills and spills once on the Congo, and if it was adventure we genuinely wanted then shouldn't we include all forms of it? That meant incorporating a local flight. Of course the very notion of Air Zaire gave me cold shivers, but that was counterbalanced by what would doubtless be an equivalent amount of trepidation when passing through more Spaghetti Western communities. The tipping point was that the latter may well take four weeks, which on the back of all that hanging around in Kigali only intensified my impatience. Like a child waking up on Christmas Day, I wanted my toys sooner rather than later. But Shaggy wasn't so hurried and, stating he didn't want to miss out on what promised to be a go-getting leg of our adventure, attempted to avoid any comebacks by going straight for my jugular.

"Bet the jungle is littered with crashed planes."

But I was two steps ahead, and slotted home the *coup de grâce*.

"Bet flying is cheaper."

"Hmm."

I further emphasised that taking such a trip would be on the cards only if we proved able to acquire something low-cost, and preferably the following day. As I said, neither of us wished to linger in Goma.

45

With understandable reservations, Shaggy agreed to at least check out the tour operator.

The next morning we departed the hotel and arrived at Air Zaire's booking office fifteen minutes ahead of its listed 9am opening, to find it already had. In the window was a sign that said they dealt with flights to two locations only — Kinshasa, the capital, and our destination, Kisangani. We entered and I attempted to talk with the assistant in French.

"It is okay, I speak English," she replied.

"Great. Is there a Kisangani flight that we can get on today?"

"I don't know."

"You don't know if there are any spare seats?"

"I don't know if there's a flight."

"Oh, right. But there is a plane that goes to Kisangani?"

"Yes."

"You just don't know if there is one that we can take today?"

"No."

"Don't you have a timetable?"

"Not until nine o'clock."

Ah, the mystery unravelled.

We waited for half an hour, but nothing seemed to materialise, so I attempted to speak to her again.

"Any update with the timetable?"

She began sifting through some papers that had been in front of her the whole time, eventually casting her eye over what may or may not have been a timetable.

"Yes, it has just come," she replied.

I shot Shaggy a look that served as a gasp, then turned back to the assistant.

"So is there a plane going to Kisangani today?"

"No."

"What about tomorrow?"

"There is one on Saturday."

"So definitely not tomorrow?"

"I don't think so."

"And nothing on Friday?"

"I'm not sure."

"You're not sure?"

"No."

I gave up. My formal "Thank you" was soon joined by a whispered "We look forward to your next sentence with much zeal" aside, as we made our way out.

And so the decision between air and land was made for us, for unless we wanted to wait three days for Saturday's flight (no thanks) the only way was obvious. We had to walk, and try to hitch.

As per our map there were three possible routes west to Kisangani. The first option was to travel eighty miles southwards towards the city of Bukavu, where an adjoining road would lead us straight to our target. The problem here lay within our mooch the preceding night, which had taken us into a nearby pub — I should say 'saloon', given the Wild West verandas and mean-looking hombres we had moseyed past. Along the way, we had bumped into an English couple, who in their own words had told us there were "bandits" operating on the southerly route. To underline this, once at the bar a brief powwow with a local (gunslinger) drew only the same guidance: going thataway was bad medicine. As this was occurring just outside of Goma, when coupling it with our sense of alarm, and the rootin' shootin' police's bad rep, dagnabbit if we lily-livered city slickers didn't quit whistling Dixie and hightail it back to our doggone cotton-pickin' room.

Of the remaining two choices, the least dicey seemed to be to head in the opposite direction of the bandits, along a passageway that went north, then west, in a kind of loop. This, we figured, should secure us some form of lift. The other overland possibility was that we head straight to Kisangani, for our map indicated there was a westbound route that at some point joined the Bukavu to Kisangani road. The problem with this option was that, while the markings implied there was a thoroughfare, half of it appeared to be either disused or under construction — almost certainly scenario one, for it was no secret that Zaire's infrastructure had severely deteriorated since independence. What had, thirty years earlier, added up to 90,000 miles of passable highway was now only a sixth of that.

Whatever the facts about the westbound road, the upshot was that it seemed to peter out long before its destination, so may have meant traversing miles and miles of near-impenetrable jungle. Then again, psychologically speaking, 'as the crow flies' was clearly appealing. Now add the fact that we would be right in the thick of the rainforest, and you have a very attractive option to two fledgling trailblazers. Mulling over the preferences, we reckoned that, although the looped way was almost twice as long, it would in all probability prove to be faster, and no doubt less hazardous. Prudence triumphed: we plumped for the lengthy hike.

I must admit that I sometimes ruminate on how the direct route might have transformed my tale, but don't let me kid you, our chosen course promised one hell of an adventure. A journey that would take us over 600 miles of the worst kind of road, through archetypal places that included Nia Nia, Avakubi, Epulu, Mambasa, Apawanza, Komanda, Beni, Butembo, Rutshuru, Rumangabo, and past several of the most beautiful sights in Zaire. Chief amongst them was the Virunga National Park — two million acres of protected splendour, where the large wildlife roamed. By our calculations, this passage could take us anywhere from four days to four weeks, depending on the traffic, the weather, our conviction and will to survive. And, of course, good old-fashioned luck. But anything would be better than plane-waiting in Goma, so come 9:30am Shaggy and I were off down the beaten track, on the road to Kisangani.

The first part of that hike was instantly liberating. Once away from the city the soundtrack of engines and people was now usurped by birdsong and chattering monkeys. Better yet, the bad vibes vanished, replaced by a feeling of optimism, even though we had never before fully entered the African countryside. In this locality, that meant that we were close to the middle of the Albertine Rift, an ecosystem that spanned five countries and whose illustrious diversity of animals was eclipsed only by its visual finery — framed by a backdrop of various mountain ranges, its vast forestry of trees, vines, fungi and flowers was interspersed by verdant savannahs. And though blue monkeys, orange weaver birds and African violets all added colour to the occasion, the primary aspect was nevertheless green, the miles of leafy forest beyond climbing effortlessly towards wooded hills and mountains. This vision of Africa was soon rubberstamped when, nestling among sumptuous undergrowth and encircled by lolling palms, we stumbled upon our first Zairian mud hut, so stopped to take a photograph. At least that's the excuse we gave each other, for while we had been happy to soak up the scenery, the longer we went without gaining a lift, the ever-dusty, once-firm dirt road increasingly rutted, like the Apollo XIII astronauts some nineteen years beforehand, we soon found we had a problem.

Travelling in a far-off land can have its effects on a person. Most notably when the persons in question were bullish enough to assume that, since they had been in Africa eleven days now, and since they had already undertaken a few rambles with no ensuing complications, once the real journey kicked in, their one flask each of water would be enough to stand them in good stead until they reached a village, waterhole or stream. And even if this took them a while, they believed that any subsequent thirst would be easily coped with. Sure, they'd 'be okay'.

What a pair of categorically brainless dickheads.

In next to no time our every ounce of water had been polished off and, parched in the extreme, we both ended up looking like a right pair of sad losers — not least your author. While at one point Shaggy was trying to lick an annoying sweat droplet from his cheek, I decided to lighten our pickle by telling him that he resembled a robber's dog chewing a wasp, only my mouth was so dry it came out, "Oou ook ike a obber's og uhewing a aasp."

"Says Sloth from The Goonies," he croaked back, his similarly frazzled throat making him sound like he had chain-smoked from birth.

The harsh reality of our situation wasn't so much that we hadn't grown used to the climate, or that we hadn't realised our heavy loads would make a physical difference. Rather it was our inability to grasp that the *combination* of these factors would have such an emphatic biological impact. And with nature taking its course we continued to dehydrate quite badly, although any belief that this was as tragic as it got was soon put to bed. Far off down what could only be described as the most diabolically uneven road I had ever walked, a group of kids began trailing us, each of them determined that their "Muzungu! Muzungu!" would out-scream the ear-piercing 'fingernails down the blackboard' cherubs of Kigali.

Although we just about managed to cope with the 'let's perforate Johnny Foreigner's eardrums' competition, how long could we suffer the intensity of the broiling sun and our ever-worsening dehydration, particularly when in conjunction with our heavy bags, the straps of which cut deeply into our shoulders? As wearisome was a real sonofabitch incline, which seemed to last forever. Consequently, our turns to carry the weighty tent got slashed from fifteen-minute intervals to five. Yet on we strove, despite our other rising problem — physical effort's partner, mental exertion — and very soon things big and small started to play on my mind.

'Why am I lugging *two* bags? Why didn't I bring more water? Why didn't I wear my shorts? Why do I have extra footwear? Why did a polymath like Aristotle formulate Aristotelian syllogism and galvanise observational and theoretical zoology, yet never once explicate his nonage with Nicomachus and Phaestis? Hmm.'

Using grey matter I thought would prove futile under this burning bright sun, I soon sorted out one of my banes. Striking up a form of sign language with the children, I got one boy to carry my holdall — a ploy quickly reproduced by Shaggy with another. For his kindness, I gave my youngster one of the books I had with me, instinctively the only (heavier) hardback — even though it belonged to my local library.

Just as we were at long last reaching the crest of the hill, a great monstrous wreck of a truck stopped and we were offered a free ride. Considering people usually paid for lifts in Zaire, the freebie was an unexpected blessing, although I did wish that he had picked us up at the bottom of the rise. Thanking the children who had aided us, we reclaimed our spare bags and leapt on to the back. Then off we went, which, owing to the undulating road, meant bouncing up and down, and round and round. A bit chaotic perhaps, but it was fun, so when we looked across from our high vantage point at the multi-layered greens of the forest silhouetted against the dramatic blue of the sky, is it any wonder that Shaggy felt compelled to punch the air?

"This is it!" he shouted. "This is where the adventure begins! This is the Indiana Jones stuff!"

Although my mouth was horribly dry, and although my trapezius ached from having carried my rucksack, I still managed to remain my usual humble self: "Indiana Jones stuff, pah. This is Sean McCarthy stuff!"

And the truck rolled and bounced on.

Forty-five minutes passed and, despite the truck's impetus causing a breeze, we were closing in on the hottest part of the day – and my dehydration escalated accordingly, to the level that I began to ponder how long I could last before shrivelling away to nothing. Another ten minutes and I was really suffering, a despair that was augmented by the driver, who, rather than having parked at Rumangabo, the small town we had just zoomed through, pulled over five minutes past it and motioned that his leg of our journey had come to an end. My dry mouth notwithstanding, I managed to grunt a thank you, then gaped forlornly as he spun the truck around and doubled back, presumably to the centre.

Doubtless his act was one of generosity, but since his destination was also our best chance of water, I couldn't help but have one of those moments, like when, in the comedy film *Three Amigos*, the main characters are riding horses across the desert. Exceptionally parched, two of the three try drinking from their waterbottles, with the result that one of them gets only a spatter of droplets, the other a mouthful of sand. Beyond dejection, they look to the third amigo, who is now knocking back floods of cascading water, after which he then gargles and spits, before tossing his still-half-full bottle on to the sand, where the rest of the liquid slowly glugs away. The miserable expression on his friends' faces, apart from being immeasurably funny, I guarantee mirrored mine.

Not ones for back-pedalling, Shaggy and I were torn between a logical about turn and bloody-minded soldiering on, so we settled the matter by other means — we plumped for a third, less energetic, option. To our left stood the last few dwellings of the community, so we decided to try for water there. Well, that's what we would have done, if not for two details. Firstly, even though only shallow, the rare sight of a puddle, straight in front of us, looked far too inviting to ignore — despite containing what appeared to be chunks of bacteria below the petrol-looking surface film — and since the equally dried-out Shaggy was already dipping his waterbottle in it, I hastily went to join him. Secondly, while we still had it in mind to call at the houses, a passing local had noticed our plight and, by way of sign language, indicated there was a waterhole not too far up the road. Thanking the man as best we could, Shaggy and I dropped purifying pills into what little 'water' we had acquired (the length of time it took for them to dissolve was unbearable), downed the smidgen, slung various bags over our shoulders and, because we no longer needed them, ignored the houses and marched on ...and on ...and on ...and on.

No waterhole.

Argh.

After another half an hour's walking we were both tremendously shoulder-sore and our dehydration had become somewhat worrying. Pausing to rest, we became aware of two girls by the roadside with, of all things, a large crate of beer. These were for sale to anyone passing, and given that vehicles seemed to be on a sabbatical, I expect the girls' eyes lit up when we desiccated *muzungus* dragged ourselves into view.

We looked longingly at the 'treasure'. Had it been kept in a refrigerator it would have been impossible to resist. Unluckily for the girls, though, it hadn't, and past experience told us that imbibing alcohol would leave us even more parched in the long run, so we declined to buy one.

"Bloody typical," rasped Shaggy.

Thankfully our misfortune wasn't to last. I was in the middle of changing into my cherished Reebok running sneakers, getting ready for another long slog, when an open-topped Land Rover pulled up. Would we like to jump onboard? I rose to my feet and joined Shaggy in squeezing in amongst ten local hitchers, the cramped conditions counterbalanced by again not being asked for any money. Excellent.

Along the way some people selling numerous items stopped the Land Rover momentarily. Willing as I was to pay a king's ransom for fluid of any description, I was forced to dream on, but Shaggy and I did manage to offset our dehydration by purchasing a couple of juicy mangoes each. A portrayal of how fabulous their moisture felt against the aridness of my tongue, I can't even start to do justice to, and for a short while at least, we managed to curb our thirst.

The next time the Land Rover stopped was at a place called Rutshuru. Then the two men in charge stood down, and while the driver greeted four ferocious-looking cohorts, his similarly tough-featured colleague let on that this was as far as they were going. He also wanted everyone to pay a Z 1,000 fee, which came out of the blue, as we had been under the impression that we were on for another freebie – regardless of whether you paid at the journey's outset or its finish, the common policy concerning fares was that they were always negotiated at the beginning of the ride. Many drivers even carried a tariff chart, and more often than not the price would be higher for a foreigner, which I thought acceptable, although I couldn't say the same for my hard-nosed companion. Not that he could grumble in this instance, since everyone had been asked to pay the same. Moreover, the (two pounds) fee was far from earth-shattering, so when all the indigenous passengers began paying up, I naturally followed suit. But Shaggy point blank refused.

Huh? I couldn't believe what I was hearing and took another look at the six bruisers in charge, and my heart leapt into mode 'Captain Kamikaze'.

What planet was Shaggy on? Irrespective of whether the fee was or wasn't unreasonable, when contemplating the bigger picture it meant nothing. Not when we were so visibly outgunned. *And* this was their backyard – another picture perfect setting for a Wild West showdown (the dusty street and overhanging upper-storey balconies cried out for a gunshot, a moan, and the earthbound tumble of a bad guy at the hands of The Stranger). But my headstrong friend remained adamant he wasn't going to pay a penny, and climbed off the back of the Land Rover – and my heartbeat cranked up to 'Captain Kamikaze plus Bad Max'.

Cursing under my breath, I realised that this may be the end and, disregarding any notion of Queensbury rules, made ready to punch, kick and bite if anyone started a fight – or wail like a baby, if I thought that would save us. The other, arguably even better, option was to act as if I had never seen Shaggy before and when they begin laying into him, basically join them. Shaggy, though, was undeterred. Apparently oblivious to the possibility of bloodshed, he casually picked up his tackle and strolled off, which left me half-dazed, half-fascinated by his actions. However, as soon as it had become clear that nothing was going to happen, I quickly took after him and we made for the open road.

"What the hell was that about?" I asked, my heartbeat returning to some semblance of normality.

"They didn't say how much we would have to pay at the start, so fuck 'em."

"Oh."

To add to the adrenaline rush I'd just been put through, bearing in mind we were still craving water, my emotions went back through the wringer when in the next two minutes we came across a tap, only to discover it didn't work. Compounding the anticlimax, not far up the road the same scenario happened again.

Purgatory.

As it was, a local man had spotted our suffering and told us that there was a fully functioning well only a minute ahead. We'd heard that one before, but thanked the man anyway. We could have kissed his feet when we learned he was telling the truth. To be fair, I think the person who had tried to point us to the last settlement's water-hole was being sincere; we probably just misinterpreted his directions.

Under normal circumstances I would be forced to admit the well's water tasted like my perception of urine, but these weren't normal circumstances, and to our dehydrated palates it was nothing short of pure nectar. We drank until we thought our bellies would pop.

Replenished and resolute, we filled our bottles and, with fairytale greenery our backdrop, once more braced ourselves for the eternally bright sun, the treacherous road, and what for us was the unknown, and marched forward, ever onward.

Soon we were deep in the forest, its shrouding walls amplifying the air's stickiness, the scent of dampness blending with fragrances of flora, earth and wood, whilst the sound of rustling leaves, crackling brushwood, and squawks and howls and barks, grew exponentially. With the sensory upsurge came the sighting of more monkeys, birds and squirrels, although, unfortunately for us, this didn't include more vehicles. An odd few did pass by, but again, despite our best efforts to catch a lift, the handful we did see did just that, passed by. In time, the all-consuming sun and pain from our heavy loads became too much and we decided to rest. My second kitbag and the unnecessary length of my jeans had preyed on my mind for far too long now and, with the knowledge that I had an extra pair of denims in my rucksack, I grabbed my penknife and cut ruthlessly at the legs, converting them into a pair of shorts. Then I took hold of what was in the holdall (my standby pair of footwear and the large space-taking blanket Ali had given me) and gave them to an old woman watching intently from a nearby hut. In the absence of a sleeping bag, handing over the blanket was a moment of madness I would later regret. Especially since, for whatever reason, I had instead kept hold of a bold-checked formal jacket I'd needlessly brought, tucked away with my belongings. At that time, though, I felt only relief to be carrying just the rucksack, my holdall now folded inside. Psychologically, that made a big difference to me. In contrast, Shaggy, always reluctant to get rid of something he might possibly need later, refused to dump anything, although he did ease his own discomfort by changing into a pair of shorts.

We walked on, only this time our small amendments had somehow changed the whole ball game. The rucksacks still cut into our shoulders, the heat was still intense, and the walk still seemed as if it would go on forever, but now we had reached some kind of accord. We were also fast becoming acclimatized, which was fortunate, as the trucks had dried up for the day and we didn't manage another lift. We were quite content not to. The walk had become more than just an experience now. More than a dogged battle of wills. More than a necessity to get from one point to another. Now there was a sense of wellbeing, a capability to enjoy, a means to take in the surroundings, to soak up their beauty, to observe rather than see, to be part of the rainforest, to rejoice in its array of greens and browns, to be captivated by the creepers, the blooming ferns, the wild orchids, and the buttress roots that grew to the size of elephants. For sure, the walk had become more than an experience now. It had become a privilege.

There was something else magnificent about that particular forest, that particular walk, that particular day. Before we had left Rwanda a few people had mentioned their reservations about Zairians, but out there, in the wilderness of the north-east, on the open road between Rutshuru and the Virunga National Park, lived the most benevolent, pleasant people you could ever imagine. Men and women of all ages appeared from archetypal little huts that dotted the forest-clad route to echo warm greetings, and children would move shyly towards us before handing out various fruits and water, which we gladly filled up on. Oh yes, these lovely people were the very antithesis of the 'Give-Me' folk who would later blight us.

Despite the enjoyable hike and the kindness of the inhabitants, it was impossible to ignore a specific harsh reality of African travel, and one that proved to worsen the longer we stayed — anything that goes in at one end goes directly through and out of the other, and doesn't stop to admire the view. So much so that in expectation I started my journey with a mammoth sixteen pairs of 'grits' — my term for underpants — correctly assuming I definitely wouldn't have so many at the conclusion (one over-used pair).

At this juncture, we had just passed a small gathering of huts when the fruits I had recently eaten decided to reappear at the other end, so I quickly nipped behind a bush. Usually I would return to hear the much-told story of how an associate of Shaggy's was competing in a half-marathon and doing well, when he felt a pressing need to relieve himself. Not wanting to blow a doable personal best by diving behind a car or wall, he simply shit into his hand and then flung it across the road (so if you recall a big turd heading your way somewhere in the United Kingdom back in the 1980s, now you know why). Upon my return, however, there was no tale, only the sight of a panic-stricken Shaggy urgently upturning his possessions.

"What is it?" I asked. "What's wrong?"

"I think I left something when I changed into these shorts."

"Your blow-up doll?"

"I wish. No, my money-belt."

Nightmare. We had walked a good three miles since then.

Shaggy's search ended with our worst fear.

"Yes, I have left it."

Another look through his baggage brought only the same conclusion.

What to do? Common sense told us that if he had indeed left his belt it would have disappeared by now, and therefore endeavouring to retrieve it would prove to be a hopeless exercise. Then again, with the contents being so important it seemed we should at least attempt a salvage mission. So, to hurry things up, it was decided that I would wait by our backpacks whilst Shaggy scampered back to the scene of the 'crime'.

This last decision infringed a self-preservation rule once explained to me by SAS top brass. A fundamental rule that, when abandoned, helped terminate the life of one General George Custer at The Battle of Little Big Horn. The rule is straightforward: do not split your group when faced by an outnumbering opponent. But the several hundred pounds' worth of travellers' cheques, the passport, and anti-malaria medication, as well as other valuables entombed in that money-belt, rendered speed essential, even though, with the heat, humidity and altitude, Shaggy's lone progress would not be very fast. Moreover, any tribesmen we had run into of late had been nothing but friendly. So, regardless of an innate instinct for self-preservation, we forsook the golden rule, hoping that nothing of any significance would come of our separation. Sure, we would be fine. I watched Shaggy fade away into the distance.

I wasn't the only one.

By this time, the children who resided in the nearby gathering of huts had congregated close by and, once Shaggy had left, they began to focus their attention on lone Johnny Foreigner here.

At first they didn't know what to make of me. Was I a friend? Was I an adversary? Was I that Tarzan bloke's runt cousin? Who was I? As beforehand when walking, some children brought fruit as an offering, only these were too frightened to draw near. Admittedly, I could have appeared more affable and beckoned them forward, but I found the whole thing far too engrossing and just adopted a non-committal posture. Fighting a natural trepidation, the largest boy, who was about twelve, and like half of his number wore only a pair of frayed shorts, tried to bring his fruit over. But an older girl, I presumed his sister, clothed like all the girls we saw on our travels in a plain dress, wasn't so convinced and talked him out of taking the risk. Arguments began to break out among them, the result being that I became too amused to suppress a giggle. So I slapped on my warmest smile and signalled for the boy to approach. The change of tactic worked and, plucking up courage, the youngster edged towards me and — at arm's length — handed over the fruit.

I was unsure of my next move. Ordinarily I would have stomached the punishment of it going directly through me, but since that meant revisiting my friend the bush — where half of the children had now congregated — it wouldn't have been very private. Yet I wanted to show these people I was grateful, so braved the consequences and ate their gift. Fortunately it had no immediate ill effect, and in next to no time I had over twenty children crowded around me — still at arm's length, mind. Their timidity noted, for a laugh I'd occasionally shout "BOO", then cackle heartily as umpteen sandaled or bare feet took off every which way. Subsequently they would turn, see that I was laughing and tiptoe their way back, tittering like the children they were.

Two hours passed. No Shaggy. Some women returned from their fruit-gathering forest sortie, their apparel typical of non-city locales, meaning African wraps and sarongs, while those with babies carried them on their backs via their binding (no maternity leave here).

The lady with the biggest smile, a full-bodied, impressive-looking woman I estimated in her mid-thirties, came straight over to me and without so much of a "Who on earth are you?" greeted me in French and shook my right hand, her left hand clasped to her forearm. At the time I had no idea this was their sign of respect, but I copied her action anyway, and with my own titbit of French relayed the situation, which, for whatever reason, only made her laugh (if her French was anything like mine, between us she may well have heard: "I wait for my dwarf, who is sniffing his limousine and oiling the backend of his left didgeridoo"). She then took me by surprise, pulling herself to me, flinging her arms around me, kissing me on the cheek and telling the children she was claiming me for herself. They all gave a great cheer, her friends whooped, and I winked at my captivated audience – in spite of the fact that for all I knew these people were cannibals and I was about to make a refreshing change to the usual Zairian pot roast.

Soon more women returned from their labours in the forest and 'my' woman explained who I was, then moved off with them into the village. Staying put, and alone with the children again, I decided to take out my notebook and, so as to describe where I had come from, drew a map of the world. Looking around I noticed that one of the smaller boys had a somewhat rotund belly and put it down on sketch. I then held the drawing in the air and pointed at the youngster, upon which everyone began roaring with laughter. Everyone, that is, except the boy, who let out a full-sized scream and ran off shrieking into the village. Of course this worried me, in particular when My Woman re-appeared with some men, and I wondered if I had taken away the kid's spirit or something – so would now myself be taken away (and pot roasted). Thankfully, their arrival was nothing to do with the boy; the first man to reach me shook my hand and invited me into the village for some food. Again I explained that I would have to wait for my friend before going anywhere, but vowed to oblige the man once Shaggy returned.

If he returned.

Time ticked by and still no Shaggy. Although I always had at least one child hanging around me, everyone else came and went (apart from the young boy whose 'spirit' I had taken – he avoided me like the plague). The most notable of these was a slim six-footer dressed in a smudged casual shirt, old trousers and sandals; it was the man who'd invited me into the village, a forty-year-old father of nine who, in my ignorance, astonished me by having the ability to speak not only Swahili and French but also pretty good English. Then again, I guess that would be only fitting for someone who had also introduced him-self as the chief, no less. Now that we were on good speaking terms, and given that the sky was becoming darker by the minute, before he went back into the village I took a chance and asked if it were possible for us to stay the night. Since I felt him to be a welcoming, generous man, I wasn't surprised when he said we could.

It was dark now. Darkness always falls at about 6:30pm in Central Africa, but a strong moon coupled with light coming from fires inside the village enabled me to catch sight of the surroundings. Suddenly there was a hullabaloo among the tribe. Then I heard a familiar voice. It was Shaggy, walking with a young man from another village, and somewhat incredibly the object of his departure.

Our being separated had paid off ...for now.

Six cat lives left.

"I've got the belt!" he yelled excitedly. Of course the villagers had little idea why he was so enthused, but empathised with his delight and clapped and cheered and patted him on the back as he drew near. "This lad's been ace," he added, pointing to his chaperon. "He saw me looking for something, reckoned it was the belt and brought it back from his hut."

"That's nothing, mate," I responded, and gestured to My Woman, now clinging to me again. "I think I'm getting married."

Shaggy beamed, but in a mumbled aside he confessed his rescuer wasn't entirely without lightness of the fingers – whilst his travellers' cheques and other valuables remained, his matches and lighter were missing.

"He probably hadn't a clue what those travellers' cheques were," said Shaggy, "or I'd no doubt never have seen them again. Not that I would have bothered. When I was going back for the belt I honestly didn't think I'd find it, and I thought, 'Bugger it, it will just add to the story I'll have to tell'."

"Funny that, you wouldn't have minded losing your passport and a few hundred quid, but if you smoked you'd be doing your nut over those thieved matches."

My chum emitted his usual chortle, but nonetheless believed the missing items were the least the young man was entitled to, so asked me to give him our trifle of pooled change. Feeling rather relieved myself (while Shaggy's lost money might well have enhanced our tale, naturally I'd have handed him half of mine), I had little complaint in disbursing what amounted to only one pound's worth of zaires. But the offer was refused.

"He wants no money," the chief translated. "It was his pleasure."

Benevolence occasionally knows no bounds. Who knows, though unlikely, maybe he was aware of what those travellers' cheques were.

Still aiming to reward the young man, I rummaged in my rucksack – thirty sets of inquisitive eyes peering and 'rummaging' with me – eventually pulling out what I hoped he would accept "as a gift, not a payment", I told our interpreter. The chief duly translated, and just as they had with Shaggy, the moment the young man accepted this new offering the villagers all clapped and cheered and patted him on the back. A few handshakes later, Shaggy's knight in shining armour vanished back down the road, his once sparsely covered body now proudly adorned by a far too large, and useful after all, bold-checked formal jacket.

With a forty-strong highly excited entourage in close attendance, the chief escorted us into the village, which resembled a children's story book depiction of 'deepest Africa': a modicum of grass-roofed huts arranged around a flattened patch of earth that nestled cosily among sentinel trees. Here, we accepted their kind offer of cooked maize cobs and haricot beans, and while this was being prepared Shaggy and I exchanged pleasantries with the chief, the questions on both sides kept fairly trivial. On our part, this could be construed as blowing a great opportunity to glean knowledge of local culture, but in our defence I have to say we were more worried about accidentally offending our hosts, so just kept to "How many children have you got?" etc. Besides, the food was almost ready, and soon we were being asked to sit ourselves on a couple of wooden chairs which the villagers had positioned next to a hut. Once we were seated, in a semi-circle all and sundry gathered around us, while the chief's wife (as it turned out, My Woman) fetched the meal. I had never eaten plain haricot beans before, only the sauced 'Baked' version, and after trying what there was of their flavour I decided I most certainly didn't want them again, particularly if accompanied by burnt-to-a-crisp maize cobs (I was gagging to introduce them to the subtleties of boiling). However, desiring to be anything other than discourteous in response to the profuse humanity being shown to us, and because Shaggy couldn't bring himself to eat much of the meal — obviously not as resilient as yours truly — protocol helped me force them down.

Keeping to his sleepover promise, the chief proposed that we stay in his hut for the night — he'd instead sleep with My Woman in hers. Accepting the offer, we decided to repay everyone their goodwill and, despite already feeling very on-the-spot, totally abased ourselves by singing 'Frère Jacques' and 'Three Wheels on My Wagon'. I have no idea what prompted that (Shaggy!) only that for both parties it had its drawbacks. For their part they had to put up with voices that would distress even the deaf. For us, midway through the last effort, we had to suffer the humiliation of everyone becoming so bored they started chatting to each other. And so, feeling even more ill at ease, once the songs were over we let it be known we were ready for bed.

Complying with our requests, the chief shooed everyone away and led us to his hut, which was precisely as one might envisage it: a clay-covered rectangular-shaped abode with a thatched roof, its sole room measuring roughly seven feet by nine. Our host opened the wooden door, ushered us in and wished us goodnight.

We entered torch in hand, and once inside my nostrils were filled with a strong aroma of earth. It wasn't unpleasant and reminded me of playing with mud when I was a child. Looking around, to our right we saw a 1950s-style bicycle, three chairs and a box full of simple clothing, whilst in front of us a little shutter, and on the left a small bamboo bed. Beyond it, inscribed on the partly crumbled walls, was some faded, inscrutable wording, whilst the low ceiling was daubed in a strangely eerie leopard effect. We put down our bags, squeezed onto the bed and turned off the torch. A minute later...

"Tell you what, Sean. Do you know what all those markings are reminding me of?"

"Go on."

"That scene in An American Werewolf in London, when they find that pentagram on the wall."

"Let me get this straight. We're in the dark, in the jungle, and you are bringing up werewolves?"

"I'm just saying that it reminds me of it."

"What a shame they didn't draw some fluffy bunny rabbits."

"Do they have rabbits in Africa?"

"Of course."

"Here, in the jungle?"

"I don't know about here."

"Bet they've got werewolves, though."

"Any chance of changing the werewolf theme?"

It went quiet. Another minute went by, then...

"Hey, Shaggy."

"What?"

"Was it a full moon tonight?"

Whilst our banter had been meant as nothing more than that, we weren't so far off the mark when it came to the villagers — we hardly knew them, after all. On that basis, despite their clear cordiality, my reasoning told me to stay on guard for all possible outcomes — were they leading the Capeless Crusaders into a false sense of security? Owning the sort of self-preservation instinct that in later years would serve me well in the security world, now in the wilds of Africa I didn't need reminding that shit happens. Ethnic warfare, lions, diarrhoea — the need to leg it was a constant possibility. For that reason, I asked Shaggy what his assessment was. Although the lucky beggar had got prime position on the bunk (my body adjacent to the doorway, he was therefore guarded against spear, machete or werewolf attack), I knew

Shaggy held much the same intuitions.

"My old man always says never trust anybody," he answered. "So while I'm pretty sure everything's okay, let's put it this way, I've got my fists clenched."

"I've got everything clenched."

"Good, no farting from you then."

"I wouldn't count on that."

Prior to our now-impending werewolf doom, the night had been sublime. I had never seen stars so prominent and the fireflies were a joy to behold, so it was something of a pity that we were stuck indoors and not gazing skyward. Yet, between the restricted environment and the sound of the chief bonking My Woman half the night, I found it difficult to get to sleep. Adding to my insomnia was a strange scraping noise that recurred only too frequently, which I supposed was some form of animal shifting around. Disturbingly, my guess was a snake. Whatever it was, the snake noises had come predominately from right beside me (jammy Shaggy on the other side, still conveniently guarded by my body). Indeed, the snake was so close that every time I heard it move, I would leap up and switch on Shaggy's torch, but I unearthed nothing.

The following morning, waking to appreciatively find that I hadn't become a pin-cushion to a serpent's or werewolf's fangs, I was tickled when I discovered the peculiar sound I had been so flustered by had been caused by a pet guinea pig.

Before we left, Shaggy handed the chief one of his shirts and I gave his eldest son — the boy who had handed me the fruit — a pair of dazzlingly coloured Tom and Jerry boxer shorts. Everyone laughed and pointed and jigged up and down as he joyously paraded around in them, for they were far too large and in this setting looked acutely bizarre.

Many handshakes later, we were back on the open road, one of eastern Zaire's key trading routes — an appallingly unkempt, bumpy, backwater lane that wound its way through some of the most glorious scenery you could ever hope to see.

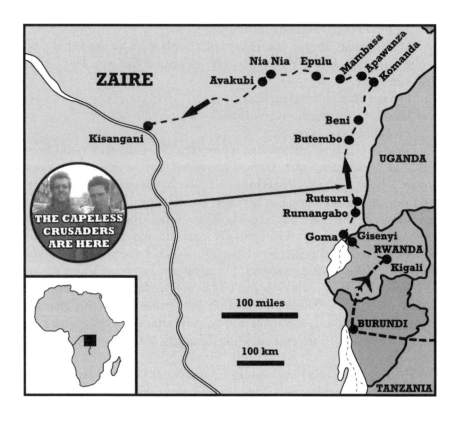

Chapter 6

THE ROAD TO KISANGANI

By now we had become accustomed to the weight of our rucksacks and were quite content to be walking among the mélange of colossal trees, heathers, groundsels and ericas. Many villagers came to the side of the road for a nosey, or to say "Jambo" (hello). Some just laughed. Then a teenage girl with a gleaming smile and matching dress approached Shaggy and, using sign language, insisted she carry his spare bag for him. Happy to let her, she walked with us for a spell, laughing and joking with the on-lookers in their native tongue. We were unable to grasp the specifics of the conversation, but it was unmistakably full of *joie de vivre*, so Shaggy and I joined in with the festivities, and beamed and waved at everyone.

After ten minutes the huts came to an end and, pointing to a sign up ahead, the teen mentioned something about being unable to carry on. So we said our goodbyes and made our way to the notice, which appeared to be written in every lingo but English, and the only thing we could translate was *Parc National des Virunga*.

"Well, Sean, this must be the start of the National Park."

"But it can't be. There would be gates and rangers."

"You'd think, but that's the sign."

"Suppose so."

Wondering how it could be possible to wander through a national park — what with all those huge, wild animals roaming around — we nevertheless took in a deep breath and walked on.

A half-mile further and our pace blatantly slowed. The sides of the meandering road continued to be littered with foliage and I had to strain my eyes to see beyond it. I had an unanticipated premonition, a feeling that a big beast was going to leap from the bush at any time. Then, without warning...

"Shit!"

"What is it?" asked Shaggy, the perturbation in his voice revealing the increased anxiety I had just caused him, his eyes avidly searching for danger.

"I'm not sure, but something very large moved over there, to the right."

"Shit."

"About thirty yards due north, moving at around seven miles per hour and weighing seven-hundred-and-fifty-six pounds, give or take a couple of ounces."

Realising I was only messing around, my comrade gave a sigh of relief, then came back with, "I didn't know one of your exes lived out here."

"Good one, Shaggy. Actually, this reminds me of that scene in An American Werewolf in London. You know, when those two hikers are walking across the moors at the beginning of the film."

"Now who's bringing up werewolves?"

"Just getting my own back."

"Tell you what, then, you can be the one who gets bitten to death. I'll be the one who ends up with Jenny Agutter."

"No way! I'll be the one who ends up with Jenny Agutter. I was the one who brought up the subject."

"Maybe, but I had dibs on her first."

"I bagsied her when I was ten years old."

"I bagsied her when I was two."

"Have her then."

"Okay, I will." There was a pause. "I'll have Miss World instead."

We both started tittering, then...

Abruptly the fun ended, as the sight of a real animal zipping across the road some seventy paces ahead took us aback.

"What the hell was that?" asked Shaggy.

"I don't know, but it was one mean-looking mother."

"Shit."

By the way it crossed, we deduced that it was some sort of monkey.

Then another one crossed. It was a monkey alright, only larger and bolder than any we had become used to.

I stared hard at the spot where the wild creature had disappeared.

"I hope they're nothing like baboons," I said.

If he hadn't before, Shaggy now looked apprehensive – giving me a 'why on earth is that?' look.

"I've heard they can be very dangerous. Have you seen their teeth? They're like lions'."

"Oh, brilliant."

Whatever the animal, both of us agreed on one thing: it wouldn't be such a bad idea if we moved back down the road fifty paces and re-assessed the situation from there.

"Trouble is," said Shaggy, "I don't think I can make it that far."

"Why the hell not?"

"Because I'm rapidly bursting for a crap."

I spluttered out a long snigger, then added, "So go and have one."

"With those mothers in the bush? I'd sooner shit myself right here!

I can see it now, I'll have just squatted down and some big hairy hand will come from behind and grab my nuts."

"Coming from your neck of the woods, you ought to be used to that."

Cross-legged, a giggling Shaggy managed to make his way back a little and disappeared into the undergrowth.

By the time he'd returned − nuts intact, I presumed − we made our boldest decision yet, and ventured on.

With eyes and ears on full alert, and penknives drawn and at the ready (really) we trod stealthily, Special Forces-like, down the centre of the road, thankfully passing the relevant area without hindrance.

Soon we reached a substantial barricade and a dozen or so rangers. It appeared that the sign we had passed made notice we were *nearing* the National Park. The 'killer' monkeys we had seen were common all over Zaire, park or no park.

"I think we need to top up our French."

"Quoi?" quipped Shaggy.

What a pity someone didn't have a *You've Been Framed* camcorder on us. It would have been hilarious to watch us executing our back to back/penknives at the ready/'walk down the rice paper, Grasshopper' manoeuvres past those innocuous monkeys, just in case one of them came out and waved at us. From here on in we would have to wait for a lift of some description. No one is allowed to indiscriminately walk through a national park, particularly if you are a couple of boneheads from England.

The day was exquisite. Anyone on holiday would have been justifiably content to copy Shaggy, who seemed glad to bask in the marvellous sunshine, but this was far from a vacation and I had no patience for such trivialities. With the Congo's call as powerful as ever, and the realisation that we were a hair's breadth away from spotting animals we had only ever seen in captivity, and viewing countryside as spectacular as anywhere in Africa, maybe even the world, I simply *had* to get going.

The clock ticked. Minutes felt like hours; when frustration kicks in, time gets distorted. Then a couple of vehicles passed by, but none that would pick us up.

More time passed. More frustration. I tried to duplicate Shaggy's lazing about, tried to enjoy the sun, tried to take my mind off the trip ahead, but then I would be up, kicking my heels into the dirt road, still champing at the bit to get into Africa's oldest national park. And still we waited.

'I tried to duplicate Shaggy's lazing about...but then I would be up...still champing at the bit to get into Africa's oldest national park'.

We had been immobile for a full hour before we got lucky. Right on the stroke of noon we were offered a lift that would subsequently take us on a seven-hour crossing, straight through the 3,000 square-mile park and on to Butembo, a major town in the North Kivu zone. For this courtesy, each of us was asked to pay Z 5,000, on arrival, which seemed a little costly, but we couldn't complain. Particularly as the pickup in which we were to travel was an excellent contraption, perfectly made for the ensuing terrain. It had an open back in which the passengers (we two, and five Zairians) sat, and were protected by bars wide enough for us to fit through but too small for a lion – a reassuring feature. The horizontal part of the bars, which generally would support a canopy, stood at about chest height and made good balancing grips for those of us who chose to stand.

What followed proved to be one of the most memorable rides of my entire existence, for the National Park was grandeur incarnate. An immense magical kingdom, its pulsating rainforest meshed stunningly with the vast golden Savannah of Virunga. And then, beyond the lush forests, grasslands, swamps and great savannah, beyond the treetops and the clouds, beyond the imagination of man, stood the legendary snow-capped Rwenzori Mountains – the 'Mountains of the Moon'. Truly astounding.

The sun now blazed down with such intensity that even the winds rushing past my face were hot. The trail itself was so irregular that I felt as though I was on a giant rollercoaster, only this one lasted for over a hundred miles and the view and aura of the whole occasion were quite simply without peer.

The first few miles had the little pickup engulfed by dense, over-hanging masses of sultry jungle, but the driver clearly knew the road well and drove it, at speed, to perfection. Then a myriad of butterflies filled the air with colour and elegance, fluttering towards us before being brushed past by the steamy wind. And on we went, revelling in the glory of a park that showcased an extensive diversity of landscapes – from savannahs and lava fields, to swamps, volcanoes and wood-land, Virunga abounded with visual riches par excellence.

In due course we were at the forest's edge, plunging headfirst into the open-plain world of elephant, giraffe, buffalo and lion, while the deep green peaks of the tree-clad mountains were at once a fantastic backdrop to the boundless yellow tract now set before us. And with it so changed the journey, for the ground was markedly flatter and we drastically picked up pace. Looking out across the unlimited miles of grassy expanse we saw warthog, then antelope, then topi, then hippo; all kinds of animals stopped and stared. And on we went.

Shaggy, standing in the back of the pickup.

The pickup had taken in what seemed like anything up to thirty miles before pausing at some kind of checkpoint. Immediately there was much animation in the vehicle.

"Look over here!" cried Shaggy, his exclamation displaying much gusto.

On the other side of the pickup was a gigantic baboon, far larger than anything I had ever imagined (encyclopaedias give their topmost weight to be around 90lbs — evidently they hadn't weighed this titan). 'Goliath' put on a bold front and sauntered over to the pickup. The next thing anybody knew the enormous monster had leapt straight into the vehicle ...and was sitting next to Shaggy! Everyone else had hastily abandoned the pickup the moment the brute had jumped in. Especially your author — sod that confronting a baboon malarkey, I was out of there at maximum warp. Shaggy on the other hand was either too mesmerized, too brave, too scared, or just too plain dumb to move. Fortunately for my inert buddy, Goliath's only objective was that of thievery, and he made a getaway with some fruit from another passenger's basket.

After, but only after, Goliath had disappeared, everyone laughed out loud (except the fruit owner, who pretended to find the whole event amusing but any idiot could see she was well cheesed off), even Shaggy, who went on to explain, "I couldn't get out fast enough. Then I saw it eyeing up my kit and I thought, 'No way are you having that!' So I grabbed my bag and sat on it."

"Bloody hell, Shaggy, I'd have shit myself."

Shaggy began to laugh. "Who said I didn't? Where's the loo roll?"

Once the excitement had died down, papers were exchanged and the roadblock opened. The driver turned the key, released the brake and started us back on the great African rollercoaster ride.

Soon we were approaching the end of the savannah. The pickup was travelling as fast as ever but for some reason the winds seemed to be getting hotter and hotter – to the point that it became somewhat oppressive. Wondering why, I suddenly noticed what turned out to be a massive grass fire miles to our left. A mile on and we were crossing the charcoal destruction where the fire had passed through. Copious amounts of vegetation had been devoured and yet, out there, where the savannah stretched for miles and miles and miles, it could have been nothing more than, as Shaggy put it, "a piss in the ocean." And on went the rollercoaster.

Now we were leaving the savannah and wound up into the mountains, once more densely occupied by thick green jungle. Up and around what seemed hardly a pathway the rollercoaster went. Up and onward, round and round, up and up. At appropriate turnings one could look out between the heavy plant life and gaze in awe at the seemingly endless lengths of savannah until it met the cloudless glare of the bright blue sky, and the contrast would be overwhelming. And on we went.

Eventually we passed over the emerald-coated hills and came to a village on the other side of the range. Here, the driver stopped for a break and went off to shop for fruits. The local who had been sitting in the front passenger seat came over and, with an outstretched hand, insisted I "pay now", rather than when the driver had decreed, which was to be at the conclusion of our lift. Doubtless this was a common trick, but unfortunately for Mr Crook, whilst I had made the odd daft decision during my Africa travels, and would do so again, handing money over willy nilly was a different proposition – I told him I'd pay the driver and no one else, after which he tried to make a case, but in time skulked off, unsurprisingly never to be seen again.

Presently we were back on the rollercoaster, but this time we were travelling through the rolling woodlands of Kivu, its milieu of broad-stemmed pink spurges standing shoulder-to-shoulder with the spiny leaves of orange-podded Encephalartos, always divine, always breathtaking. We passed through countless villages: Kanyabayonga; Kayna; Mulinga; Kasegbe; Matembe; Alimbongo, each clothed and enveloped in the picturesque green hills and trees that seemed to stretch forever. And when the people of the forest noticed us Johnny Foreigners they would drop their wares and shout for their friends to come and look. Then their pals would rush over to see what all the fuss was about, the routine chorus of "Muzungu! Muzungu!" stifled only whenever we ground to a halt while one of the other passengers exited.

One of these occasions is etched in my mind. Following the initial "Muzungu! Muzungu!" hubbub, the villagers had appeared *en masse*, bar one late arrival, who couldn't take in what the now-silent crowd was pointing at (should have gone to Specsavers). In attempting to grasp the situation, he proceeded to strut around the pickup like 'ten men', his arms splaying as though carrying invisible water buckets, accompanied by the equally typical 'I'm hard' pecking head. It was only when right in front of me that he became aware of my presence, whereupon his eyes metaphorically 'stalked' and, tail between his legs, off he shot. Everyone else, the villagers and those in the pickup, burst into laughter, and I held my hand out in a 'high five' gesture, which the nearest local cheerfully reciprocated.

The pickup departures continued until, come early evening, only Shaggy and I were left. Shortly darkness fell, and the once-hot air rushing through the bars turned to a deathly cold. I was wearing only shorts and a T-shirt and it became impossible to stand. Lying down was the best way of saving any warmth, but I was positioned on something that jabbed painfully into my side, which in time caused me to ache all over. I thought about altering my posture, or obtaining more clothes from my rucksack, yet the cold was so insufferable I just didn't want to move from my hunched position. Instead I bit into my lip, the mix of pain and cold so demoralizing it was all I could do to stop myself from drawing blood. The ride had turned into a nightmare.

As keen as I was to make Butembo, I wasn't alone in my anguish. Although the other passengers had gone, any surplus space had been filled by a plethora of merchandise loaded en route, hence Shaggy was unavoidably sitting on a metal box, and the pickup's violent bounces caused much throbbing to his backside. Then the temperature dipped again but somehow, in spite of the tribulation and mounting pain, we managed a brief conversation.

"Sod the budget," I said. "Once we get there I'm going straight to the best hotel. I want a comfy bed, a bath and a bloody good meal."

"Preferably steak," rasped Shaggy, so aching and frozen he ditched his usual penny-pinching and kept his concurring deliberately short.

We finally reached our destination at 7:30pm, but what agony. Despite having a population of 100,000, like most places in Zaire, Butembo had no electricity. It was pitch black.

To add to the disappointment, even with a concerted effort not to, we ended up in another hovel. No bath and rock hard beds as well. At least the two pounds charge reflected the lack of home comforts.

The dearth of facilities notwithstanding, my frustration came more from youthful ignorance and daydreaming of somewhere luxurious, brought on by the dreadful ending of our pickup trip — diabolical in comparison with Five Star lettings our room may have been, but it was no worse than we should have expected. Besides, we did manage to procure a reasonable meal, albeit eaten by the light of a candle, and even though we were slightly put off by the, although very friendly, proprietor. After taking our order, he exited to the adjacent room, upon which followed much squawking, then a sudden silence, and later our chicken meal.

I slept well that night, my general fatigue overcoming the rigidity of the bed, and was woken only once, briefly, by someone wielding a pillow and flashing a torch. Surmising it to be Shaggy, I mumbled an enquiry in his direction, subsequently discovering he was chasing a bothersome fly, so I went back to sleep.

Poor Shaggy. Whilst I had endured some discomfort that evening, I had finished the day with a satisfying meal and, although jaded, felt fit and healthy. Not so my sidekick, who had acquired fierce stomach cramps and complained bitterly about his now-chapped lips.

Friday, 23rd June. It was the morning after, and I rose ready and fully replenished for a good day's journey.

"It's surprising but I actually had a decent night's sleep. Did you catch that fly?" I was shadowboxing as I spoke. I felt good.

Shaggy was sat on the edge of his bed, torch in one hand, pillow in the other. He looked across at me. His eyes were red, drawn and had great bags hanging beneath them — his chapped lips so inflated one would have assumed yesterday's face-off with Goliath had continued in a dead-of-night, one-sided, losing rematch.

"Don't mention that bloody fly. I got to sleep alright, but then a buzzing noise woke me. It kept buzzing, so I got the pillow and torch and went after it. Then it buggered off and I was just getting back to sleep and the bloody thing came back. Anyway, I went after it again."

"What happened this time?"

"It buggered off again."

"And?"

"I reckoned I'd be getting back to sleep and the little shit would come back, so I sat and waited for it."

"And did it?"

"No."

"How long have you been sat up?"

"All night." He started to chuckle. "I just sat here praying it would come back so I could swat it. But it didn't. The little shit."

Shaggy's day was no better than his previous night. Along with his chapped lips, stomach cramps and dehydration, he began to suffer a painful blister. Worse still, he sustained the first bouts of an affliction that was bound to have an effect on him, since it already had me — excessive loosening of the bowels.

We had been walking for quite a while before my troubled friend was relieved of his blister torment by two huge trucks. That they were travelling in convoy from Kenya was a further bonus, since, according to the drivers, Kenyans always gave hitchhikers lifts out of kindness rather than for profit.

Heading towards Beni, approximately forty miles up the road, with only the solitary spare seat in each truck, Shaggy had had to sit in the passenger seat of the one up front whilst I followed suit in the other. Being so large, and the road so bad, these trucks dawdled along at a brain-deadening 'speed' of 8mph, although at one point my truck overtook Shaggy's (at the one feasible passing spot the entire way) at but 6mph! Hence, even though Beni wasn't half the distance we had covered the preceding day, we eventually took at least as long getting there as we had reaching Butembo.

Once safely at our destination, we thanked our respective drivers, debussed, and took stock of our surroundings. Oh dear. Were it not for a handful of vehicles, Beni's central thoroughfare of trampled dust and raggle-taggle rows of wood, plaster and clapboard buildings, all added up to another place that very much looked like it was awaiting the odd rolling tumbleweed and the leisurely ride into town of The Man With No Name — i.e. another Spaghetti Western settlement in the mould of Goma. The difference was that I thankfully didn't sense any bad vibes. Nor apparently did someone else: citing his ailments, upon arrival my too-lazy mate was keen to wait around until a truck bound for Kisangani passed by. The problem was, my urge to keep moving now bordered on fanaticism, and I insisted we walk on. To compromise, while Shaggy stood by the road waiting for a lift, I went round to every parked truck whose driver could be found in order to ask if anyone was heading north. If so, would they mind us jumping onboard? But no one was going our way. So we hung out by the road, both of us believing something would pass by, but come another half an hour, nothing had.

What now? If we had waited, even up to a day or two, it should have been possible to grab a truck heading in Kisangani's direction, yet I maintained we walk on. My philosophy was simple: if we were at some point able to cadge a lift at Beni, then that same truck would still pick us up later, should we be hitchhiking on the open road. Conversely, if for whatever reason no trucks were due for months, not walking meant we would be stuck in Beni. At least travelling on foot guaranteed we would arrive sooner or later in Kisangani, even if we had to walk the entire way. So walk we did, thumbs at the ready, eager to flag down anything that might pass us by.

Despite the sense of my theory, Shaggy continued to petition for hitching from a fixed spot, and I was in the process of re-explaining my (patently more sensible) way of thinking when our luck changed. A Portuguese gentleman in his mid-thirties and dressed in shorts and a T-shirt, offered us a lift in his brand new 'deluxe' four-wheel-drive.

Now we were travelling in style, and although the dead ringer for British actor Trevor Eve wasn't going far, only two or three miles, any disappointment with the lift being brief soon abated as fortune again smiled our way. Would we care to stay at his house for the night? For my part I was a little reluctant, as my inner spirit told me to carry on until I dropped, but I relented. There was only one more hour before dark anyway, and warranted or not I realised Shaggy's resolve had, of late, not been up to scratch.

Whilst the vehicle was a something of a giveaway, what we hadn't realised was just how affluent 'Trevor' was. Not until, that is, he spun into a sizeable coffee plantation and let on that the entire acreage, the manpower, the servants, and what turned out to be an enchanting homestead, with its own generator, were all his. A half-mile on and we came to rest in an isolated but spacious dusty yard, dotted around which were some outbuildings and Trevor's residence — a large, white, single-storied house.

Once out of the four by four, Shaggy and I followed our host up a short flight of steps — and into a world of clean sheets, good food, hot and cold running water, electric lights, television, and even a valet. What a windfall! From nowhere we appeared suddenly to have everything to hand. Our bedroom even had an en suite bathroom, which was the most welcomed facility of all. Bliss. Well, nearly, as there was one aspect of the stay that proved to be less than heavenly — while Trevor spoke French, he did so very quickly. And because our French was at best basic, we were hard pressed to comprehend him. Rather than appreciate there was a language problem, however, Trevor would become annoyed whenever he was asked to repeat himself. So we just nodded whenever he spoke, which seemed to appease him. But hey, who were we to object? We each had a hot bath and snug bed, drank a bottle of chilled lager, and attempted to absorb a foreign-tongue video. Who would have predicted that a couple of hours beforehand?

After a pleasant sleep on soft pillows, another relaxing bath, and a belly filling breakfast, it was time to go. While this could have been construed as a shame for indolent Shaggy, the worst aspect of leaving, as far as he was concerned, was the way in which it was effected – not by the plush car in which we had travelled yesterday, but by an open-backed pickup.

To return us to the main road, not only did Trevor have to drive a half-mile back along an extremely rough, pot-holed dirt track, but he also decided to cut a few corners, making the journey even bumpier. Unwittingly, Shaggy had consented to sit in the open-back section, whilst I, enjoying the comfy passenger seat, was told to fasten my seat belt. This wasn't because buckling up was a legal requirement (who would impose it?), but because Trevor fancied himself as a rally driver, something he'd neglected to show off in his new car.

So off we set, me all buckled up in the front, and in the back the unrestrained dupe Shaggy, sat on a hard corrugated floor, with only the sides of the pickup to hold on to. Which is precisely what he had to do – with all his might – as at speed Trevor proceeded to bounce his 'stunt-machine' in all directions. Oh what fun, as now and again we would BANG hit a mound or BUMP go over a crater. But Trevor was undeterred and, foot to the floor, would just look round at me with a nod and wink as if to say, 'How do you like that wheel spin?' or 'Brace yourself, here comes another gargantuan ramp.' With my seat-belt and protected sitting position, I revelled in it. Alas, not so the un-tethered Shaggy, who ended up being smashed all over the rock-hard metal back – on numerous occasions he almost bounced out of the thing altogether.

Twenty bangs and bumps later – Shaggy still flying through the air in the rear – we were again by the main route, and our chauffeur slammed on the brakes and violently skidded the pickup to a halt. Thanking our Portuguese friend for his charity, I undid my seatbelt and bounded enthusiastically from my secure comfort, only to witness a battered-senseless Shaggy crawling agonisingly from the back. Now bruised left, right and centre, my colleague still had the good grace to thank Trevor – although no more was he punching the air with his, "This is it! This is the Indiana Jones stuff!"

One more day's journeying and maybe we could be in Mambasa, a noteworthy milestone, as it was halfway between Goma and Kisangani and would prove to be a good incentive for both of us, particularly the waning Shaggy.

We walked and walked and walked. Three hours passed. Nothing. Again my friend swore he was suffering too much to continue, and we were in the process of debating how much of a break the big girl's blouse needed when fortune again sprang to our aid. Another huge truck was spotted heading in the direction we wished to travel. In flagging it down, we learned it was going to Bunia, which was to the north-east, not to the west as was Kisangani, but the driver was happy to take us as far as the crossroads at Komanda, some sixty miles. We accepted the lift and jumped onboard, consequently with the same agreement as Trevor's pickup. By this I mean that, because the truck was loaded to the brim with both passengers and commodities, one of us had had to sit in the front, the other the back. That it was I who again managed to opportunistically attain the seat next to the driver, while in the back Shaggy was forced to sit on a small bag of nuts and bolts the entire *eleven* hours, which he later admitted were the most torturous of his whole life, may appear to be the product of a hidden agenda on my part — especially since he'd already perched on a metal box through to Butembo, and of course there was also Trevor's pick-up — but I assure you it just turned out that way (cough).

The journey was a drawn-out affair and the hideous, undulating road hadn't aided Shaggy's grieving undercarriage any, although the sighting of pygmies, their males alone averaging less than five-feet in height, briefly cheered him.

Along the way, the driver had to stop occasionally to drop off or pick up and pack in various produce and passengers, and it was most likely one of these characters who added to Shaggy's growing list of grievances. Upon arriving in Komanda, he discovered his (borrowed) tent was missing.

Red with anger, blister-footed, lacerated-lipped, battered-bodied, numb-buttocked Shaggy demanded the entire truck be stripped so he could find it, but the driver didn't want to unload his many supplies until he'd made Bunia, seventy miles to the east, and closed his case by saying it was too dark to see anyway.

"I'll soon bloody well sort that out!" snapped Shaggy, tearing open his rucksack and producing his torch.

The driver again protested, but when Shaggy remained unmoved he instead asked us to accompany him to Bunia, claiming that only there would they be able to search the truck properly. To further the idea, he offered to waiver the fee for the extra mileage: a humungous wrong move. After eleven hours of having his arse mangled by a bag of nuts and bolts, Shaggy wasn't too keen on repeating the experience and, with figurative steam flying from his ears, reacted accordingly.

"WHY THE FUCK SHOULD I WASTE MY TIME TRAVELLING TO FUCKING BUNIA, PROBABLY PICKING UP A FUCKING HERNIA ON THE WAY, WHEN I'M ONLY GOING TO HAVE TO PAY FOR SOME OTHER FUCKING SHITHEAD TO FUCKING WELL DRIVE ME BACK?!!!"

I had got on well with the driver and couldn't help feeling sorry for him — although this didn't stop me from erupting with laughter — but Shaggy was having none of it and insisted, once again, that they move the entire cargo, or he would get the police (not that there were any). So they started to unload it.

Attempting to use logic, I assumed the tent would be located in a corner that had recently been covered with hundreds of bananas. I tried relating this but couldn't recall what 'corner' was in French (le coin, Sean, le coin), which resulted only in the crew staring vacantly at my "dans la corner", even though I was vigorously pointing *at the corner*. Yet each time I looked at any of the crew to get confirmation of what I was trying to explain, I'd just find myself being gaped at by some completely nonplussed 'dopey' face.

Frustration spilled over. Now it was my turn to lose my composure and grasping Shaggy's torch I brutally ripped open my bag, threw half its contents across the floor, then with a salvo of gratified laughter maniacally grabbed my French phrase book and tore open the pages.

There was no word for corner.

Dejectedly, I gave up.

Despite my failings and the complaints of the other passengers, Shaggy made the driver carry on searching until he got so bored he proposed to return our fare and call it quits. Whether the tent was still under some freight or had indeed been stolen, no one found out, as the vexed Shaggy decided to accept the deal and took back our Z 2,500 fare. Minutes later, the truck was reloaded and restarted, and we watched it melt into the night.

Once the truck had disappeared Shaggy began grinning.

"Why the smile?" I quizzed.

"Oh, I knew the tent had been stolen."

"You knew! Then why on earth did you make him shift all those goods?"

"I reckoned that if I kicked up enough of a fuss I'd get our money back. Worked didn't it."

"You crafty..."

With the truck gone and our pockets refilled, we looked around. Hmm, Komanda seemed familiar. Very familiar indeed. Ah yes, that's because it gave me the same sense of unease that I had felt at ...Goma.

Groan.

"Tell you what," said Shaggy, "have you seen the film Papillon?"

"Course I have. Steve McQueen on Devil's Island."

"Think of the parade ground."

I had a hazy recollection of Henri Charriere's eponymous hero on screen, but Komanda's central square, a plaza of compressed dirt and encasing single-storey, canopied units, did have some semblance of the Devil's Island image I had in mind.

"Oh yes, I see where you're coming from."

"Oh yes? You mean, oh no."

Double groan.

The sense of unease was heightened when a couple of locals began pestering us for freebies, although our anxiety was probably owing as much to the want of light — only a few campfires lit the village. Either way, it was time to make a decision, and although we contemplated walking on, it was decided that our best bet was to stay where some form of protection was offered. So we sat by the crossroads hoping to thumb another lift, but none materialised. Come midnight, we gave in and rented another fleapit, the worst so far, its decaying walls and lack of windows contributing to the stale air and B.O. stench, while the principal look of grime was compounded by the two ancient beds' half-sticky, half-crusty covers. At least the door had a reassuringly strong lock.

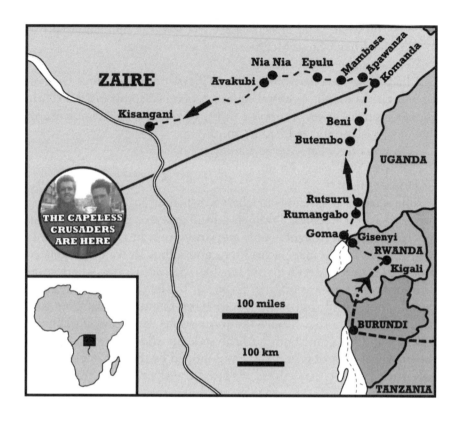

The map shows the route through ZAIRE including Kisangani, Avakubi, Nia Nia, Epulu, Mambasa, Apawanza, Komanda, Beni, Butembo, Rutsuru, Rumangabo, Goma, Gisenyi, Kigali in RWANDA, and onwards to BURUNDI, UGANDA and TANZANIA. An inset shows the location within Africa, labelled THE CAPELESS CRUSADERS ARE HERE. Scale markers show 100 miles and 100 km.

Chapter 7

THE QUIET MAN

In addition to a mutual though diminishing-by-the-day ignorance of Africa, as friends Shaggy and I naturally shared a number of interests and traits. Rainforest adventure aside, the interests included a love of sports, books, movies, debate, and also humour — whether bawdy or innocent, adult or adolescent, our humour ranged from wicked and exceedingly adult in content, to childish sniggering; Shaggy was always giggling. Our shared traits on the other hand included sheer bloody-mindedness. Another obvious similarity was a tendency to swear, and whilst I don't excuse Shaggy or myself for our bad language — toned down here, to tell the truth — it is an element common to many like-minded men when away from the general public, in particular when as young and full of beans as we were. Add this to our being in an environment that wasn't exactly a haven of creature comforts, and any habit you have becomes amplified.

A third shared trait was an offshoot of the last two — a temper. Don't get me wrong, we were both very easy-going people who could be pushed and pushed without a reaction, but push that one time too often and, as chip-thief Limpet and this last driver had discovered, believe me you are going to know about it. Now bear in mind that even the closest of friends disagree every now and then, so when two stubborn alpha males find themselves plonked in a setting to which they are unaccustomed, blood may boil. In England, Shaggy and I had lived under the same roof for over a year and had never had one dispute. In Africa, where our emotions were taken right to the wire, it took just over two weeks for all that to change.

The altercation began when Shaggy again insisted we stay put. He said he was struggling with his chapped lips and blistered foot and wanted to hang about in Komanda for a lift. My itchy feet, however, wouldn't let me wait around doing nothing. Not when we could be walking, and certainly not for something I regarded as trifling. Did he have a broken leg? A punctured lung? Malaria? What is more, I knew from our training camp days that whilst Shaggy had a Mach One turbo-boost starter kit to what was a very formidable V8 engine, this was counterbalanced by his tendency to regularly switch off his motor altogether. Hence I expressed the opinion that he was just using his afflictions as an excuse for being a "lazy twat", which kind of put the cat amongst the pigeons.

A slightly ticked off Shaggy launched a retaliatory tirade, but I was having none of it, and to settle matters I simply upped my gear and set off — adding the odd "diddum doos" and "aww, has poor baby got blisters".

Incensed, Shaggy groped for his bag, dragged it on to his back and scampered after me. Discontented with the outcome, he pressed his case.

"Why are you so pigheaded? You should consider every option."

"I have considered every option. Yours is a load of shite."

"You didn't bloody well consider it long."

"It was that shite, I didn't have to."

"This blister's killing, you know."

"It's a blister, not a fracture. Get over it and stop moaning."

"What! You're the one who's always fucking moaning."

"Yeah, and don't you just keep fucking moaning about that."

The spat continued, each sentence laden with more venom, more antagonism, and more lewd words, until finally it concluded with the inevitable.

"Right then, Sean, when we get to fucking Kinshasa you go your fucking way and I'll fucking go mine!"

"Too fucking right!"

At that precise moment a vehicle rolled into view, and with it the argument was long forgotten and never mentioned again.

We never bore grudges.

The truck that rolled towards us did just that — rolled. This was due to the excessive overloading of merchandise, and to cap that, a throng of Zairians had somehow squeezed into a holding pen on top, like sardines in a tin. Thinking our chance of a lift more improbable than Albert the Bore winning a personality contest, I lamely dropped my thumb. But, hold on, what was this? Taking us both by surprise, the truck pulled over. Surely we couldn't fit aboard this lumbering mass? Not only that but, on this undulating, pot-holed road, it would also be far too risky to travel atop such a contraption. Yet we were wrong, for the closer of two men sitting on the passenger side hung his head out of his window, plainly expecting us to start the negotiations.

"Où allez-vous?" I asked.

Apparently they were heading to a place called Isiro, in the north, but we could be dropped off where the truck turned, at Nia Nia.

"Combien de kilometres?"

"Cinq cents," the man answered.

500 kilometres equalled 311 miles. So far so good.

"Combien zaires?"

Unlike the "pay now" fraudulent passenger on the ride through the Virunga National Park, this man was evidently part of the team, and he proceeded to take out a tariff chart. The fee would be Z 5,000 each – in advance. Ten pounds was another fair old sum, but then again the probability of obtaining another lift seemed low. Even if someone else did come by, for all we knew they might want to charge more, and anyway, covering 500km would mean we would have to travel only half as much again and we would be in Kisangani. I took another look at the truck, which was a ten-tonne, six-wheeled Isuzu. Commonplace in Africa, they had a reputation for being robust and reliable, but this one's goods were packed ludicrously high and, atop the cockpit, in a 'sardine tin' holding pen, sat ten locals, six of whom were very generously proportioned women.

"What the hell," I said, looking at Shaggy for conformation and getting an acquiescent shrug back.

After paying as requested, we somehow burrowed in amongst the disgruntled passengers, all audibly grumbling at the thought of more sardines crushing into the tin.

The driver, a stocky Zairian in his mid-thirties who appeared to be mixed-race due to his more European features and lighter skin tone – and who, for reasons that will unfold, I shall refer to as 'Duke' – slipped the gearstick into first and, with a heave and a splutter, the Isuzu chugged off down the potholed backwater road, which was even more churned up and dangerous than the one to Komanda. So much so that we constantly tottered all over the place; on many occasions the truck literally tipped over on to its outer wheels, leaving everyone to pray for a brief moment that it would fall back in the right direction. Thankfully it did, and we passengers would look knowingly at each other, unanimously gasping huge sighs of relief.

As if that wasn't bad enough, in various spots the 'craters' were so bad that it was impossible to get out of first gear, which only fuelled my impatience. I wanted to go–go–go, but my frustration found new heights when Duke stopped off at Apawanza. Powerless, I watched in horror as he dismounted the truck, placed a rug on the floor, himself on top, then fell asleep – for three hours.

Argh.

To add to the frustration, a quick scan of the area rekindled the wrong memory.

"We're back on Devil's Island," I said to no one in particular.

Even so, with the arrival of necessity, and the reassurance that we were with the crew, I told myself to deal with it and went for a walk.

'Zaire's infrastructure had severely deteriorated since independence'.

Presently, I asked a local the whereabouts of a toilet, but he declined to tell me unless I put Z 100 in his hand (Shaggy later told me that I should have just shit in it). Sadly for him I was here as an explorer, so kept my cash and soon found relief in a nearby hut — I assumed it was a lavatory due to the hole in the ground. If not, my apologies to the owner. Thereafter I continued my ramble, but Apawanza was unfortunately no more than a hamlet, so all of five minutes later I rejoined Shaggy for a mind-numbing three-hour stint of marking time.

During those long Apawanza hours we just lay around, under the scorching sun, listening to the heartrending screams of a lone monkey enclosed in a cage, not twenty paces from the wagon. Its crime: being caught. Its punishment: solitary confinement, probably for life.

Finally Duke woke and remounted his vehicle, and we were back on the road to Kisangani.

We had travelled quite some distance and had long since passed Mambasa, the halfway point, when Shaggy forecast, "If we get a move on we'll be in Nia Nia by twelve. That means we'll be in Kisangani by Monday night, with a bit of luck."

The Isuzu instantly blew a tyre.

Now then, in the 'normal' world with which I was familiar, at this juncture one would merely substitute the defunct tyre with the spare — or call the breakdown service. Of course this was rural Zaire, so out came a 'quick fix' repair kit. This meant that, as well as the obvious fiddling about, we would also have to wait for the glue to dry. The whole shebang took no fewer than *eight* hours to fix. Eight painfully boring, watching-paint-dry hours.

Aaaaaargh.

Throughout that seemingly endless period we were, for part of the time, gratefully relieved of our boredom by a passing, well-travelled local who, belying the appearance of his tattered trousers and shirt, luckily spoke several languages, including English. Being something of a linguist wasn't the fifty year-old's only boast, for he also claimed to be a gold prospector, which straightaway made two Englishmen's ears prick up — especially those of Indian Jones wannabe Shaggy. Upon hearing that 'Goldfinga' was every bit as intrigued by our presence, he readily kick-started what turned out to be a lengthy chitchat, which had us relaying not only our Congo plan, but also an account of our lives to date.

"Growing up my only interest was sport," said Shaggy, closing out a dialogue of his upbringing and why he didn't take A-Levels, strange as it was to hear anyone talking of such things deep in the jungle. "I did a few meaningless jobs but was then offered the chance to become a full-time athlete, which was how I met Sean."

In telling his story, I have to say that Shaggy sold himself a little short. After leaving school he had actually blended his "meaningless" jobs with the obtaining of sports-related qualifications – orienteering, gymnastics, swimming, weight-training, you name it. He was even licensed as an Oriental Concept of Fitness Tutor, whatever that was, before eventually becoming a track instructor at his local athletics club. Nor did he just coach; Shaggy participated too. But his preferred sport of running overshadowed a great natural ability in other fields, at one time or other reaching competitive standards in both football and cycling. As a matter of fact, when I first met the then nineteen-year-old Shaggy, not only was he a county 1500m champion (and threw so fluently with a set of 'manky' – one of Shaggy's pet adjectives – darts that I often wondered how he might fair with bespoke ones) but for a laugh he would also soon enter an inter-counties javelin tournament and, with no prior training, win.

Shaggy's finale signalled my turn to spill all. Without wanting to shorten my account (we were trying to kill time, after all), I still glossed over a whole slew of specifics. Of how, as the son of a former RAF serviceman, I had spent toddler-time in places that included France and Holland. Of how over later years I had mixed numerous college courses with a range of backpacking episodes and meaningless jobs of my own. Of how, like Shaggy, I had indulged myself in a number of sports during my life, although it was athletics that had brought us together, in the shape of 'Bournemouth'. Named after the town we had at the time moved to, Bournemouth was our shorthand for the athletics camp that we had been part of. The brainchild of a senior British athletics coach, Jim Arnold, the four-year project had started in 1984, "with the intention of getting a few half-decent athletes to live and train together, in the hope that at least one of us would make it to last year's Olympics," I told Goldfinga.

"And did either of you run in these Olympics?"

"I wish," said Shaggy. "I was only there for a couple of years. I kept getting injured, so I went back home and ended up working at the local sports centre."

"I was booted out after fifteen months," I confessed.

"Booted out? As in, asked to leave?"

"As in, he was shit," joshed Shaggy, which caused much chortling between the two of them, though he in time got round to appeasing me. A "personality clash" had been the real reason.

Killing time aside, the good news concerning Goldfinga's presence was that he also helped instigate a better connection with our trucking companions. Although we had previously had a tad of discourse with a couple of them, by this time translations were being asked for, and with Goldfinga's assistance we thereby found ourselves drumming up a more in-depth conversation. Apart from passenger-seat financier 'Barclay' — a skinny thirty year-old who underlined his position by carrying a portfolio — up until this point we had been unsure as to who were or weren't actual crew members. It transpired that Duke's team included two engineers: twenty-eight-year-old head mechanic 'Ferrari' and his equally short and stocky twenty-two-year-old helper Jerome, both of whom had taken turns sitting up front with Barclay. There was also Jerome's little brother, Pepe. Shy at first, Pepe became more gregarious throughout the journey, as you would expect from a fourteen year-old. This left eight actual hitchers: the six generously proportioned women (who kept to themselves, so we never really got to know them) and two twenty-year-old students, the always smiling 'Hitch' and his slight, even shorter pal 'Ike', who were heading home to Isiro. I came to look upon them as being part of the crew.

The upshot of the enhanced chat was that a mutual harmony was struck between foreigner and crew. A solidarity that, once Goldfinga had gone, was sealed by an exchange of gifts. Hitch and Ike handed Shaggy and me a loaf of bread and some sardines, whilst yours truly did an over-the-top impression of the singing crazy man who had passed by minutes after we had broken down.

Before he departed, Goldfinga also satisfied our curiosity on the subject of gold. From our schooldays, Shaggy and I knew that gold's chemical symbol was Au, the atomic number seventy-nine, and that its highest purity was twenty-four carats. Other than that, it was a deep yellow. Ten minutes of listening to Goldfinga and we also knew that gold was so malleable that one ounce could be broadened into a sheet the size of a tennis court, and that president Mobutu had taken personal control of the largest of Zaire's gold mines, estimated to hold over one hundred tonnes.

Goldfinga also delighted in showing us a couple of small nuggets, which he stored about his person until he had the opportunity to swap them for cash. We did toy with the idea of offering to buy one from him, but being inexpert in the authenticity and value of gold, not to mention the apprehension of getting it through customs, we suppressed any such fancy. More crucially, we would need whatever hard cash we still had for future fares; so we placated ourselves by continuing to absorb Goldfinga's wisdom — and his tales. Seemingly, jobs in the industry were split between those who received a weekly pittance by working for big companies in minefields, and those who went it alone via 'panning': a method of placing a dish into running water, then agitating it so that lighter contents of sand and gravel are sloshed over the side, leaving, hopefully, gold. Whilst Goldfinga was then a panning man, at some stage in his career he had undertaken both activities, and told us all sorts of wacky stories of how miners had hidden a portion of their day's takings (only to complement their measly wage, he affirmed), which included cramming their booty into more than one orifice. Although the majority of these chancers got caught out, said Goldfinga, I was more than glad to remain ignorant of how this was effected.

Whilst this cranny-stuffing might not have been for us, the notion of slinking off to a tributary and having a go at panning was suddenly quite attractive, until we were discouraged by Goldfinga insisting the profession was infinitely more laborious than romantic. He finished by saying that whilst the unearthing of gold nuggets was very rare, for someone such as he the emotional reward of that elusive find far outweighed the potential economic security.

There was an air of melancholy about me when Goldfinga waved goodbye. Sure, this was mostly due to his being an obvious source of killing time, but then again part of the reason was simply because it's nice to meet people who are, in a good way, different from the norm. He certainly was, and not just because he was a pygmy.

After dark another truck's headlights were spotted in the distance and, as it drew near, I heard the 'opposition' crew mocking our woe. Fatal. If ever there was an argument for the veracity of Sod's Law, this was it. As their truck drew out to overtake, guess what? Yep, it too blew a tyre (our return banter was terrifically zealous). And guess what else? Yep, they also had but a repair kit. At least it took them 'only' two hours to mend their puncture, and they were away yonks before our boredom was relieved.

When we eventually got going, the sun had long gone down and the night winds blew effortlessly through my T-shirt. Too cramped to reach into my rucksack, for a while I was very uncomfortable and cold, but with a little persuasion I managed to hunch down atop the two heads I now found resting on each knee. Contentment at last, and with the people huddled around me now keeping me warm, after a long and frustrating day I finally felt myself drifting off to sleep.

Who was I trying to kid? At the very moment of peaceful slumber, the Isuzu pulled up.

It could not have been worse. We had arrived at Epulu, the site of the main rangers' headquarters by the Epulu river, but the first of two bridges was falling to pieces, so they had closed it down. To add insult to injury, whoever had sanctioned this had supposedly made their judgment only moments before our appearance. If we hadn't had that puncture, if it had been fixed quicker, or had happened later in the journey, we would have been across.

With nowhere to go, we were forced to bed down for the night. Frustrated but unable to do anything about it, while the generously proportioned women vanished to wherever, Shaggy and I stayed with the Isuzu and its crew. Here, I sought out the warmest place possible, laid my mum's once-clean towel on the floor, myself on top of that, added my thinner-than-thin sheet and mosquito netting, shut my eyes and, since I was now laying beneath it, prayed the truck's hand brake was a lot more reliable than its tyres.

Monday, 26th June. We had landed at three o'clock in the morning. It was now ten o'clock, and all fifteen of us were back by the Isuzu, eagerly watching a few rangers laying planks across the derelict bridge. Once this was achieved, they allowed the barmiest volunteer (Duke) to try to cross it. At long last we could get on our way. Well, that was the objective. With Duke ready to set off in nanoseconds, a jobsworth official arrived on the scene and announced that the bridge had to be fully restored before anyone was allowed on it, and all the planks were taken up. The repairs, we were told, would take all of two months to complete.

TWO MONTHS!

"Bloody typical," moaned Shaggy.

Despite the wealth of vulgarity that has survived my partial censorship, my opinion as expressed remains unsuitable for print.

I couldn't believe our bad luck, nor indeed abide the idea of being stuck for weeks on end in the same place. But stuck we were. Not that we were the only ones, for as the day wore on the number of trucks that ended up waiting on either side of the river soon had us baffled as to where they had been in the run up to this lift. Yet there they were, at least fifty of them sitting around doing nothing.

In a way it was quite fortunate that Epulu was situated near the bridge, as it was a Third World version of a motorway service station. Even when the crossing was fine, the drivers would stop here to use the facilities, despite its being no bigger than a village. It comprised two rows of clay huts, one either side of the roadway, and a tiny market at the other end of the settlement. Directly across from that was an official building, which we correctly presumed incorporated a police station. There was also a modest zoo and campsite, both located on the other side but away from the road — these had been built by the rangers to help raise funds for the surrounding 8,000 square-mile Okapi Wildlife Reserve.

With time to spare, Shaggy and I took to wandering through the village with the crew, the generously proportioned women going their own way, as was customary. In the centre we purchased food from one of six little 'café' huts, all of which had their own makeshift signs outside, with a menu and price list. The menus generally consisted of rice, eggs, and what I found to be the most common meat throughout our journey, goat, which to my uneducated palate tasted like a cross between mutton and beef. You could also buy a beer or a cola, and one hut even had its own (generator-powered) refrigerator, which, given the tremendous heat and humidity in this part of the world, understandably attracted the most business.

Next we sauntered down to the campsite, but it was deserted so we instead visited the zoo, the fee for which was surprisingly pitiful, the equivalent of sixteen pence. I soon realised that the outlay reflected the goods, as its sole occupants were two zebroids (the offspring of an interbred zebra stallion and any other non-zebra equine mare), four chimpanzees and one snake, albeit a very imposing but beautifully marked viper renowned for having the longest fangs in the world – an awesome two inches! Having over the years been a regular visitor to the animal section of the *Guinness Book of World Records*, Mr Smart-arse here confidently asserted, "It's a Gaboon viper."

"Oui, c'est vrai!" came the impressed ranger's reply, which milked pats on the back from the crew, and helped increase my already large hat size. That said, I was greatly saddened to see this exotic creature being kept inside a two-foot by two-foot box.

After the snake we moved on to the two zebroids and then the four chimpanzees. Housed in independent enclosures and penned off by chicken wire, both species were mercifully given a little more space than the viper, and in an effort to entertain everyone I mimicked the seemingly friendly chimps. But my teasing wasn't to last. Unlike in England, where there is either a wall of glass or much space between the section in which you may stand and the penned-off area, here there was only a small gap between two wire fences. The result of this was that the chimp I had been mocking somehow managed to get its hand through the wiring, at which it made a swift 'pay-back' grab at my family jewels. Fortunately aware of the situation, I rapidly proved that Superman wasn't the only life form capable of travelling faster than a speeding bullet, although the sight did draw a big "Oooooh!" from the onlookers, each wincing at the thought of the near-disaster.

Zoo visit over, the crew separated and Shaggy and I ambled down to the market with Hitch and Ike. Here, one could buy bread, fruit, vegetables, nuts, and peanut butter (mashed peanuts), a spoonful of which would be placed inside a leaf, which was then folded and, hey presto, packaging. We also spent time at another café, at which point Ike decided he liked Shaggy's Nike running shoes and wanted to swap them for his plastic sandals. Shaggy chuckled and told him he wasn't interested.

"Pourquoi?" asked Ike.

Deadly serious, he wanted to know why Shaggy wouldn't exchange with him. Before then, anyone asking my not always tolerant ally such a question had been met by one of two reactions: either a 'I can't be arsed with this conversation' attitude — frequently backed up by an abrupt "piss off" — or else a lengthy debate, which more often than not culminated in the same two words. On good terms with Hitch and Ike, Shaggy decided on option two and asked Ike how much his sandals had cost. Establishing they were worth two pounds, my fellow Brit disclosed that his beloved trainers had cost him seventy. "And I had to work a lot of hours to afford them, so no, I won't be swapping, thank you," he concluded in a mixture of sign language and as much explicable French as he could muster.

Despite having had this explained to him in simplistic detail, Ike turned to Shaggy and asked, "Alors, on échange?"

Shaggy looked at me in amazement. My 'only in Africa' shrug preceded his telling Ike once more that he didn't want to swap, and to nullify any riposte he adopted the most palpable way of drawing the discussion to a close. At six-feet-two Shaggy towered over five-feet-five Ike, so they measured shoe sizes — they were like snuggly peas in a pod. It was impossible not to laugh at Ike's raised-eyebrows look of kismet. Even Shaggy tittered, though he of course had other ideas about the destiny of his prized trainers, so carefully re-explained how much of a fiscal difference there was between the contrasting footwear, adding that he'd stick with his running shoes even if the sandals were worth more. He was a trainers, not a "manky sandals", man.

Evidently not one for being fobbed off, in reply Ike insisted he had understood in the first place and that there was no need for Shaggy to repeat himself. But did he want to swap anyway? Shaggy was all but speechless, though finally made his point clear with a firm: "Non!"

"Pourquoi?" asked Ike.

Later, Shaggy went swimming in the river with a handful of the crew while I busied myself with my camera. A minute into this and the Epuluan I was set to photograph began shouting "Frère! Frère!" whilst beckoning me to spin around. Upon doing so, instead of being met by a similar-looking African, I quickly realised that 'Brother! Brother!' was his way of telling me there was another *muzungu* heading our way. A moment later and I was shaking hands with a big Australian.

"Can't stay long," said the backpacker. "Heard you were in town, thought I'd say hello before heading off."

A brief chat ensued, which ended with my 'brother' informing me that he had stayed the night at the small campsite.

"We checked that out earlier, there was no one there."

"Yeah, bit dead now. The guys staying there are probably off seeing the okapis. Anyway, I'll say g'day. Got to go, got a pickup waiting."

"Which way are you heading? Nia Nia?"

"No, the other way, Bunia."

"Pity."

We shook hands again and I watched the big backpacker depart.

Although understandable, it was ironic that the Aussie had been referred to as my brother. After all, geographically speaking he must have lived twice the distance from me as did the Epuluan. More note-worthy was the fact that Shaggy and I had only gone to the campsite because we had nothing better to do and were bored. In all honesty, the last thing we wanted to do right now was spend time with non-Africans. This wasn't because we had "gone native", as one character puts it in *Lawrence of Arabia* — a film that helped instigate my wander-lust — but more so because after knocking about with the crew we just wanted to 'belong'. Not forever of course, just for now, for this one moment, this one journey. No longer were we 'Shaggy, Sean and the crew'. Now it was only 'the crew'.

By the time Shaggy had come back from his swim, the Aussie had disappeared down the road to Bunia, so we took another stroll to the campsite, where we at last came across other Johnny Foreigners — an American geology student and a couple of Scandinavians, who had indeed been to see the okapis, which they recommended. They also advised us to visit a nearby village of tourist-friendly pygmies. While both proposals were obviously attractive, the fact remained that if we were away from the immediate vicinity and they somehow fixed the bridge, we might miss the Isuzu's departure. A distinct no-no.

With his girlfriend, the American was gathering facts for a book on rainforests and had been staying with tribesmen in much the same way as we had done post-Rutshuru. Now they were heading to our chosen destination, but first he had come alone to the closer Epulu, as he'd been told that he could get his bicycle gears re-adjusted here. Quite clearly he'd been misinformed and, tempted to follow him, we watched enviously as he cycled off down the road we wanted to tread, towards Kisangani.

Having witnessed the recent exodus, Shaggy and I figured it a wise move to revise our alternatives. If the Isuzu was forced to remain in Epulu indefinitely, rather than hang about, one option was purely to walk on, despite this meaning we would unhappily be abandoning the crew. A still more interesting possibility was to obtain a pirogue here and then paddle it down the river, which in due course flowed into the Congo. We examined our map. As far as the tributary idea went, things looked promising. It would bring us out at Basoko, downriver of our intended Kisangani starting point. Although this would mean omitting 120 miles of our predetermined 1,000-mile Congo voyage, since we would have to paddle 460 miles just to get there, we would hardly be missing out. Then we spotted a snag. Tiny blue lines drawn every so often across the tributary spelt one thing only: like the Congo upriver of Kisangani, it had waterfalls. Back to the drawing board.

"Let's think about walking again," I said, running my finger over the map. "It's about seventy miles to Nia Nia..."

"With no adjoining roads until then, so there are going to be no trucks to cadge a lift from."

"...Fifteen miles minimum a day, let's say twenty, we could easily do the whole lot in less than four days."

"Seventy miles, though."

"It's better than being stuck here for two months. That's what they said, Shaggy — two months."

"I suppose a truck could always turn back."

"Or someone in a pickup could pass by."

"Or they could fix the bridge and then our truck will pick us up."

"Now you're talking."

After more debate, as much as it pained me we agreed to stay put for twenty-four hours and see what transpired. If, as rumoured, it looked like weeks of stalemate, then we would walk the seventy miles to Nia Nia (where we would have been leaving the crew anyway) and attain another lift from there, if not beforehand.

Our itinerary clear, we had one last matter to straighten out. Back in Apawanza, with Duke asleep, Shaggy and I had had time to assess our state of affairs, and as per usual had been eying the map. Upon inspection, we had found that the real distance from Komanda to Nia Nia was in fact much closer to 250km. Yet we'd had to pay Z 10,000 after being told the trip totalled 500km (remember Duke's financier Barclay had identified our payment from a tariff chart). In this case, a 250km lift should have been cheaper. We tightwads wanted some of the fare back. Now was as good as any time to ask, and having by this time gained Barclay's friendship we felt no unease when bringing the issue to his attention. Unfortunately, he had other plans and refused any such repayment. So we took him to 'arbitration' in the form of an impartial ranger, who listened attentively to both sides but couldn't decide who was correct and abstained from any further proceedings. Hello square one.

Doubtless Barclay had presumed this to be the end of the matter, but alas, he had another think coming when the hitherto engaged Duke arrived on the scene. His accountant hadn't got twenty seconds into explaining the debate when Duke stopped him in mid-flow and ordered him to hand back Z 4,000. We two stupendous politicians hadn't actually asked for such a bountiful sum, but willingly took the reimbursement and celebrated by blowing it all (and a bit more, after we had acquired the habit) on one or two chilled colas. Of course we simpletons came to regret this, if only because once we had stopped abusing our bellies all that remained in cash for future fares was a combined total of Z 7,000.

Turning out to be a bit of a hero, Duke confirmed his new status that very evening. Sleeping under the Isuzu again, I was awoken by his shaking me and, although I had never heard him speak in any other tongue but his own, he whispered, in a clipped accent, "Come on, I will try tonight."

Apparently the police blockade on the other side of the river had been left unguarded, so Duke had decided he was going to try to drive across the unstable bridge during the dead of night — even if the extra planking had been pulled up. Worse still, so had half of the originals, no doubt done in a bid to prevent the very exercise Duke proposed — which left two old beams only.

Gulp.

The thing was, the surviving beams were about the width of a truck wheel apart, and that was just too tempting for our hero.

Duke was going for it.

Hence, so was his crew.

Hence, so were we.

There was an additional inducement in this new escapade. Aside from being able to get back to the journey, those of us who had sat atop the Isuzu rejoiced at the thought of travelling without the poky conditions, for with no knowledge of their whereabouts, Duke had no choice but to leave behind the generously proportioned women. Even though I felt sympathy towards them for this quandary, at the same time I wasn't complaining.

* * *

Crack. The ignition fired, Duke slipped into gear and slowly aimed his heavy vehicle towards the broken down, half-eaten, rickety bridge. The rest of us, afraid of it collapsing, bottled it and walked a good few strides behind. We were also feverishly shushing ourselves, for this latest adventure had brought forth a succession of nervous giggling all round. Not Duke, though. He stayed calculating and composed, and seconds later two wheels were perched against what was left of the bridge's timbers. With no space on them to manoeuvre, the truck had to be straight, and Duke checked with both Ferrari and Jerome, now standing across the other side. His engineers gave a thumbs-up. He had executed it first time. This was it, do or die, and everyone held their breath as Duke eased his foot down on the gas and nudged the Isuzu on to the beams — they let out an ominous creak as the front end crossed the point of no return. But Duke remained steadfast, and with fortitude cast in iron he inched his vehicle forward until finally its full weight was borne.

Now to take the truck out to the middle.

Incapable of helping, the rest of us watched anxiously as our hardy driver crept towards the daunting make-or-break centre, playing the clutch in such a manner that the truck could only crawl forth, as one inch, two inches, three inches, smidgen by smidgen Duke eased the Isuzu along a bridge that croaked and creaked and buckled with every nail-biting second, a ten-foot drop into the swirling waves beckoning him to a sorry end. Yet our hero ignored such peril and soldiered on, his surgeon-like precision guiding the truck beyond the gaps, while wheels teetered on beams that bowed ever more under the vast force being exerted on them, as closer to the centre Duke edged until eventually he was there. He had made it.

Then... from somewhere on the bridge came the distinctive sound of splintering wood, which could only mean one thing: the old beams had had enough and were in the processes of shattering.

Uh oh.

Refusing to be bested, upon seeing his engineers' frenzied waving Duke floored the accelerator and the vehicle shot forward. Again he showed outstanding deftness, as at pace he navigated the rest of the skeletonised bridge, its few planks continuing to squeak and creak as he did so ...but they held fast. Duke had done it. What a star.

Reminding himself that he was still stuck in Epulu with all to play for, once across the bridge Duke banished any thoughts of celebration or hesitation and, by James Bond-like swerving through a hedgerow and traversing the bordering field, straightaway rounded the police blockade. He then drove back on to the thoroughfare and was seen chuckling to himself, as the rest of us ran after him, one and all doing our own 007 impressions as we leapt on to the back of the moving truck. We were also forced to suppress our returning sniggering, each of us marvelling at the exhilaration that this little jaunt had created.

Now then, at this stage the best tactic would have been to park the Isuzu among the other trucks on this side of the bridge and hope the authorities didn't have photographic memories. Having blended in, we could wait until, say, mid-morning and then make out that we had simply had enough of hanging around, so would now be 'turning back' to Kisangani. The catch was, there was a second barrier at the other end of the village, close to the police headquarters, and while the authorities were keen to let any trucks in through the blockade, they weren't as eager to let them out (I had no idea why, though my cynical side suggested money was on the agenda). Consequently, our dead-of-night quest was only half complete.

Shortly we approached the centre of the village, and Duke turned off the headlights whilst the rest of us listened for any unwelcome movement, our eyes vigilant for any sign of the law. If Duke could just get to the other side of the village, if he could round the second cordon, then maybe, just maybe, we might be able to get away with it.

Like the others, at this point I was crouching on top of the truck, the anxiety unbearable. Would we be heard? Would we make it to the barrier? Would we get past it once there? Of course nobody knew if there were any policemen on duty and the pressure mounted with each passing second, primarily because everything was deathly silent. Everything bar the engine, that is, which ticked over relatively quietly but in the calm of the night still sounded as though it were a bloody marching band. Yet on we strove, as the snail-paced truck sneaked towards sanctuary, our hero Duke continuing to tease the accelerator, while my thoughts were saying, 'Keep going, buddy. Don't make any blunders. Everyone else – no talking. No one move. No one breathe. And can someone please shush this goddamned engine!'

Closer still we drew to the other end of the village ...and closer... ...and closer. Surely we were going to make it. Hold on, yes, we were there, for certain. Almost home and dry we had only to cover a few more yards and we'd be at the barrier. Oh my word, we'd done it, we had made it. Hello blockade, goodbye creeping through town. Goodbye tension. Goodbye to waiting around. Goodbye to Epulu. Hello Kisangani! What joy. Hallelujah.

Ha—lle—lu—jah!

Huh, what was this? A voice had called out; there was a torch, then a man, and the Isuzu was stopped. It was the police. Moments later Duke was arrested and detained. The upshot of this was obvious – we would have to stay in Epulu.

That night the rest of us slept on benches, usually used as a picnic area.

Come morning, the escape story had been passed around so many times that Duke might well have been considered a national super-star. Bar none, everyone had heard of his courageous crossing of the bridge, and upon his mid-morning discharge scores of crews clapped and cheered and paid homage to him – so much so that even a John Wayne character couldn't have been deemed more valiant.

Wayne, who played the hero in classic movies such as *The Quiet Man*, was nicknamed Duke, hence my driver's pseudonym – that, and the fact that if I ever knew his real name, I'm afraid I can't recall it.

The crews continued to give a standing ovation to John Wayne as he swaggered back towards the truck. Noting Duke's newfound fame, those of us connected with him quickly jumped on the bandwagon, following him closely and joining in the bowing and waving to 'our' fans, of which there must now have been no less than one hundred, for the trucks were virtually wall-to-wall by this time. If this praise wasn't enough, Duke's laudable actions also convinced the jobsworth official who'd caused the whole debacle that the bridge was, for the time being at least, safe enough to cross. So they decided to abandon the cordon and re-lay the extra planks (they lasted for twenty years, eventually disintegrating under the weight of a ...drum roll, please... truck. It took twenty-six days to fix).

Talk about irony, although he had already spent the night in jail – wangling a bunk rather than a bench, so it wasn't all bad – Duke was informed that whereas everybody else was free to leave, he would be permitted to go only on one condition: he would have to consent to transport the official who had stopped us crossing the bridge in the first place! Raring to get on his way, our hero jumped at the chance, and we gleefully leapt on to the Isuzu – only to find the generously proportioned women had squeezed back into the sardine tin.

Irony indeed.

Further irony occurred when we were made to wait while everyone else left first.

Groan.

When finally we got shifting, a relieving exit was preceded by our stopping outside the police headquarters, where Duke had been asked to collect 'Jobsworth'. With the generously proportioned women now squashing us again, the entire outfit cringed when we saw the size of the most incalculably huge, enormous, hulking, ponderously gross vat of blubbering walrus fat-filled, whale-featured, wobbly bottomed 'I can block any toilet' official we had ever needed wide-screen vision to set eyes on. That guy was big! The best sight of the day, however, was Shaggy's expression when he realised Jobsworth had decided he was going to fashion a deckchair out of his rucksack ...CRUNCH! Later on, Shaggy checked his belongings and found that every remotely fragile article had been flattened. And all he could picture was Jobsworth's big beaming smile as he'd sat on it.

Our trip had taken us into the overflowing forests of the north. Here, where the road narrowed slightly, the tree branches would hang over significantly. Okay if you are inside the Isuzu, not so clever if you're propped on top. And especially if you are sat straddling the sides of the sardine tin, which, bearing in mind the generously proportioned women and the even more colossal Jobsworth were sprawled all over, was exactly what the rest of us were forced to do. This also meant we were obliged to play a game, which I shall name: Dodge The Branch Or Die.

My favourite moment occurred when another truck decided to join in. Aside from looking out for the branches ourselves, whenever an oncoming truck came by it would be as much fun to watch their crew also playing Dodge The Branch Or Die, and vice versa. From all passengers there were many moments of unified drawn-in breaths, as someone on their side or ours just about got away with dodging a branch. But this wasn't always the case. In the one event I mentioned, a member of an opposition crew had ducked beneath a particularly awkward, dangerous branch. So perfect in his technique was he that he drew rounds of applause from our crew, and to reward his new fans he gave us a small, though somewhat conceited, bow. Ha, the mug. What a great ploy on our part, for it took away his focus, and the one thing you could never do while playing Dodge The Branch Or Die, however good you were, was lose focus. Yet we had suckered him splendidly, and Mr Mug turned from his rather smug little bow directly into another equally awkward and dangerous branch — only this time he wasn't so fast, and it veritably caught him right in the kisser, sending him flying. We pissed ourselves laughing. No one beat us at Dodge The Branch Or Die.

Other games and more laughs abounded with the crew. The most memorable was when one of them winked at us cronies, then in a whisper and sign language asked who would "jiggy-jiggy" with the lady he flashed his eyes at, the big momma of the big women. Desperately trying not to giggle, everybody feigned nausea at such a notion, apart from Mr Slapstick here. Pretending to size up Big Momma, I joked (inadvertently far too loud as we went over a bump) "Moi". Those in on the clowning creased up with laughter at my faux pas — while Big Momma's nose went straight into the air.

Needless to say the potholes were every bit as bad as the branches. On one occasion, we passed a truck which had fully toppled over on to its side. Told this was far from uncommon, it was just good fortune there had been no passengers, who may well have perished, especially if they'd had a few generously proportioned women and an elephantine official ready to land on them. Still, this omen couldn't persuade Duke to abate his cavalier driving methods and, as usual, he had the Isuzu agonisingly balanced on its outer wheels here and there.

Eventually we reached the crossroads at Nia Nia, which, despite being touted as one of the large gold-mining districts, appeared to be nothing more than a small community. To support this, the handful of domiciles that lined our south-westerly route ended long before the next bend in the road. But that was the least of our concerns, for here we were to carry on without the likes of Duke and his crew, as destined for Isiro, they would be turning north. I for one had become quite attached to these men, our 'brothers', and couldn't help wishing that they too were heading towards Kisangani — not least because we had so little hard cash left for lifts. Nevertheless, we said goodbye to all and shook hands with Duke, Barclay, Jerome, Pepe, Ferrari, Hitch and Ike, and departed their company.

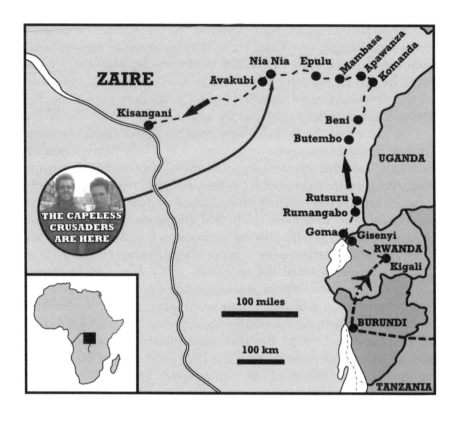

Chapter 8

MEN OF HARLECH

Once more Shaggy and I had the choice between waiting for a truck and thumbing one whilst on the move. We shouldn't have had far to walk, as there would be plenty heading towards Kisangani from Nia Nia. Or so we had thought, because once the die had been cast and we were out walking once again, we found that, like the thousands of years before technology arrived at Africa's door, the metal beasts may as well have been non-existent. At least Shaggy was now feeling a lot better, and for the first time in days both of us were quite content to just mosey along, amongst the ever-exquisite flora, on a beautifully coloured, sunny African afternoon.

Two hours came and went. By this time we had passed a couple of settlements and crossed over what our map-reading told us was the bridge on the river Aruwimi-Ituri, its waters encased by an equatorial rainforest so heaving it threatened to overrun our furrowed pathway, the thick tangle of trees alive with squabbling monkeys and twittering birds, while gigantic creepers and scented flowers intermingled with fruits that dangled appealingly from their slightly too-high position and goaded us to 'have a go'.

"If you give me a leg up, I reckon I could grab that one there," said Shaggy.

A swift hoist and the papaya was in his hand, although any happy ending was negated by its being unripe. But it mattered not, for food and water was soon on hand when we came across another gathering of mud huts, which, again as per our map-reading, was the village of Avakubi.

"Do you know how they make these huts?" I asked Shaggy as we approached.

"Yeah, they're made in Hong Kong and then flown in."

"And there's me thinking it was Monaco. No, you knob. What you do is take some long branches and cut them to the height of however tall you want the walls to be. But you'll need an extra twelve inches..."

"I could provide that."

"I said inches, not millimetres. So, you need an extra twelve *inches* because you have to dig holes into the ground. Then you put in the stakes and pack everything down with stones and dirt. Before that you have to coat them in a special sap, a sort of preserver. Then you put the holes about a foot apart, in a quadrangle, or whatever shape you want your hut, and once you've got your uprights in, you just inter-weave thinner branches through everything. Then you get some mud and grass, and mix them up with water and then rub it all over. Voila, a hut."

"So the roofs get there by themselves?"

"Alright, I forgot that bit. *Obviously* you then interweave some long grasses and vines to make the roof, and then coat that too."

"I could have guessed all that."

"Sure you could."

"So where'd you get this from?"

"I read about it."

"You can read? Wow."

In spite of the folk of the village staring at us as though we had just beamed down from Mars, they were all the same friendly, so we rested briefly and bought and devoured water, a pineapple and goat meat. Shaggy's opting to offset the sting of the pineapple's juices by holding tissues against his improved but still blistered lips caused more gaping — and demonstrated that his wellbeing still wasn't on a par with the magnificent specimen of superhuman virility that was his exploration partner. Then we were off again, on the road to Kisangani.

We walked and walked and walked. With the exemption of two un-cooperative pickups early doors, not one vehicle passed. Soon daylight was drawing to a close, and while the night brought about a natural unease, with a decent moon to guide us, we quickly learned to handle it. We were enjoying the walk. Life was good.

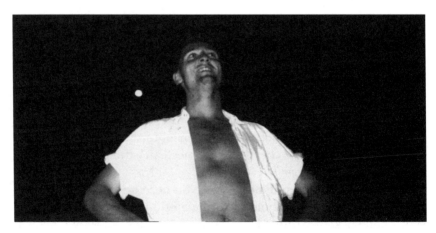

The debilitating darkness of many of our African nights was thankfully punctuated by several with decent moons.

Even so, there was something amiss. A cog that wasn't in place, but I couldn't work out what it was. Something to do with the whole 'Africa' thing, of that I was certain. More often than not, when you watch a movie that's located in the depths of the rainforest you will see remote tribes living a primitive existence; you will observe ritual dances; you will behold witch doctors, and a picture will take shape in your mind. Of course this spectacle would have been nice to see for real, yet the settlements we had passed on the journey through Zaire's eastern provinces, although archaic by big city standards, had thus far all but embraced modern society. Indeed, the only settings where we had seen anything 'other worldly' was at villages like My Woman's and this last community. But this still wasn't 'natives in headdresses', wasn't men of a bygone age, wasn't tribesmen wearing loincloths or performing ceremonial dance. And, to be straightforward, as much as it would have been thrilling to come across these people, this wasn't a problem to me — it wasn't the cog that I'd been missing. No, this time around I just wanted to see the jungle on my way to the Congo; wanted to be part of the rich green shading I had been so enthused by in an atlas when I was a schoolboy, while keeping myself as far away from harm as possible.

So what was it that I had been missing? As it was, that mysterious cog was about to fall into place.

Yes, I was getting the sights, and the aromas, but the missing link lay in another sense, for the component that finalized the picture was *sounds*. I should say 'sound', singular, as the elusive cog was one very specific sound — one that was about to become a stark reality to us, as at long last we got a taste of my image of Africa.

Once night had fallen, in the distance somewhere, we began to hear natives chanting. With this came that one very precise sound I had been subliminally waiting for. It sounded like this: Boom–Boom–Boom. Boom–Boom–Boom.

Tom-tom drums.

Gulp.

* * *

Boom–Boom–Boom. Boom–Boom–Boom, went the drums.

There was a sudden mixture of emotions. Elation, in that I finally had a sound that went along with the vision I had previously held of Africa. Excitement, in that I might actually spend a night with my idea of a remote tribe. And apprehension, because my fear of the un-known refused to allow my positive side any leeway. After all, who knew what the drums meant? As ignorant as I was, for all I knew we were close to a hostile tribe and the Boom-Boom-Boom decoded as: 'Two strangers approach. They are bad juju. They must be punished. Make sure the dark-haired one suffers in particular.'

Whatever the message, the drums and the chanting were, without question, enthralling.

Boom-Boom-Boom. Boom-Boom-Boom.

There is a famous scene in the film *Zulu*, the 1964 classic based on the true tale of the battle of Rorke's Drift, where 120 British soldiers somehow repel twenty times as many combat-hardened Zulu warriors. In the film, the warriors surround the small encampment and begin their war cry in an effort to unnerve their foe. Not to be outdone, the men of Rorke's Drift counteract this with their version of the Welsh battle song 'Men of Harlech'.

If you are partial to rousing scenes and haven't seen this one, do so. It is electric.

Boom-Boom-Boom. Boom-Boom-Boom.

The tom-toms were getting closer.

Boom-Boom-Boom. Boom-Boom-Boom.

I decided not to be outdone either, and I burst into the first verse of 'Jerusalem': "And did those feet, in ancient times, walk upon England's mountains green..."

The men of Rorke's Drift would have been proud.

Boom-Boom-Boom. Boom-Boom-Boom.

Bless him if Shaggy didn't join me: "And was the Holy Lamb of God, on England's pleasant pastures seen..."

Boom-Boom-Boom. Boom-Boom-Boom.

This carried on for some time, as we leaped from 'Jerusalem' into what lines we knew of things like 'Men of Harlech', 'Land of Hope and Glory', 'God Save The Queen', and a few rugby songs to boot.

Life was still good.

Though late, the drums continued to beat incessantly, and while our tonsils had yet to reach the 'nigh-on expired' stage, we decided to stop singing. The tom-toms were getting too loud and, oblivious as to what they were actually signalling, our insecurity told us to be mindful of worst-case scenarios. Whatever the conclusion, it made sense to be completely aware of the situation, and that meant sticking a sock in it and pinning back our lugholes.

We had timed our silence to perfection, for within the next sixty seconds three things happened that required our being as receptive as humanly possible. Firstly, the chanting and tom-tom beat concluded. Presumably unable to hear our singing beforehand, whilst my positive side urged me to cross the cultural barrier and announce our arrival to men who would probably treat us with nothing but kindness and respect, an innate feeling of self-preservation kept me on high alert. 'Why attract potential adversity? Maintain your silence. Play it by ear,' it told me. Secondly, it was at this moment that the warning issued by Ali's friend Larry X, way back in Nairobi, loomed ever larger: "Never travel at night. Africa can be an amazing place to be during the day, but at night — beware." Thirdly, we heard another sound. A sudden one that invaded our senses like an arrow whistling past the ear — it was a vehicle, closing from behind. Of course we had hoped it would be a truck, but quite quickly it became apparent that it was a motorbike. The engine's whirr drawing closer and closer.

What to do? A motorbike would be of no use to us, and since we were guarding against all prospective danger, the thought crossed my mind to employ our pre-determined 'stay safe' stratagem of moving twenty paces into the cover of the forest, returning only once all was clear. The problem with that little trick was that we had devised it during daylight hours, when implementing it hadn't meant walking blindly into a pitch-black thicket of alternative peril. Weighing up what ended as a fifty-fifty choice, I whispered the options to Shaggy, who unfortunately came back with the same indecision. So we just hoped for the best and kept walking. Besides, the more I mulled it over the more I decided the biker would likely be another traveller, in the vein of Dean, the Australian who, on the flight from Moscow, had regaled us with the story of his motorbike expedition across the Sahara.

Almost immediately we detected the dimness lifting as the headlights neared, and we no longer needed to strain our eyes to see the way ahead. The bike was close now but the instant we were caught in the beam, instead of sweeping by, it slowed dramatically, then crawled past us at a snail's pace, whoever was on the seat staring intently. By this I don't mean the one rider I was expecting — or two. I mean three. Three Zairians.

Although concerned, I decided not to worry too much because one would presume they would be curious. Two greenhorns hiking through the jungle in the dark, I doubt many others of the same ilk had ever been so intrepid (so stupid!). As odd for me was the contrast in sounds. One minute I was listening to the beat of tom-toms, the next to the drone of a motorbike. One symbolised perfectly the old world Africa, the other the new; I just hadn't ever put them together. Be that as it may, I stayed composed and continued walking. So what if three locals showed some curiosity towards us? It was only natural. Sure enough, the bike passed by.

What was this? Not far up the road the motorbike turned on itself and circled back, slowly passing us again, the three men making more acute eye contact. We didn't respond, but watched every single movement out of the corner of our eyes. It was curiosity. Yes, that's what it was, just curiosity.

Or was it?

Behind us the bike turned again, and again came to us, crawling past even slower. I wasn't exactly happy about this, and was even less so when the practice was repeated, each sweep looming ever nearer.

This time I made eye contact. I wanted to know who and what we were dealing with. Curiosity is the easiest thing in the world to cope with, provided that's all it is. And yet — fuck. I didn't like the look of these guys. I really didn't like the look of them, and I mean really. Their whole demeanour, the intense eyeballing, the furrowed brows, the inflated masculinity, the scarring, the bike drawing closer, all told me the same thing...

We are bad.

Once past us, the bike moved on a little but then ground to a halt. Then one man dismounted, yet simply stood by the bike until we had walked by.

Bad indeed.

Then the bikers repeated the procedure. This time a second man dismounted, the first now walking behind us.

Fuck indeed.

My heart began to pound harder and harder. No way were they just 'being nosy'. This was proper bad. They were weighing us up for sure. How strong were we? Could we put up a fight?

Fuck, this was bad.

Now what to do? Do we run? Do we drop rucksacks and run? Do we drop rucksacks and stay and fight? I assessed our circumstances. Not only did they outnumber us, and knew the area, but they doubtless also guessed that no one had a clue that we were walking along this particular road at this particular time. Into the bargain, they were likely to be carrying far deadlier weapons than the measly stick Shaggy had just picked up — an action that only validated my fears, and sent my already high adrenalin into overdrive. Now couple all that with a lack of witnesses and, oh yes, we were right in the shit. Real down and out, straight to the core, no messing around, hard–fast proper shit.

Fuck!

This was it. Fate had arrived. In readiness I flicked open my pen-knife and dropped one of the rucksack's straps from my shoulder.

Then it happened.

In the distance, a heavy shaft of light of shone deep into the night. Talk about a million-to-one lucky break — after hours of nothing, it was a truck, heading our way and surely our only possibility of a lift. Better yet, it stopped the bikers in their tracks.

For now.

As the truck neared, I fretted about all manner of possible negative outcomes. Maybe the driver wouldn't stop because it was night-time? Maybe he wouldn't stop because of the sight of the motorbike gang? Maybe he wasn't interested in picking up passengers regardless? Either way, I couldn't help but picture the truck sailing past. If that were the case, I was sure we would find ourselves in the unenviable position of having to defend our lives. We needed this lift to happen like no lift we had ever had before. Especially as the bikers were visibly remaining within striking range, no doubt hoping our salvation would pass by.

The truck drew closer. My whole being now centred on getting a lift, I willed the thing to stop, and if it looked as though it wouldn't, I told Shaggy we should leap on the back.

Presently it was upon us. The moment of truth had arrived and I metaphorically crossed my fingers and flailed my arms at the driver, who fortunately for us couldn't have missed anyone in his headlights on such a narrow, slow-moving road.

The truck pulled to a stop. Result. But would we be allowed on-board? An English-speaking passenger atop the truck interpreted for the driver.

Yes, they were heading straight to Kisangani.

Yes, they would give us a lift.

Yes, they wanted Z 12,000.

Hang on ...Z 12,000?

Shit.

One of the things we had learned in our short time here was the cost of hitching, and at over double what Duke had charged for a similar distance, this was far too high. But faced with our disagreeable circumstances we could hardly refuse. The problem was, after our wild cola-buying spree at Epulu we had only those Z 7,000 left.

Uh oh.

With the bikers still loitering in the background, I maintained that without this lift we would soon be swapping our *muzungus* title to 'the deceased'. And since we hadn't Z 12,000 on us, therefore pleaded with the driver to let us have the lift for what we did have. The answer was an emphatic "No!" — the sound of which registered in my brain like the chime of a 100-decibel bell.

FUCK!

Our goose was cooked. Goodbye sheltered lift, hello fight to the death.

In desperation, I was about to offer to clean the truck as part payment when the words cascaded out of my mouth: "What about taking seven thousand zaires cash and the other five thousand in travellers' cheques?"

A debate ensued, and with it my pulse fluctuated accordingly, as one second the lift was on, the next it wasn't. But fortune swung our way, as the driver finally assented to escort me to a bank in Kisangani to get the cheques cashed (not that I knew if any would be open — or cared). The important thing was that, at least for the time being, we were safe.

Now we had five cat lives left.

Now I needed some toilet roll.

Tout de suite, Shaggy and I leaped into the back.

Surprise, surprise — a zillion other passengers.

Between the dimness and the fact that the rest of them were all under blankets laying down sleeping, it was near-impossible to know where to wriggle in, and I heard the odd grunt and groan, followed by my "whoops, excusez-moi" as I stepped on a few bodies. Eventually Shaggy slipped in alongside the others, whilst I, the human footrest, ended up down by everyone's feet.

Although we had gained a lift, I had worried that the bikers may follow us, or else go off and obtain reinforcements. In reality, though, they were more likely opportunists who had merely come across two potential victims in the dark. But then again, were they? Think back. Was it really nothing more than a coincidence that the tom-toms had concluded at roughly the same time as we heard the motorbike?

Food for thought.

Whatever their intent, as the minutes turned into hours it became apparent that neither they, nor any others, would return. And thank heaven for that, for when I look back on this occasion, a chill runs down my spine. Had that truck not appeared from out of the blue, I am convinced that whoever might have won blood would have been spilled that night.

As if the lift and the departure of the bikers wasn't pleasing enough, someone smiled down on us again, for the driver decided to travel all night.

"Hey, Shaggy. If he keeps going at this rate we'll be in Kisangani tomorrow morning," I said (although perhaps I shouldn't have. Not after his "We'll be in Kisangani by Monday night" had heralded the last puncture).

Whilst the idea of reaching our ultimate destination gave me some solace, journeying at night had its downside, for it also meant the cold night air would again rush through my mum's once-clean towel and my thinner-than-thin sheet and mosquito netting, and again I regretted not keeping hold of the blanket Ali had given me.

Despite the cold I didn't sleep too badly, until a painful throbbing located somewhere around my shins woke me. This, I discovered, had been caused by a fellow passenger's tootsies, or rather the footwear to which they belonged – hobnailed boots – now embedded into my shins, thank you very much. Hence, although it was still rather chilly at this time in the morning, and therefore lying flat was definitely the preferable option, I nonetheless opted to liberate my tibias and rose to my feet, fervently awaiting the exposure of the blanket-covered, shin-crushing fiend.

Impatient as usual, I started drumming my fingers. Awake since 6:30am, it was now 8am and I hadn't a clue how far away Kisangani was, although one of the crew let on we would be there before noon. Certainly we were near, for the road was both wider and flatter, and the sides of the route were far more colonised (by shacks and little stalls) than during the previous day. This, however, served only to rile me, as the driver persisted in stopping, seemingly every other minute, to purchase various items – notably dead porcupines and monkeys, the latter strung up on stalls like handbags, a small slit in the end of the tail with their heads popped through.

Quite why the frustrating git couldn't wait until Kisangani before obtaining such paraphernalia, who knows? "It's probably cheaper" is an obvious assumption, but then again simple *sociopathy* could also explain not only his willingness to leave Shaggy and me to the bikers had we not the fare, but also his decision to splatter some poor kid's pet dog, a sickening incident that, to be honest, would have been very easy to prevent.

As our truck drew closer to Kisangani, my attention began to focus on the hobnailed fiend who had gouged my shins to pieces. Whoever it was, they were still fast asleep under a blanket that masked their identity, which irked increasingly the longer it stayed there. To the point that whenever we reached Kisangani it didn't matter now, I *had* to see who it was. Not that I was after revenge or anything like that – although that would have been perfectly satisfactory – I just wanted to know who the hell had mangled my shins. Another half an hour and my patience was rewarded. For the fiend slowly stirred, until, a moment later, the culprit sat bolt upright and the blanket dropped, revealing all.

Crikey! There in front of me was a sight too unreal to believe — sodding Jobsworth! The self-same rucksack-squashing, incalculably huge, enormous, hulking, ponderously gross vat of blubbering walrus fat-filled, whale-featured, wobbly bottomed 'I can block any toilet' official who had cut short our Epulu progress. Shaggy, who had been watching the events unfold, cracked up laughing — he later joked that he had wanted to cry but it came out wrong. Still half disbelieving the probability of such a painful coincidence, I looked at my mate as if to say, 'Only in Africa, my old cock sparrow. Only in Africa.'

An hour later we were in Kisangani. 28th June. 9:30am. It had taken us one week to travel from Goma to Kisangani ...to the minute.

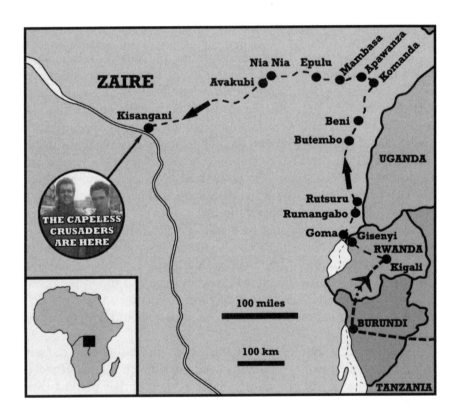

Chapter 9

DEN OF INIQUITY

At 220 metres, the depth of the Congo is four times the height of the Leaning Tower of Pisa — it is the deepest river on earth. And with a drainage basin that encompasses well over a million square miles it is utilised by man in numerous ways, fishing and hydro-electric power amongst them. Mainly, though, it is used for the transportation of goods and passengers between the capital, Kinshasa, near the mouth, and Kisangani, 1,000 miles upriver. With an overall length of almost 3,000 miles, travelling further is practicable, but not by boat, as the journey would be impossibly hampered by the occasional waterfall and, if a history of sporadic violence plays its part, guerrilla warfare. Back in 1989 cannibals supposedly thrived too, although apparently that was the case in either direction. With these factors in mind you would find that most individuals passing through Zaire to East Africa normally took the riverboat from Kinshasa to Kisangani, and then either flew to their destination or, if deranged, hitch-hiked. Since we had travelled the opposite way, it seemed logical that all we had to do to satisfy our hunger for achievement and travel down the illustrious Congo was to wait for the riverboat to turn back. But not Shaggy and I, oh no. We weren't going to make things so easy by catching a cosy boat. No, we had decided, long before we had set foot on African soil, that if we arrived at Kisangani we were going to paddle a pirogue the entire way.

And here we were — Kisangani, the geographical centre of Africa, and a critical place because it connected Kinshasa with trading routes from adjoining countries. So much so that in the 19th century both Henry Morton Stanley — the Congo's first conqueror — and Arab slave traders had based themselves here. It was also the Inner Station in Joseph Conrad's fêted 1902 Congo novel *Heart of Darkness*. By the time we landed, Kisangani was Zaire's third largest industrialised city and benefited from many mod cons, including something we hadn't seen for a week — street lighting. Another godsend was that I felt no unhealthy vibes, *à la* Goma. Whether this was down to Kisangani's appearance being less 'Wild West', who knows, but throw in a half-million population and a few Johnny Foreigners, and you also get a variety of cheap cafés and hotels. So, after changing some travellers' cheques, paying off the truck driver, and then being fleeced at one of these so-called 'cheap' cafés, we made for what was the most popular accommodation used by travellers, the Hotel Olympia.

The Olympia was owned by a middle-aged Greek couple, who seemed to sit around all day eating and playing cards. It comprised a large central yard, which was used by travellers who were either happy to 'rough it' or simply had limited finances. Luckily for them, it was partly covered by a downpour-defying veranda and had communal washrooms and toilets. Both were putrid, and only one of the toilets flushed. Encircling the yard were some cheap and some costly cabins, the latter not because of any luxury, but because they had their own bathroom – the ill-fated occupants of the cheap (one-room) cabins were obliged to use the shared amenities. There was also an indoor dining hall, with bar, and an outdoor dining area, also with bar. This was favourable for any beer lovers who had emerged from the jungle, such as a group of lager-guzzling Kiwis who had arrived there several days before us.

Other travellers came and went. An American pair, both geology students, the man of whom we had already met back in Epulu, here to have his cycle gears realigned. An English lady, on her way to The Sudan, who had been travelling in Africa for some two years now. A bunch of Germans, who had run out of cash and were hoping to sell their truck. An English schoolteacher, here only briefly, taking time out to see the world.

Being in his late forties, the teacher was by far the oldest traveller at the Olympia. Apart from an early thirties member of the Kiwi backpackers, every other traveller we met was, like Shaggy and me, in their twenties, seemingly the norm. My guess for this generality is that, unlike the teenager who is still finding his or her adult feet and looking forward to things like university or relationships, the person in their twenties might have done all of this but has not yet gathered responsibilities. With no spouse, children or mortgage, and still on life's learning curve, they haven't yet hit that stage of 'family', a time where it might be deemed irresponsible to wander off. Alternatively, the more mature, post-twenties person interested in seeing the world usually does so as a quick break, by means of a tour operator. Steeped in responsibilities, they have commitments, children, mortgages, time constraints. They are also at a period in life where they have perhaps seen parents or friends pass away, so are less likely to be carefree. They possess more fear. They no longer feel unbreakable. Everything won't 'be okay'. This being so, they believe a tour operator offers not only a faster and more comfortable way of seeing the sights, but also presents the safer option, particularly in places of perceived danger – like Africa. To support my point, I saw this fear in my parents' eyes when I advised them of my do-it-yourself Congo intentions. Where I saw an opportunity, they saw problems. Where I saw adventure, they saw danger. Just the same, I vowed I was indestructible: I would 'be okay'. Ironically, they tried to persuade me to go to China instead. Had I done so, I would have been rocking up around the same time that their authorities were cracking down on Tiananmen Square protestors. Good job I picked Africa.

So far.

The abovementioned managed to move on before our departure, excepting the Kiwis, with whom in due course we became quite congenial. Forced to stay on a few days longer because they had tickets for the impending riverboat, they thought Shaggy and I were stark raving bonkers to even contemplate paddling down the Congo.

"Take your pick," they told us, "crocs, hippos, cannibals — one of them's bound to eat you!"

Others awaiting the riverboat included an American student, Dan, and also Paul, an English solicitor who had forked out for a pricey 'top of the range' cabin, something the Kiwis would never have done. Indeed, having arrived over a week before the riverboat's listed date of arrival, like Dan they hadn't even opted for the inexpensive cabins, saving money by roughing it out in the yard, regardless of not having a tent.

As much as Shaggy and I were on the side of thrift, we nevertheless plumped for a cabin. I won't pretend that being without sleeping bags or a tent didn't come into the equation, or that we hadn't had our fill of cold, uncomfortable nights, but primarily we needed to be able to leave our stuff somewhere secure whilst searching for a pirogue. To appease our prudence, we chose a cheaper cabin, which was lucky for our budget, as a couple of complications eventually expanded our stay from a calculated two nights to an unforeseen five.

Our first priority had been to pay a visit to the immigration office — in spite of having three weeks remaining on our existing permits, we estimated that it would take between four and six to reach Kinshasa, so we would need additional visas. Since these were sold in one- or three-month durations, there was no advantage in paying extra for the lengthy one. Of course there was something else we definitely had to do — go see the Congo. How could we not?

Sniffing around for directions, we decided to head to the famed river on the way to immigration, and fortunately had far less trouble finding it than we later did their headquarters, although something as enormous as the most voluminous river in Africa could hardly go unnoticed, despite its being 'only' a half-mile wide here at Kisangani, compared with ten at its widest.

Soon we were standing by the water's edge, gazing at and listening to the rumble of "an immense snake uncoiled, with its head in the sea, its body at rest curving afar over a vast country and its tail lost in the depths of the land", as Conrad described it in *Heart of Darkness*. Our initial words were every bit as eloquent.

"There it is, Shaggy."

"Aye, there it is."

Well, maybe not.

Our brevity may have been due to a cauldron of mixed emotions. On one hand, as bizarre as it seems there was a feeling of anticlimax. After all, we were but staring at a large body of water, something we had done many times before bearing in mind our athletics camp had been positioned close to the coast. On the other hand, a far more upbeat surge of excitement came from both a sense of pride in having got this far, and that old passion-inducer, anticipation. Better than the act? In the Congo's case, only time would tell. All in all, the sense of occasion quashed any feeling of anticlimax, the intoxicating expectation of destiny rubbing shoulders with that of history. Henry Morton Stanley; Joseph Conrad: how many other people had carved out their finest hour here? Now the Congo was set to be more than 'just' a large body of water, as it entered the life story of that little boy gazing at an atlas.

And what of the Congo itself? Blue in numerous photos one sees, and indeed blue many times when we were finally on it, at Kisangani the river's colour would better have been described as gunmetal grey, although the backdrop medley of trees that would line our journey completed a portrait that included tones gleaned from a galaxy of wenge, agba, iroko and limba trees, their greens and browns standing side by side with, and enhanced by, the more renowned ebony and mahogany, each helping to form a towering rainforest whose canopy peaked at well over a hundred feet.

The closing transcript of my first impression of the Congo may well have covered a visual description of its Kisangani waterfall, had we been standing in the right spot. Positioned a little further upriver, later on we did view the last instalment of the Congo's famous series of seven cataracts, although to be fair, Stanley Falls, as it is commonly known, wasn't reputed to be anywhere near as breathtaking as its cousin, Victoria Falls. Hence our preliminary inertia.

Our dalliance with the Congo over, we headed off to immigration, the locating of which turned out to be a mission in itself and we were forced to ask one of the countless soldiers on hand for the correct directions. Rather than tell us, the private stopped a local and instructed him to escort us there, which he duly did, even though the bureau transpired to be a fair old distance. Disobeying someone in the forces, we surmised, was decidedly inadvisable.

As if we hadn't already spent a small fortune on visas, at the office we were told that obtaining added permits was viable but, contrary to what we understood were the usual terms, you couldn't select your start date; the visa simply began upon payment. Our remaining three weeks would be redundant.

"Bloody typical!" snorted a displeased Shaggy. "That means that if we really need up to six weeks to get down the Congo, we'll have to buy a full three-month visa. Another big dint in the wallet."

Wishing to retain as much money as possible, we had a brainwave and sought out a person whom we hoped might help us bend the (dodgy) rules: the British Consul. Years later I was to learn his name was François Seneque and that his long service in the region had at some point earned him an OBE, but at the time I knew nothing of him except that he was supposedly a Belgian, which I guess accounted for his apparently French accent. There was nothing inherently wrong with his being Belgique, of course, as long as he did his job. But a lack of patriotism, I suspected, led to him spending all of his time trying to get a buyer for the German travellers' truck.

The UK, Belgium or Germany — whichever country the Consul was working for, word had it that his conduct had nothing to do with allegiance, rather he was just trying to get his hands on a percentage of any sales going. Of course these assumptions might be doing him a disservice; suffice to say that when eventually we pinned him down, he did give us a letter to take to immigration asking for leniency. And so, armed with the all-powerful note, we headed back to the relevant office. No sense in waving it at the desk lady, this time we asked to see the personage in charge, the Big Cheese. To my surprise, our wish was granted and we were guided into a rather plain, dimly lit office that smelled of old wood. Here, we found two people. The first was a dead ringer for Huggy Bear from the TV series *Starsky and Hutch*, and I don't just mean because he had a comparable face and build, as he seriously looked like a 1970s pimp, transported in time and place from the streetlife of New York; his white, embroidered and sequined ensemble, with its humungous lapels and even wider bell-bottoms, would have put Las Vegas Elvis to shame.

Shading our eyes from the suit's glare, we looked beyond Huggy, where we saw a hefty wooden desk. On the other side sat the chief of immigration, patiently waiting for our requests. Both Shaggy and I took one look at him and thought the exact same thing: 'We're going to get sweet-FA here'. For the Big Cheese, with his heavy-set frame and brooding expression, was so much the spitting image of Uganda's dictatorial ex-president Idi Amin that we began to wonder if he really did abscond to Libya. Even his clothing was evocative of Amin's non-military fashion, a tailored suit with cravat.

"How may I help you?" asked a now-smiling 'Cheesy', his English perfect.

As politely as we could, Shaggy and I explained the situation and showed him the note from the sales rep, I mean the Belgian/British/German Consul. At odds with his appearance, Cheesy seemed very caring and unexpectedly agreed to our terms, telling us to have our visas lengthened by the woman in charge of such transactions.

"Is there anything else I can assist you with?" he asked, a picture of kindness.

We declined any more help, but thanked him for his benevolence.

"That's a turn up for the books," said Shaggy, after we had exited his office. "It just goes to show, you never know."

"You mean, don't judge the cheese by the wrapper."

The woman Cheesy was talking about was the same one who had first rejected us, and we again found ourselves staring at, as Shaggy presently described her, "a sour faced, bumble-bee-type piece of shit, hanging from a sick dog's arse." His portrayal had its merits. Rotund of body and wearing a yellow and black dress, since we had gone over her head, by this time 'The Bee' was already sulking, and as such I was amazed that the pout on her sour face didn't worsen when I told her the 'supplementary visa to begin in three weeks' update. Sticking to protocol, she handed us various forms, which we filled in, but when I looked at the stamp she'd given us, it read one month to start from this very day. I wasn't best pleased.

"Le directeur parlez oui," I said in my broken French.

It made no difference. She was adamant these were the rules, that it couldn't be done any other way and that this is what we were going to get.

"Mais le directeur parlez oui!" I insisted.

Now she wasn't best pleased, and her sour mug went into overdrive as she snatched up the papers and buzzed off to consult her boss. Five minutes later The Bee returned to her hive, a sickly sweet 'Limpet smirk' now plastered on her face, as though she had taken part in a debating competition and won a pot of honey. Following her was the Big Cheese, only he wasn't smiling. He was also minded by five rifle-toting guards.

Uh oh.

Luckily the extra security wasn't for our benefit, for they all rushed off to an awaiting car. The problem was, before this happened Cheesy stopped to apportion us a moment of his time.

Uh oh.

Quite what The Bee had said to him we didn't know, but whatever it was she certainly stung any chance we had with our appeal.

We didn't try reasoning with him, or question his change of heart – not with five rifles on hand – we just stood there listening to him rant and rave, this time in French, about how we must comply with the rules and regulations (must acquiesce to being swindled). After the mauling I watched Idi Amin disappear out of the building, and mused about how nice it would be to have a genie offer me three wishes, which I would have picked thus... One: Cheesy's family jewels become fruit scented. Two: Cheesy is picked up and taxied by Bad Max. Three: Cheesy is dropped off at the dwelling of Goliath, the fruit-loving, teeth-like-a-lion baboon. Likewise, it would be poetic justice if the same genie bequeathed another three wishes to Shaggy, who would no doubt have used them in a similar fashion on The Bee, as she'd still got that smug Limpet-grin stuck on that waspish mush of hers. Oh my giddy aunt how I yearned to tell her where she might thrust her pot of honey, but thought better of it and snatched up my belongings, appeasing myself by muttering a few obscenities under my breath on the way out.

Still faced with our predicament, we dolefully headed back to the Olympia, our only solution now, apart from paying the small fortune for a three-month visa (sod that), to hope that somebody else could come up with a suitable alternative.

Thankfully, someone did.

Rescue came in the mould of the Kiwis, who had gathered a useful array of information while they had been in town and were of the opinion that we would be able to renew our visas at Bumba, one of the riverboat's stops, 230 miles downriver. If this were true, we could paddle there on our existing passes – which we guessed would take no longer than two weeks – and then purchase a one-month extension. Hopefully, with the distance we would have travelled already, that month's validity would be all we'd need in order to get right down the Congo and out of Zaire. This sounded such an excellent idea that we instantaneously went and sought confirmation with The Bee (so was relieved I had kept my diatribe to a mumble, and to be frank she was awfully nice to us second time around – probably just revelling in her 'victory'). We were in luck: yes, it was possible to renew the visas at Bumba. There and then we decided that this was what we would do. If, for whatever reason, we didn't have time to get out of Zaire, it was just tough. We couldn't care less anymore and adopted the outlook *que sera, sera*. If we ended up in bother, or even jail, then so be it, we would merely have another story to tell, so we washed our hands of the subject.

The Kiwis were an engaging lot who had travelled from the north and were on their way to South Africa. With them was the equally charismatic Tony, a pony-tailed Australian who apparently had been born in the same Tasmanian hospital as the author of one of the books I had brought, Hollywood icon Errol Flynn. For the purposes of the forthcoming passages, however, I hope he'll forgive me (should he ever read this humble tome) if I band him hereafter in the group 'The Kiwis', the rest of whom consisted of: Heinzy, Tom, Pricey, Goods, Greeny, and Jack, who was short of statue but never slow to provide a friendly ear. This didn't stop him from telling it like it is, though, a quality he very much shared with rugged-looking Greeny. A veteran traveller for the last five years, he embodied the proverb, "if you don't ask, you don't get." Bearded Heinzy was also no-nonsense. Whether or not this was just his way, I supposed the trait might have been due to his being, at thirty one, the 'old man' of the team. The others, like Shaggy and me, were aged between twenty and twenty-five, although I was shocked to learn that well-spoken Pricey and fellow prankster Goods were younger than me, as was the seventh and final member, Tom. Reminiscent of the older Kiwis, however, they were nonetheless as outgoing as they were laid back. I reasoned these traits were forged by a blend of unspoiled childhoods and years of international roving, the latter unsurprising, as Antipodeans are famous for being the great modern-day travellers. Wherever you go in the world, you are always likely to run into someone from Down Under.

These go-getting Kiwis brimmed with all kinds of claims to fame. Brilliant raconteurs, I found myself absorbed by their company and listened intently as they swapped stories of their wide-ranging voyages and exploits both past and present, and of how during their travels they had bumped into just about everybody; half of the stories seemed to have a celebrity attached to them. Such as when, in America, one of them got talking to Oscar-winner Michael Caine, star of *Zulu*, who had then invited him to a party. These anecdotes were by and large

Top Left: *The flight from Moscow, with Ali and fellow passenger Meredith.*
Top Right: *With Albert the Bore, Nairobi.*
Above: *Boating in Nairobi, with Ali, his cousin Sayeed, and Shaggy.*
Left: *'Visitors throwing litter into this pit will be required to retrieve it', says the sign. Shaggy and Ali, by the crocodile pen at Snake Park, Nairobi.*
Below Left: *With Mr Cool Larry X & Suzette, Nairobi.*
Below Right: *Shaggy, standing by the door of our budget room at The New Kenya Lodge, Nairobi.*

Above Left: *My Rwanda visa, issued in Nairobi.*

Above Right: *The New Kenya Lodge, Nairobi. I still have and use the Ron Hill holdall to my left!*

Right: *The Hassans' compound, Kigali. The apparent frivolity belied Shaggy's real feelings towards Snooty.*

Below Left: *Claver and next door's maid, Magolitte, Kigali.*

Below Right: *Posing in Ali's Mercedes. I never really drove it. The shots beneath tell the true tale of our time in Kigali, kipping on a concrete floor and using that toilet.*

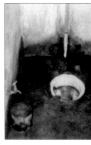

Above: *Shaggy lazing in the compound, Kigali.*
Left: *The jacket I gave away, Kigali.*
Right: *Shaggy and Sajid's secretary, Felicité, the downstairs office, Kigali.*
Below: *The road to Kisangani, Goma. We soon learned that we should have taken more water!*

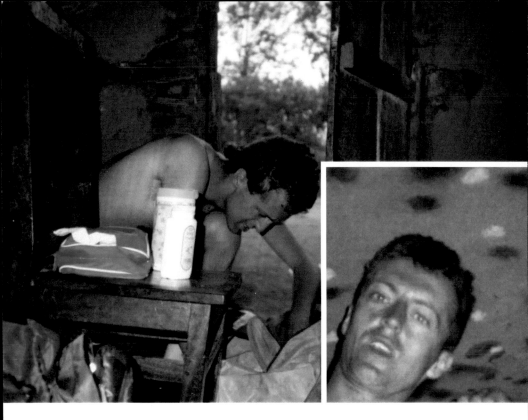

Above & Below: *The chief's hut, somewhere in Zaire.*
Inset: *'the low ceiling was daubed in a strangely eerie leopard effect'.*

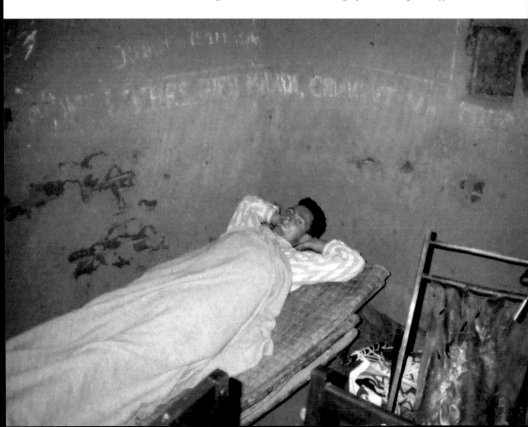

p: One of the rock-hard beds at Butembo. The room was practically 5-star when compared to ...e of the places we stayed at.

...ove: Shaggy frequently switched off his motor. This time (left) on top of the Isuzu — lying ...-down in the background is Duke — and (right) in its sardine tin interior, Apawanza.

...ow Left: 'Shaggy and I followed our host up a short flight of steps — and into a world of clean ...ts'. Trevor, at Beni.

...ow Right: Shaggy, on the second bridge at Epulu. To our right is Hitch. To Shaggy's right is Ike ...who had the same size feet!

Top: *Jerome and his little brother, Pepe, with the Isuzu, at Apawanza.*
Inset: *Squashed into the Isuzu's 'sardine tin' holding pen are (front)*
Pepe and Jerome, and (back) Ferrari and Ike, somewhere in Zaire.

Left & Below: *'for the first time in days both of us were quite content to just mosey along, amongst the ever-exquisite flora'.*
Right: *'Everything comes at a price.'*

Above: *The hottest day yet. You can just make out Shaggy's green tape on my nose, to stop it from burning.*
Left: *His tape also came in handy when fixing the paddle, but don't be fooled by Shaggy's "posing" stance. We paddled sitting down.*
Below: *Cal.*

Below: *Only rarely did Shaggy risk his feet to the jaws of The Bollock–Muncher.*

terribly droll, definitely adventurous, sometimes sad, and occasionally cringeworthy, but the Kiwis weren't the only people with a tale to tell.

They might not have hung around long, but the two American geologists related the most memorable narrative. Whilst staying with a tribe out in the wilds they had been offered monkey for tea. So as not to offend anyone, they had accepted the otherwise unappetizing meal, but instead of being handed something cooked, they soon grasped they would have to watch a live monkey being skinned. Repulsed not only by the sight but also by its sickening screams, the geologists had requested the tribesmen kill it instantly, thereby ending a nightmare of slow torture and its desperate, ineffectual, effort to break free. The natives, however, misunderstood their guests' plea and, thinking only that the noise had disturbed them, just cut out its tongue. Then they resumed peeling its skin, and although its resistance became less frantic, it still took what seemed an age to die.

The chronicles often carried on far into the night, and adventurers one and all would gather around the bar area playing chess — with a made-up board and thirty-two beer bottle tops — telling tales, and topping themselves up with an omnipresent Congolese brew called Primus. It went some way to avoiding my top ten best-tasting lagers, but was nonetheless an integral part of where I existed, in this strange, distant land, at the core of a vast frowning jungle, over 4,000 miles away from home.

Shaggy and I had no sooner rid ourselves of the visa fix than another ace cropped up. It was after the first night, when I rose to find I was itching far more than usual, that I should have taken the hint. On further inspection, I discovered some large red blobs had mottled my arms and ankles, but if I was galled by this, I certainly wasn't prepared for the sight that was to meet me whilst rising from the adjoining bed — Shaggy crawled with the ravages of something that had fed on him. Being amateurs we too-quickly dismissed what transpired to be the real problem, figuring only that we had been victimised by a raiding party of some sort of flying insect, and stomached the consequences until the following morning. This time Shaggy woke to what looked like several hundred bites on his back alone. For whatever reason my back remained untouched (probably too grimy), although I now had additional 'teeth marks' on my arms and ankles, and these itched so much one couldn't help but want to scratch incessantly. Not Shaggy, mind. Despite his itching being tenfold, man that he was, he swore scratching would only make his bites worse and somehow resisted. Balls to that, I tore at mine until blood flowed.

Still too blinkered to appreciate the true cause of our anguish, we decided to show our war wounds to the Kiwis.

"Looks like you've been dined on by bedbugs," said Greeny.

"Sadistic little bastards," uttered Jack.

"No question, bedbugs," confirmed Tony, who went on to explain that the pinhead-sized bedbug is a parasite that lives in mattresses and feeds on you while you are asleep, after which really itchy lumps are installed. "Were there any old bloodstains on the sheets or walls?"

Shaggy and I both gave him a sheepish nod, because in all honesty we had already done our homework about bedbugs and knew all the signs. So did we take heed? Obviously not.

When Larry X told us "at night — beware", we didn't factor in bedbugs.

In attempting to defend our inability to take steps after that first night, whilst in hindsight the clues were there, the room was no less comfortable than anywhere else we had rented so far — better than some, to be fair — and we had never before had a bedbug crisis.

Miffed that we had been given a plague-infested room, which we would later no doubt be expected to pay for, with Pricey winding us up to take action (not that we needed motivating) we barged into the manageress's office.

"Look at my back!" cried Shaggy, lifting his top.

The manageress — a slender, businesslike local of about thirty — replied with an understated "Oh là là", tendered her apologies and moved us into a different cabin. We later saw an orderly taking the mattresses out of the old one and beating them, upon which they were then put back — and other victims moved in.

Even though the new cabin appearing to be bedbug-free, the bites remained and I continued to tear at mine, while Shaggy, rising above the expectations of any normal man, still refused to scratch. That's in spite of the agony in his face, and the torment in his words.

"I-will-not-scratch. Aaaargh! I-will-not-scratch. Aaaaaaargh! I—will—not—scratch. Aaaaaaaaaaaaargh!" ...all night long.

Revenge of a sort came two nights later when the evil bedbug had been replaced by the ever-irritating fly. Impossible to sleep among the buzzing (and itching), unluckily for them, these specific flies weren't nearly as nimble as the usual species and, although outnumbered, we two 'avenging angels' doggedly set about our foes. After a while the main light was turned on and scores of "thirteen nil!" "fourteen nil!" "fifteen nil!" could be heard victoriously ringing out into the night.

When finally we turned off the light, I couldn't get back to sleep, what with maddening discomfort fuelling my customary insomnia — even back home, in familiar surroundings, I always had a problem with sleep. To be out here, though, deep in the tropics, when all was dark, my incapacity to drift into the unknown that vengeful night increased. Just as frustrating was the shortage of alternative diversions. There were no televisions or radios, and my books I'd already read to distraction. Even so, despite the worry over my sleeping patterns pre-Africa, mercifully this night's experience wasn't repeated too often.

Irrespective of whether my sleeping or itching troubles would be here for the duration, the one problem that was indisputably a constant annoyance, and indeed gradually worsened, was The Shits.

In spite of the odd close shave, up until now diarrhoea hadn't led to anything awkward for me, as there had usually been a large tree or bush to escape behind. However, now that I was out of the rainforests and in a town, I decided it would be much safer to embrace a more cautious approach and stayed as close to the hotel toilets as possible, a strategy endorsed by similarly suffering Shaggy. That isn't to say we didn't visit the market, the post office or the bank, we did, but these rambles were always well timed and generally began after a soothing clear out. No, the real problem arose when my sweet-toothed buddy noticed some townsfolk scoffing ice cream and ill-advisedly conveyed this to a man who could, in one sitting, easily gorge a couple of family tubs (and then some).

Drawn by its irresistible appeal, after a short search we soon found the shop from which our 'fix' was peddled. Alas, this proved to be, if you'll forgive the pun, my Waterloo, and while I should have seen it coming, for me the shit was really about to hit the fan. Well, hit something anyway. Although the store wasn't too far away, it was far enough, and our original policy swiftly became more of a guideline than a rule, as we two dessert-worshippers frequented the ice cream parlour just a bit more often than was sensible — with the result that, during one of these simple sprees, yours truly again felt an alarming turbulence building.

What to do? Head back to the sanctuary of the hotel toilets? Yes, of course. But how? Should I sprint back and risk overburdening the metabolism, thereby creating more waste and forcing out what I now urgently tried to keep in? Or should I ease my way back bit by bit, periodically holding my breath (and buttocks) but running the risk that I might not have the time to fight against gravity's natural effect? Either way it didn't matter, for having separated from Shaggy, in the heat of the moment I turned down the wrong alley, got lost, and my quest for the Hotel Olympia suddenly failed, as I felt my overtaxed grits expand with that warm, soggy feeling that in the event threatened to — but thank God didn't — break the elastic. Shitting yourself is one thing, but to have it run down your leg when wearing shorts in public is a whole new ball-game.

Embarrassed but concealing my pickle reasonably well (not least because the garbage-pong of Kisangani's back streets helped mask my own stench — I hoped), I eventually located the Olympia and headed straight to the toilets, which were situated directly past the outdoor dining area. Typical of my day, the bar was packed with customers, including most if not all of the travellers I had come to know, no doubt wondering why I had taken to walking as though I was trying to clutch a cactus between my butt cheeks — then again, for foreigners visiting these parts, Montezuma's Revenge would be the rule rather than the exception. As if this wasn't suspicious enough, no sooner had I reached the nearest toilet and squatted down, than I realised I had made my second mistake of the day: I hadn't checked if it was the one that flushed. Fortunately for me I had chosen correctly, although unfortunately for me it had no loo roll. Thoroughly suspect, I surfaced a full ten minutes later without not only my grits — now jammed behind the cistern — but also no shirtsleeves. Still, as I can certainly testify, and practically speaking, since cotton definitely offers more grip than toilet paper, the method of cleaning one's arse with sleeves should not, if you'll forgive me another pun, be sniffed at.

Chapter 10

ENTER THE DRAGONS

Friday, 30th June. Finding a pirogue wasn't much of a problem. Finding the right one, however, was. When we had initially arrived at the Olympia, the first people Shaggy and I had run into were the hustlers, who stood outside the entrance selling sculptures and clothing, etc, while also promising to get us whatever was accessible, for a price of course. Even if you didn't want anything, they would still be in your face pestering until you bought something to rid yourself of them. To avoid these people I used to just walk past, ignoring them, although at times I would be compelled to back them off by shaking my head and saying, "No! No! No! No!" Shaggy, on the other hand, would have a field day with them. Teasing them to the limit, he would make believe he was highly interested in, say, a T-shirt. He would then try it on and tell them it fitted perfectly, and add that his dad would also love one, and so on. Next he would ask if he could look at a sculpture, as he had lots of gifts to buy. Continuing to act as though he was just as attracted to other things, his next move would be to profess to having no money on him, but if they would bring the items he would meet them "in two hours" outside the bank — always one that was furthest away. Quite miraculously, every time they went to meet him, Shaggy wasn't there.

As luck would have it, it was these hustlers that we were ultimately forced to turn to in order to find a pirogue. Believing they were even dodgier than Limpet, I hadn't wished to consult them at all, but a particular Kisanganian, who we had been hoping would help, had let us down too often, and time was ticking by.

Eugene, the man in question, was quite the minor celebrity in the area and well known among travellers after being mentioned in the only guide book which at the time dealt with Zaire — Lonely Planet's excellent *Africa on a Shoestring* — as a sort of all-purpose Mr Fix-it. Although the title appeared to fit (he had helped change our capital on the black market — and it was he, not the consul, who eventually brokered the Germans' truck), as yet he'd been too busy to solve our pirogue problem, and so we approached Shaggy's best mates.

The hustlers informed us that they would have no problem getting us the cheapest pirogue possible (predictable sales patter, I know, but we were desperate) and led us, for what seemed like miles, to a village downstream of Kisangani. Here, we were introduced to a very shady-looking local – his killer breath so bad I swear his teeth ducked whenever he exhaled.

'Halitosis' endeavoured to sell us an astonishingly pathetic, teeny weeny pirogue for a whopping Z 60,000. To justify this price tag, he affirmed that we would not find one bigger, or indeed cheaper, which was strange, since, unbeknown to the hustlers, Eugene had advised us we would have little difficulty obtaining an adequate dugout for no more than Z 30,000. He even went so far as to insist that not only would this amount be expensive, but anything higher would also be an unmitigated rip-off. Now relating this detail, I bartered against Halitosis for quite some time, starting the price at a more equitable Z 10,000. However, backed up by the hustlers' denunciation of Eugene, the 'I need a mint' pirogue owner was adamant that we wouldn't find a better bargain and stuck to his bullshit price. So, realising I wasn't going to get the cost any lower, and irritated at having had my time squandered on something that looked pared from a twig, I closed our dialogue with a flagrant hint as to where he may shove his pirogue.

Occasionally waxing lyrical about how he fancied owning a market stall, Shaggy held too much of a fascination with haggling to leave it at that, so tried to make a deal himself. Given that I had bartered Mr Poop Breath to a standstill I assumed nothing would change, and sure enough my wrangling colleague also found himself telling Halitosis how he might better park his diddy twig.

With time still passing us by, we at long last managed to persuade Eugene to give us a hand, and come the early morning of our fourth day in Kisangani, we were outside the Olympia shaking hands with this short thirty-five year-old, although he looked a decade younger, who wore designer jeans and a chic sweatshirt, which was edged up at the sleeves, enough to showcase a massive-faced watch – an ensemble that screamed 'wannabe-A-list' personality. But I cared not. He held a wealth of regional knowledge, was affable enough, and since he had stated that he didn't want a penny from us, who was I to complain, or label?

Like the hustlers beforehand, Eugene planned to take us miles away, albeit in the opposite direction, upriver, to a fishing village sited on the banks of one of the Congo's tributaries. In spite of our desire to walk, with Eugene being pushed for time and holding all the cards, we allowed him to talk us into catching a taxi down by the market – subsequently a truly weather-beaten, suspension-free, hole-ridden old jalopy that so poured with fumes we were only too glad to get out of the darned thing alive. It was about to leave with a woman inside, but minor-celebrity Eugene stopped the cabbie and asked how much she was paying. Apparently she was journeying a few blocks away (Z 500-worth), whereas we would be travelling further (Z 1,000), so the driver booted the woman out.

In these parts, the highest bidder definitely got the dinner.

Soon we were by the tributary's edge, looking at pirogues that were much bigger, much smarter and much better than Halitosis' twiglet. The dugouts, however, weren't the only things being scrutinised, as two *muzungus* pricing up a pirogue was a must-see novelty, and within a minute the whole village had crowded around us. Another minute and, via English speaker Eugene, we were back to bartering, this time with a fisherman who looked remarkably like a shorter version of Hollywood actor Woody Strode, the champion gladiator in the 1960 classic *Spartacus*.

Woody offered us a big eighteen-feet long, two-and-a-half-feet wide, strong-looking pirogue for all of Z 16,000, and although it had a twenty-inch circular piece of metal riveted to our side of the hull, it nonetheless floated. Moreover, unlike Halitosis' shitty twig, this was a decent-sized, robust vessel, and we had little objection to sacrificing streamlined speed for a craft that would offer better security against probable storms – whilst we had for the most part enjoyed blazing, dry weather throughout our time in Africa, even when overcast, here in Kisangani we'd had our first taste of equatorial rainstorms. These may have lasted only ten minutes at a time, but take it from me, those deluges, not to mention the booming thunder and forked lightning, made you think twice about your pirogue's dimensions.

There was another reason why it made sense to get a sturdy craft. Although we weren't expecting a visit from the superstar of *Jaws*, large predators undoubtedly abound and the last thing we wanted running through our minds was, 'You're going to need a bigger boat.'

Pleased with the pirogue and its low price, its acquisition wasn't all plain sailing, as there was only one paddle. This meant we would have to pay an extra Z 1,000 for a second. Also, as this tributary was on the wrong side of the waterfall, the pirogue would have to be transported past it by land, which would cost a further Z 2,000. We skinflints did ask if it was possible to navigate the cataract, but were told, not with something so weighty.

While it seemed Woody's expenses would keep mounting, the tax never materialised and we eventually shook hands on Z 19,000, which we agreed to pay on departure, fixing a time for the next morning. All we had to do now was turn up. The Congo was beckoning.

Excited by the prospect of our pending adventure, we headed back to the Olympia, this time on foot, in spite of Eugene's bellyaching for another taxi — very grateful for his assistance we may have been, but there was little sense in drowning ourselves in more exhaust fumes. Especially since we needed to mark out the correct route by which to return. That, and the fact that with Eugene no longer holding all the cards, Scrooge Shaggy refused to cough up another Z 1,000.

As expected, as soon as we had reached the Olympia the first folks we came across were the hustlers, who had no idea that we had found a pirogue and inevitably tried re-hustling us to acquire Halitosis' shite offering.

"You won't get one cheaper."

"You won't get one better."

"You won't get one."

Having spent quite some time haggling with them after I had left the previous day, Shaggy insisted I let him do any talking. Then he waved his hand, summoning the hustlers around him.

"Do you remember yesterday, when you dragged us miles away and showed us that pirogue?"

Sensing a sale, the hustlers crowded in. Did we want to inspect it again? Had we changed our minds? Were we going to buy it after all?

"And do you remember telling us how sixty thousand zaires was a very cheap price?"

The hustlers all nodded.

"And you're still saying we won't find one cheaper, or better?"

Again, more nodding.

"Well, you're *wrong!*"

At this, the hustlers moved to protest, but Shaggy was faster: "No, no, no, don't say anything. Let me just tell you something. Today we bought a pirogue. And guess what? We only paid sixteen thousand zaires for it. That's right, *sixteen* thousand. A big difference from *sixty* thousand, don't you think? And ours is twice the size of that manky piece of shit you showed us..." Again the hustlers tried to cut in, but once more Shaggy wouldn't let them: "Hang on, hang on. I haven't finished yet. I want to tell you slimy toe-rags what you can do with your manky pirogue. Do you know what people do with suppositories? If not, then I shall enlighten you. I want you to go back down to your manky little fishing village, and one by one take hold of that manky little pirogue you showed us, and shove it, sideways, right up your fucking manky arseholes!"

After Shaggy had reprimanded the Olympia hustlers we returned to our cabin and braced ourselves for what turned out to be a future-changing pow-wow. Despite our being elated at attaining a pirogue, its acquisition had nonetheless come at a price, and I don't mean vis-à-vis the extra cash for the paddle and transportation. The price I'm talking about arrived in the shape of a giant bombshell delivered by Eugene. It appeared that a territory beyond our visa-extending town of Bumba was occupied by the Ngombe, a clan of thieves who always covered their tracks by murdering their victims. These lovely people posed no threat to the gargantuan riverboat, but entering their waters as a two-man job without some serious backup was as good as signing one's own death warrant. "Do you have some guns? Can you afford more manpower?" our mediator had asked. Of course many people had endeavoured to steer us from our objectives, but this was different since it came from the oracle Eugene. It wasn't guesswork either; this was something he *knew*.

As much as we trusted Eugene's information, it didn't hurt to get a second opinion. So, giving immigration a miss, we decided to return to the consul, who practically said, "Oh yes, the Ngombe will for sure slay you." Gee, thanks for telling us first time around.

Decision time. As we saw it we had a number of options — the first being to magic some cash from midair, buy backup and weapons, and resume our task with an all-guns-blazing "Do you feel lucky, punk?" methodology. As enticing as that was, it was also less realistic than Bad Max passing a driving test. And so to the more feasible choices, which included basically turning back, or binning the pirogue and catching the riverboat. Both equalled game over, so were instantly discarded. This left two more alternatives: to hope for the best and stubbornly soldier on towards Kinshasa, or else implement Eugene's proposal of merely changing the end goal to Bumba, which, although frustrating, made sense on several levels. For one, the last time we had flouted good counsel it had resulted in the "at night — beware" confrontation with the motorbike gang. Did we really want to keep pushing our luck with marauders? Moreover, it wasn't as if we were against flexibility considering that, when back in Goma, we had ditched plans to travel on the southerly pathway to Kisangani because of bandits. There was also the question of our being the first documented people to paddle a native canoe from Kisangani to Kinshasa. It wasn't our *raison d'être*, but we liked the concept. This, however, was negated by the fact that Kisangani to Bumba would still be a 'first'. Furthermore, it wasn't as if we were going to scupper a source-to-sea attempt, since the cataracts pre-Kisangani had put paid to that thought long before the off. No, the goal, our quest, was to experience, by paddling, a section of the Congo. That I had picked out Kisangani to Kinshasa simply made sense at the time. Kisangani was the first major port after the waterfalls, while Kinshasa was where we would be heading back to England from. The literal length between the two was not the question. The target was purely to paddle a respectable distance. And Kisangani to Bumba — for two novice paddlers, anyway — was a respectable distance.

Everything seemed to favour a modification of our finish line, with one exception. Eugene was quite certain that, even with the riverboat scheduled to set off two days after us, we would still miss its exit from Bumba. This meant that, to get to Kinshasa, as opposed to jumping on the boat for a cosy 'feet up' finale, we would now have to hitch-hike, which didn't exactly thrill me. Not because I disliked walking — I loved hiking through the rainforest — but because I had visions of having to hang around days on end waiting for lifts. As unpalatable as that sounded, being bored senseless still trumped being slaughtered. Grudgingly, we chose Eugene's advice and changed our focal point to Bumba.

Before I continue with the story, I should give a special mention to Eugene, because had it not been for him this book might never have come to pass. Without an alternative, Shaggy and I would most likely have shelled out to Halitosis, and then either capsized and drowned or been slain by the Ngombe. It was therefore frustrating to later read, in the following year's version of the guide book that had so lionised him: 'A man called Eugene...used to be the usual contact, but mention in the last edition has gone to his head and it seems that he's resting on his laurels and doesn't have a lot of useful information these days'. Had they known our story, I doubt they would have been so hasty to print this. Eugene may have taken his time over our dilemma, but he still sorted it. And for no charge.

With our set off time planned for the morning, Shaggy and I headed into the centre for provisions, subsequently bumping into four highly energised Kiwis. Seemingly there was a wonderful café at the market which actually served a real beef dinner.

"It was like eating a Sunday roast," claimed Heinzy.

"Seriously?" asked Shaggy.

"Oh yes," said Goods. "And proper steak. Wasn't it, Tom?"

"Totally. Proper vegetables, too. Potatoes, peas, carrots and gravy."

"Nah, you're kidding," I chipped in.

Apparently they weren't. In fact, they had only just returned from having a juicy platter themselves and they were on their way to inform everyone.

"It was a taste of home," concluded Jack.

Shaggy and I shot off to the marketplace. We wanted our portion of wholesome, much-loved, too-good-to-miss, Sunday roast.

Once there we found Kisangani's main market to be no different from that of Kigali, only this one was enormous. Here, you could buy virtually anything that the town had to offer, from everyday utensils, clothing, fruit and vegetables, to your more elaborate and newly slain, roasted or smoked: fish, goat, antelope, monkey, snake, and even rat.

We didn't buy much food (a pineapple; a tin of corned beef; a loaf of bread; margarine) as we felt we would spot plenty of fruits growing wild en route, so would save cash by scavenging from the land. Before buying any supplies, however, and still licking our lips in anticipation, we had sought out and found the relevant café.

Hmm. We had a nasty feeling that someone was having a laugh at our expense, for a large tent was hardly what we had been expecting. All the same, hunger, and a sign that indicated the meals cost only Z 500 (plus a growing, if unrealistic, vision of Yorkshire puddings), got the better of any sound judgment, so we decided to follow the Kiwis' advice and spoke to the smiling man standing by the entrance, whom we took to be the manager.

"Avez-vous le boeuf ici?" asked Shaggy. "Manger la vache."

"Oui."

"Avec légume," I added. "Moo-moo avec légume."

"Oui, oui," came the reply, together with much beaming and hand beckoning.

Although still dubious, we gave 'Smiler' a chance and followed him inside. Apart from a local couple, the place was deserted, and we parked ourselves at one of the empty tables Smiler had motioned us to. He then disappeared into an adjoining area, concealed from our position, presumably where the chef grappled with the food. With time on our hands we glanced around the room, which wasn't overly unlike a marquee set-up back in Britain — no flooring, just ground, and a collection of benches pulled under a few wooden tables. Yep, we were sceptical alright, and like the chicken back in Butembo, half expected to hear some form of commotion while the chef went toe-to-hoof with whatever it was he was going to cook.

"There is no way this is going to have a happy ending," I declared.

"I think you're right. Shall we tell him we've changed our minds?"

"We need to eat something, so whatever he brings, he brings?"

"Okay, but only because it's cheap."

We had the routinely long wait before discovering our fears were merited, when Smiler reappeared with two battered metal bowls, the contents' overpowering 'rotting corpse' stench forcing us to reel, and he hadn't even reached our table yet. When he did, we could see that each bowl held a lump of something or other.

Trying not to gag, with streaming eyes Shaggy and I looked at the cargo, and then at each other with a twin 'what on earth?' expression. They were peculiar-looking steaks. The reason for this was obvious — although we were sure our French had been fairly graspable, Smiler's understanding of the language was perhaps a tad suspect, and we were given something that undoubtedly was not steak. Not the kind we were used to, anyway. Nor did it come with potatoes, peas or carrots, or any sort of vegetable — and definitely no Yorkshire puddings — just 'gravy'. But, the big question, precisely what did we have? We had no idea, but whatever it was it tasted every bit as foul as it smelled. Even mixing it with some gravy proved pointless, as the flavouring was, in essence, just the blood and juice of whatever creature it had come from. To make matters worse, although the chef had evidently cooked the shit out of it (since it was nigh-on burnt to a cinder), this applied only to the external flesh. The innards, though, were as tough as old leather, and as such proved almost impossible to swallow.

Still not swallowing, and chewing very slowly, we two *haute cuisine* gourmets looked at each other again, our faces each giving away the vileness of the 'what on earth' now being masticated. To add to our misery, Smiler had decided he was going to ogle the proceedings, so we couldn't even spit it out. Not without upsetting him, that is, but his sparkling 'please like me' grin was so passionate that both Shaggy and I felt dutifully obliged not to disappoint. Worse still, he appeared to be so deliriously happy to have pleased his guests that it looked like he was going to watch us devour the whole thing — right up to the last ghastly fragment.

Strewth!

"I really don't want to eat this," Shaggy finally mumbled through a mouthful of 'what on earth'.

"I *can't* eat it," I mumbled back.

"Tell you what, I wish I had my hat. I'd slip whatever it is in there and make out I've scoffed it."

"If he wasn't watching we could maybe spit it out somewhere."

"Ask him to bugger off then."

"Will you ask him? He's beaming at me so hard I wouldn't want to offend him."

"That's two of us."

"I know what, I'll sneak mine into your bowl when he blinks and pretend I've finished."

"No way. I'll sneak mine into your bowl and pretend *I've* finished."

"I'll give you five quid if you eat mine."

"Tenner if you eat them both."

Momentarily we forgot the lump's horridness and erupted into a fit of giggles.

Smiler asked if everything was okay, that 'please don't hurt me or I'll start crying' beam still stamped on his face.

Damn.

"Oui, oui. Magnifique," I said, still unwilling to upset him – not easy when you're half-wretching.

Shaggy employed his own white lie by stroking his abdomen and making approving "mmm, mmm" yummy sounds.

Embarrassingly I joined him: "Mmm – très bon – mmm."

We went back to mumbling.

"Sean, I'm going to throw up."

"That's not going to look too good, is it?"

"I'll bet it looks better than this shit."

"I'll bet it bloody well tastes better too."

We descended into another bout of sniggering, but in due course composed ourselves.

"What do you think he's given us?" I asked.

"I have absolutely no idea. Not sure if I want to know either."

"Probably a wildebeest."

"Warthog."

"A warthog's balls."

"More like his own balls."

After more cackling, we two *former* roast-lovers agreed to tolerate half the meal and then pretend it was so filling we couldn't consume another morsel.

Later on, having procured the machetes and rations, we managed to corner our fabulous 'friends' at the post office. After hearing our gut-wrenching account, the Kiwis bellowed with laughter, and then explained we had both been victims of a wind-up (golly, we hadn't yet realised), adding that we had eaten...

"Rat."

Despite the authenticity of this confession, whatever it was, it most definitely might well have been.

Regardless of all manner of communicative gadgets these days, a post office can still prove to be a useful means of keeping in touch with people when abroad. Certainly it was back in 1989, when there were as yet no email facilities, and mobile phones were in their bulky, un-reliable and astronomically expensive infancy.

Although I was sending postcards from every major town, I wasn't getting anything in return. But this didn't have to be. A pre-planned itinerary means that friends and family can dispatch their letters "care of" the main post office of the town you will be arriving at. All the traveller needs to do is present their passport and ask for any mail bearing their name. Simple, and at that time I couldn't help wishing that, like the Kiwis, I had done this. Especially since many of them had received letters, even in Kisangani, which they generously showed us. I read all correspondence with both pleasure and envy.

Our last night in Kisangani was spent in topsy-turvy land. The other travellers had bought their riverboat tickets and, although it wasn't expected to show up for another two days, everyone was eager to celebrate ...Kiwi-style. This incorporated two items. The first was, unsurprisingly, lager. The second was a particular object Goods had brought with him. As for the identity of this, let's just say it's funny how some people, remembering the time-honoured rule to 'always travel light', might insist on carrying a spare blanket, or an extra pair of jeans, or a second novel in their rucksack. Not so Goods, who had planned to travel the entire length of Africa – and much of the Congo – with a rugby ball. Then again, he did hail from the realm of the All Black.

Of course it's no good having a rugby ball if you're not going to use it, so, young and high-spirited, we booted it all over the place. If truth be told, it was rather a privilege to have a kick about with the Kiwis (their legendary team bordering on gods within the world of rugby union). That said, having played league for my town team, brat here I had to outdo everyone and started hoofing the ball too hard — and it landed on the proprietors' dinner table. End of game.

Now that the physical pastimes had been abandoned, our group of adventurers turned to a new activity — cards. Unfortunately this too had to be discarded, as it was the loser's punishment to drink a whole pint of lager; hence, once the rules of the game had been sussed out, everyone was so hell bent on losing that they just downed the booze anyway. Too drunk to continue, the well-oiled crew decided to return to the warmth of the campfire on which they boiled their daily stew. As usual this was stoked on bits of wood, a few pieces of charcoal and, provided by a couple of the Kiwis who smoked the stuff, lashings of marijuana, which was supposedly illegal but could be purchased by seemingly anyone, and at a ludicrously cheap price. Although Shaggy and I abstained from smoking of any kind, and elected to sit upwind of the fumes, we nonetheless joined in the telling of tales and jokes, briefly forgetting we were a long, long way from home. Between the beer and the strenuous day, soon the entire bunch of us were lying flat out around the fire, a million miles from anywhere.

The following day was our fifth and last in Kisangani. It was time to leave. A time to embark on our ultimate quest, down the Congo river. Shaggy and I bade farewell to Tony, Greeny, Pricey, Goods, Tom, Heinzy and Jack, then marched into the manageress's office. Lucidly remembering the anguish of our first two nights, we had already decided we were going to pay only for the other three, and reminded her that we'd had to change cabins. Despite her earlier apologies, it quickly became obvious that she couldn't have given a tinker's about our two nights of martyrdom (which still had us suffering the itches for the next three nights), as her previously friendly manner changed immediately to that of a right dragon, and she demanded we pay for all five. Shaggy, whose refusal to scratch these past few days had by now taken his patience to the limit, was incensed. With raised hackles he explained that, as a matter of courtesy, we shouldn't be expected to pay for one night, let alone five.

"You ought to be grateful we're offering you anything!" he ended.

But 'The Dragon' wouldn't have it. The expressions 'fair play' and 'public relations' were not in her vocabulary, and she gave him a dose of flaming verbal. In retort and merely agreeing to play by her rules, Shaggy countered with words comparable to his earlier, "take hold of that manky little pirogue...and shove it, sideways!" Alas, she wasn't too happy about this (maybe there wasn't a pirogue to hand) and hit the roof, again insisting we pay for five nights and no less. Too angry to persevere, Shaggy simply slapped the price of three on her desk and turned to go. The Dragon, however, was not the defeatist kind and, barking more verbal flames at him, seized his rucksack and refused to release it. So the only way he could leave now would be to (a) haul her out with him, (b) pay for five nights, or (c) snuff out her puff. Sorely tempted by the last option, Shaggy remained the gentleman and just snatched up the cash, though did let fly with a few more, "and shove it, sideways!" But his antagonist refused to budge and hit back with yet another fiery tirade, the resulting slanging match continuing until Shaggy changed his approach and persuaded her to let him speak to the husband and wife owners instead; he was duly led to where the latter could to be found.

Sat in her cabin stuffing her fat chops as seemed usual, the wife was reputably an even bigger dragon than The Dragon. With this in mind, once Shaggy had been given the green light, I decided it best to wait outside, as you do. After a short while I heard another argument, upon which Shaggy's voice came ringing out loud and clear.

"And fuck you an' all!"

Then he came flying out of her cabin, face like thunder, rushing past me and The Dragon, and then off out through the hotel's exit so fast it took me a while to catch up with him.

"What happened?"

"The fucking bitch."

"What? What?"

"The fucking bitch. I wasn't even halfway through the story when she just cut me off and said, 'Oh, I can't be bothered with you anymore, pay what you want.' Then she waved her hand for me to go and carried on shovelling food into her fat fucking face. Fuuucking bitch. Just ignored me like I was some kind of insignificant piece of shit..."

"Which of course you are."

"Tell you what, I felt like taking every last zaire I had on me and stuffing them straight down her fat fucking, slimy toe-rag throat. Oh, I'd have loved it. Big handful of cash. Right down her fucking manky throat. Eat that, you fat git."

"Then what?"

"I stormed out here, didn't I?"

"But you didn't pay, right?"

"Of course not. I'm not that daft." Shaggy started to laugh. "Once I'd left the fat fuck's cabin, I couldn't have given a shit about her anymore, but I figured that that manageress bitch might come after me, so I just kept my anger going and buggered off as fast as possible."

"You crafty..."

"Well, what do you expect? Right pair of fucking dragons."

Although we had remembered the route back from Woody Strode's fishing village, once we began closing in on it we still managed to lose our way. Rescue came in the form of a small group of youths, who in the event only had to lead us around a set of bushes, yet maintained we pay them for their energy-sapping labours. Still smarting over his treatment at the Olympia, Shaggy just politely told them to "Fuck off" but after having saved some accommodation cash I was feeling charitable and gave them a small tip. Besides, the last thing I wanted before paddling 230 miles in a sawn-off tree was for some whipper-snappers to take the hump and go jinxing us.

The problem now was how to set about shifting the pirogue overland to the banks of the Congo, so as to circumvent the waterfall. Deciding he'd had enough discussion for one day, Shaggy wandered over to the water's edge, leaving me to wade in amongst at least one hundred villagers, all of whom had decided they were going to help. The trouble now, apart from the pirogue being incredibly heavy and any means of transporting it plainly limited, was that there were just too many people determining how it should be moved. I even found myself having to referee one or two minor scuffles, such as in the case of one small boy who was particularly keen to lend a hand. So much so that when we finally heaved the pirogue from the water (tug-of-war-like, with a rope and many bodies lined up, pulling it in unison), the boy did everything he could to squeeze in the line. Unfortunately he just kept getting in the way and, despite his good intentions, ended up being whacked all over the place. Every time he approached an adult to offer his services, it would culminate in their giving him a dig and telling him to get lost. Remaining resolute, he'd move on to the next adult, and sure enough they would give him a clout too – to the point where it actually became funny to everyone, myself included, and even the boy started tittering. Soon he was getting a wallop left, right and centre, all the way down the line. To add to his woes, in an effort to emulate the adults, all his friends came rushing over with their own elbows, cuffs and pushes. Having witnessed this and not to be outdone, when he eventually came to me for assistance, I slapped a mock look of contempt on my face and pretended to backhand him, which had the whole village and even the boy hooting with laughter – thankfully.

Once the pirogue had been dragged from its mooring and on to a cart-like set of wheels, the villagers transported it overland, until we had passed the waterfall, where it was placed – almost symbolically – on the waters of the Congo.

It had been pre-decided that we would pay only at this juncture, and scores of people counted loudly as one by one I handed over nineteen of the Z 1,000 notes that Shaggy and I had pooled. Upon the last thousand, everyone gave a terrific cheer. Then we exchanged goodbyes and climbed into the pirogue – with me at the back, where I had always pictured myself. As for why Shaggy had straightaway gone to the front, when later queried he told me, "So that I could see any danger first and get out first!" (thanks, friend), before admitting he had, "No reason really, I just got in."

When settled, we took up the paddles and requested the villagers to push us as far into the river as they could. At long last, we were on the Congo. Seconds later we were away from the bank and heading for our new finish line of Bumba.

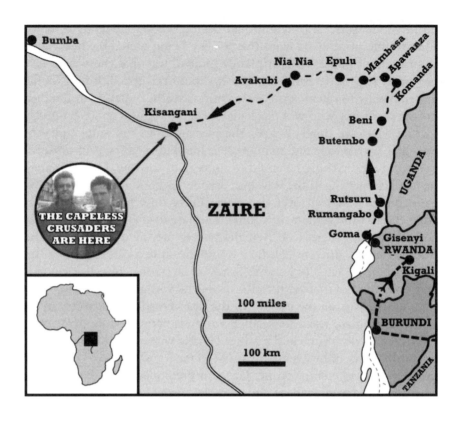

Chapter 11

THE WRATH OF THE CONGO

I suppose the fact that neither of us had ever paddled any form of canoe didn't matter to Shaggy and me. We were adventurers in a land awash with the possibility of derring-do, after that we didn't care. On the other hand, when you are in what is essentially a whittled-down log, on a titanic ocean-like river, and you're anything but Olympic swimmers, it might prove to be a pretty bad idea. Especially when we at once realised we hadn't the faintest clue how to keep the pirogue from spinning in circles – we later sussed our new toy had a natural leaning to the right, although I'm convinced we would have been all over the place during that first hour regardless. To really rub it in, the crowds on the bank began howling with laughter, as the pirogue spun firstly one way and then the other, erratically criss-crossing the waters irrespective of our best efforts. The result of this was obvious – deep embarrassment – and Shaggy and I swapped countless insults, both furiously blaming the other. But there was no escape, and the villagers kept on howling.

Fortunately some fishermen were passing in their pirogue, and one offered to show us how to paddle correctly. We were happily about to let him, until we learned he wanted payment for his time – clearly he didn't know that fifty pence coins are that shape so they can be prised from Shaggy's hand with a spanner. So on we carried unassisted, and while there seemed to be little we could do to fix our dire technique, besides time and practice, once out of everyone's sight we had enough nous to change something we did have control over. Whenever there appeared a village – which invariably meant a gathering of mud huts – to save face we would down paddles and pretend to be taking in the sun. Only once we had floated past would we go back to looking like Laurel and Hardy in a remake of *Dumb and Dumber*.

After a couple of hours of rotating every which way, smacking into the banks, and travelling backwards half the time, we finally mastered some kind of direction to our strokes and succeeded in keeping the pirogue in a straight(ish), forward-facing line. Now our only problem would be newly blistered hands. Well, that and wild animals. And the heat. And a worry that we hadn't brought enough provisions. And, to cap it all, the realisation that our sluggishness was due not only to the cumbersome pirogue and our distinctly amateur paddling, but also a lethargic current. Combine that with the ever-worsening ache in our backs (I would hate to think how excruciating the pain would have been without our rucksacks to use as makeshift stools) and the idea of the escapade being exhilarating soon turned sour, as paddling sank from glamorous notion to downright boring pain in the arse — and back. No fast adventure. No romantic ideal come true.

Another hour passed. No current. No rapids. No speed. More pain. Still no 'adventure'. I look at my map. Bumba: *sixty-trillion light years*. Needless to say, we began jesting about how we were glad we'd binned Kinshasa. And that we should have stayed for the riverboat, despite the fact that the latter started to sound like a genuine wish. Of course, simply catching the riverboat would have gone utterly against not just our central objective, to literally paddle down the Congo, but also our hunger for excitement, for true adventure. Taking a boat was a breeze. Real adventure came in the mode of one's own bodily endeavours, of daring to risk the elements, of sheer physical effort, of being right in the thick of nature, of being part of it, if not the battle against it. And this meant doing precisely what we were doing. At least that's what I told myself, since I was now desperately clinging to the belief that we had done the right thing, even though in my heart I knew we had. Evidently the war of attrition that had started on my body had now moved to my psyche, the very place where wars are often won or lost.

More time passed. More listless currents. More pain. More mind games, as again I was forced to tell myself that one cannot live an adventure by ducking the tough stuff. Anyone could do that — and I wasn't just anyone. I was the little boy with big dreams and aspirations. The little boy who was going to be different. The little boy who was going to boldly go.

The pep talk didn't work. There was something wrong. But what?

Whatever the answer, it didn't lie with fatigue and a crippled back, though obviously these things didn't help. Stuff like this I could cope with. I was an athlete after all; I had a gift for endurance, a history of handling pain. No, the solution to the problem was something else, and my mind harked back to scenes of Tarzan swinging through the jungle, Indiana Jones dashing from the huge boulder, Enid Blyton's characters fleeing down the slippery-slip. There was a common theme running throughout — they each had excitement, had pace, had an edge to them. Like a tennis match that goes into the last set, naturally there is always going to be exhaustion, be aches and pains, but these are equalized by the passion of the moment. At this moment, however, the passion just wasn't there. It was so slow and laborious I'd have found more pleasure in rolling a square boulder up a hill — and we had another God knows how many days of it.

What to do? Call it quits and return to Kisangani? No, that was never an option. Okay, what then? Regrettably there was no answer other than to arrive at Bumba ahead of the riverboat, and that was beyond our reach. Or was it? On our visas we had sixteen days to get there. In spite of the leisurely speed, I didn't see that as too great a test. Making Bumba before the riverboat however? Hmm ...was it truly so unattainable? It was certainly a challenge. In fact, it was a veritable race — my game. Suddenly my zeal picked up, and with a new way of thinking there was just one part of the problem to deal with: putting the stratagem to my unhurried friend.

"Listen, I've been thinking about something..."

"Ouch."

"Ha, good one. Anyway, what I was saying was that, I know that Eugene said we would never get to Bumba before the riverboat, but if we give it everything we've got, you never know."

I hadn't expected a resounding "Yee-ha, let's push on!" but then again I wasn't prepared for the deathly silence that did follow. Even so, I could tell Shaggy was mulling over the idea, so tried to help sway things my way by using the same 'shouldn't we include all forms of adventure' line of reasoning as when plane bargaining back in Goma.

"Let's face it," I resumed, "if we ever get home we may never come back, so I reckon we would be far more satisfied with ourselves if we can take the riverboat, rather than do the same-old, same-old hitch-hiking."

My near-duplicated "more satisfied" tactic didn't fool him one jot.

"You mean you're pissed off with this pirogue and you don't fancy waiting for lifts at the end of it."

"Where on earth did you get that idea?"

"Well," said Shaggy, the sigh in his voice betraying his own disappointment, "let's just see how it goes. If we get to Bumba before the boat, we can get on it. If not, we'll hitchhike."

"Either way makes no difference to me."

"Yeah, right."

With the thought of missing the riverboat at Bumba and having to spend another however many days sitting around waiting for lifts, I then pressed Shaggy to go on paddling as far beyond sunset as possible — something I later came to regret. Being in the jungle when it's dark is one thing, but floating in the centre of the Congo at night opens up a whole new can of worms, particularly if you have a serious case of overactive imagination.

It was practically pitch black. The mainland we guessed was about a quarter-mile away, and with my faith in our ability to remain afloat about as valuable as a second-hand toilet roll, my nerve started to ebb 'Captain Kamikaze meets Bad Max' style. Thankfully not alone in my dread, Shaggy's courage followed suit when the strange, unidentifiable noises that often accompany darkness began to envelop us, especially since they were magnified by the Congo, a river whose banks were filled with every type of wildlife and creepy crawly – the worst was the shrill of what sounded like a banshee being tortured.

"What in the world *is* that?" I asked.

"Don't know, but it's got severe constipation."

Shaggy's witticism did little to offset our fear of either upending in the dark, being attacked by a large creature, or plunging into an island bank crammed with overhanging, scary jungle. Even later, when we discovered the 'banshee' noise had come from some sort of primate, it still managed to put the frighteners on us.

Another hour passed, and we decided our best approach would be to find a clearing along a bank somewhere, preferably an extensive one, and set up a big fire – to discourage any inquisitive animals – then resume paddling when dawn broke, at around six o'clock.

Our eyes now slightly more accustomed to the dark, we noticed the faint outline of an island to our left and decided to head for it, but succeeded only in making the pirogue spin in circles. With a bit of luck, though, we managed to travel in its general direction. The trouble was, not only did there appear to be no clearing, but neither could we stop. More alarming for me, it looked as though my end of the rotating pirogue was about to be selected as jungle fodder – and dinner for whatever lurked within.

"Get your torch out!" I hollered.

"Hang on, I'll just find it."

"You haven't got it to hand?"

"It's here somewhere. Could have sworn..."

"Bloody hurry up!"

"I can't see it anywhere."

"FEEL FOR IT!"

"I am, I can't find it."

"Oh shiiiiiiit!"

The next thing I knew, yep, my end of the pirogue had delved into the island's overhanging trees, and while smacking into these banks and being engulfed by the forest during daylight hours had proved frightening enough – I mean, who knows what's in there – at least I could see. To have it close in around you at night, however, feeling the thicket about your body while effectively blind, is another thing altogether. Yet all Shaggy could do was look on with despair, as my cowering outline disappeared under a shroud of dense, 'life ending' jungle.

Up until now I had managed to act fairly cool and had kept a tight grip on my feelings of terror. Not any more, as this new predicament cast a grim shadow over any gallantry, and proved to be another cause of any remaining 'tough guy' image heading straight out the window. Petrified in the extreme, all I could think about was whether I would be landed on by a snake, creepy-crawlies, head-hunters, or varying combinations of all of them, and I let out a volley of abuse, screaming at my comrade-in-arms to get me the hell out of there. True to form, rather than panicking, Shaggy found my hysteria far too funny to pass up on and started to roar with laughter.

Fuck that.

Paddling frantically, my trepidation refused to let up until we were heading away from danger (although now moving towards the centre of the Congo, as if that were a safe haven), where I managed to reflect on my silliness and broke into a hearty chuckle. But Shaggy wasn't so quick to let me forget.

"You soft bugger."

"Hey, I was just fooling around. Can't believe you fell for that."

"Yeah, right."

Soon we were inventing stories about an imagined colossal killer fish lying in wait below the surface, which we fittingly christened: The Bollock-Muncher. Who would it grab first, and who would somehow scramble to safety, proving he was the real action man hero? As it was, we weren't so far off the truth given that a giant piranha-like species known as the goliath tigerfish populated these waters, its 150lbs bulk and two-inch teeth not something you'd want to dangle your jewellery in front of. Fortunately for us, this assassin inhabited only the upper reaches of the Congo, although its mention was fuel for angst. Subsequently, it crossed our minds that we were still in the dark, haphazardly floating on the deepest river on earth, in the middle of a vast, snake-infested rainforest. Not surprisingly, we began to wonder if we had our 'upper reaches' facts right — maybe a gilled man-eater really was stalking us — and our sense of fun soon turned to dismay, fear, and a great worry for the fantasy-turns-real Bollock-Muncher. Yet each time we made towards land in the hope of finding a clearing, we would be met only by swathes of sinister, pirogue-gobbling rainforest. And the only let-up for me, between the fear of the jungle and that of the now-vivid Muncher, was when the unwary Shaggy had his end of the pirogue plunge headlong into the bank's foliage. Especially as he reacted — to my immense delight — in much the same hysterical manner that I had.

"You wimp," I mocked.

"I was just doing an impression of you."

"Yeah, right."

The pants-shitting score stood at an equitable one-all.

Four hours beyond dusk we finally located a bank with a clearing, levered ourselves alongside and made ready for our first night on the Congo. Rather than sleep on land, with the pirogue being eighteen feet in length, Shaggy had ample space to stretch out at one end and I at the other, thus offering us a smidgen of protection against whatever may walk, crawl or slither our way. And so, with the torch now found, I grabbed my rope and set about mooring for the night.

"Told you this rope would come in handy. Now you just relax, Sonny, while the amazing Sean sorts everything out. First, I will fasten the rope that only I had the foresight to bring along, to this tree, like so. Then I will tie the other end to the pirogue like...er...like..."

Whilst my "amazing Sean" attempt at humour was in this instance as much my way of dealing with acute fear of the coming night, the joking ended when I realised there was no means by which I could attach the rope to the pirogue — no eyelet, no tow-ring, no anything. Bewildered, I thought back to our earlier toilet breaks and it dawned on me that we hadn't actually moored, but had taken turns to lever and hold the pirogue against the banking with our paddles.

"Wait a second, how did Woody Strode anchor it at the village?" asked Shaggy. "I'm sure it was by a rope."

"I thought so too, but now I'm thinking about it, I don't know. I'll bet there was something wedged behind it."

"Bloody typical."

Undiscouraged, we set about the hull with forensic determination, whilst also speculating which our best backup plan was — securing the rope's free end to a large stone and popping it into the pirogue, or attaching it to ourselves. Neither of these seemed particularly safe (or appealing), but fortunately neither proved necessary.

"Bingo! It's here, Shaggy."

"You've found it?"

"Yes, there." I aimed the torch at the bow end. "See, right there where the light is."

"Eh? Where?"

"Bloody hell, get some glasses. *There*, that little hole, three inches below the rim."

"Ah, right. That's why we missed it, it's tiny."

"Bet you can get your knob through it, though."

I handed Shaggy the rope's free end, which he just about managed to squeeze through.

"Tell you what, Sean, I'm glad you're a cheapskate. No way would a normal-sized rope fit through here."

"Your use of *cheapskate* is ironic, and that rope might look like one of those nylon washing lines but it's actually a state-of-the-art rope that Q designed for me."

"You mean it cost you fifty pence."

"A pound actually."

"A quid! I'd have borrowed one."

Our pirogue now securely fastened, further security would come from the fire I proposed to make and, trying to establish I still had some of the he-man about me, I headed inland (not too far, mind!) to gather wood. A couple of minutes later I returned with a stockpile of dead branches, which I then built into a small stack.

"Stand back," I said, utilising my best 'hardy guy starts fire' pitch while I placed a lit match into the timber.

It failed miserably to ignite.

Several botched efforts later, salvation appeared in the mould of three young fishermen who, having noticed our pirogue pulled up in theirs. Fortunately one spoke a little French and, after explaining the problem to him, he offered to light the fire for me. Feeling something of a wuss, I was nonetheless eager to glean what I figured would be a mysterious technique honed and passed down through generations of tribal bushcraft. Well, you'd think. In reality, I put a match to wood: nothing. He put a match to wood: inferno.

Although we did come across the occasional tribesman who wore nothing but indigenous garb (wraps akin to those worn by the ladies, who almost universally wore traditional clothing in this locale), the fishermen's well worn clothes more or less mirrored what we would see for the rest of our pirogue journey. Two of them wore a raggedy T-shirt and shorts with sandals, the other a raggedy vest and long pants, with bare feet. Given their sparse togs, it was no wonder they were good at starting fires of an evening.

The three of them stayed but a few minutes and the conversation followed what proved to be a routine pattern during our forthcoming Congo adventure. Our mixture of dodgy French and sign-language went something like: "What is your name?" "How old are you?" "Are there any fruit-bearing trees here?" (apparently not), and "What the hell is that banshee noise?" Whereas, accompanied by a finger point, theirs seemed to be stuck on anything beginning with: "Give me..."

'it dawned on me that we hadn't actually moored, but had taken turns to lever and hold the pirogue against the banking with our paddles'.

Tuesday, 4th July. Our night's sleep had luckily gone without incident and we were up and paddling by dawn. Even so, all was not well in the world of Sean and Shaggy. Whilst folks across the United States were waking to an Independence Day feast of pancakes and waffles – their thoughts drifting to that evening's lavish banquet – since we had yesterday eaten our meagre food stock, unfortunately for us, our breakfast consisted of nothing more than a swig of water. We had intended to make sandwiches pre-departure; however, that plan had gone up in smoke when we realised that not only was the bread we'd purchased soaked in petrol, but also the corned beef was so foul we could eat only a couple of mouthfuls each. Hence we had discarded everything, including the margarine. Of course it made sense to do this *after* our chief scheme to acquire wild fruits had prevailed. Sadly for us, though, our IQ had fallen to single figures that day – meaning we dimwits had whizzed our stash up front. Sure enough, once again Sod's Law came calling – the wild fruits never materialised. Almost certainly they did exist, but not from our viewpoint. Not yesterday, nor today. So, to address our hunger, we later that morning bought a pineapple from a local passing in his pirogue, an occurrence that unfortunately failed to become a trend.

By 8am the sun was already insufferable and the repetitive back-breaking strokes, which seemed to carry us nowhere, had us both feeling exceedingly low. Then Shaggy complained of his lips cracking again, and he contemplated whether the rest of him would follow suit. Opportunely, our despondency found a brief respite when two of the fishermen from the previous night reappeared – a surprise, since we had set off over two hours ago – and the one who spoke a soupçon of French offered to hop into our pirogue and gift us a paddling lesson. That it came without a price tag gave us another shock following the untold "Give me"s we had received after he'd sorted our fire, but it merited our acceptance, and soon we were zipping along at thrice our usual speed. Not that it was to last. When at five minutes into the assist we playfully asked our paddle tutor to take us all the way, his unexpected "Oui" was followed directly by his leaping back into his mate's pirogue, and off they went! Plainly he'd misinterpreted our ropey French "will you take us all the way" to mean "will you now go away", which deprived us of I dread to think how many extra minutes of added paddle-power. It also taught us a valuable lesson – to keep the gags in-house. Still, his kind support had been a nice touch, and one that helped redeem the preceding night's myriad "Give me"s.

We later attempted to copy his style of paddling, standing upright, the typical Congolese method conducive to the design of their dug-outs. It was the foremost reason why they were so much quicker than us – and why their backs weren't crippled. Try as we might to master the skill, however, time and again we nigh-on capsized, so decided to knock that idea on the head, despite its meaning we'd have to return to our limited pace and pain of back.

As time passed, our paddling technique began to improve, but that didn't stop the Congo's flow remaining wearyingly laboured and it depressed us to watch the upright Africans whooshing past in their smaller, much more streamlined pirogues. Even the reeds floating on the surface moved faster than we did, but the fascinating aspect of this befuddling sight was that most of them appeared to be heading *up*stream. After observing some of the resident fishermen, though, it became evident that floating logs had trapped these reeds, which were in turn dragged by fish caught up in the attached netting. That said, one mega-mound of earth the size of a small island sped upriver at such a tempo that for some time we were left questioning its identity. Shaggy's "it was propelled by an invisible force" theory was of course preposterous, especially when weighed against my wholly plausible, "a disguised mini-submarine."

Disheartened by the mundane paddling, the ache in our backs, the lack of speed, and the heat from the sun, it came as no surprise to find that by mid-afternoon we had scoffed the pineapple and drunk all of our fresh water too. Food we could theoretically do without, but if we were to survive this ordeal we would definitely need liquid, and the reasons we hadn't brought more were as follows: Firstly, we were young and we were male. That made us stupid. Secondly, when going for supplies we had of course intended to obtain extra water canisters, but alas, our frugality kicked in when we saw the shameful fees being charged, so decided to make the water purchase en route to Woody's village. In the event, however, we came across no such merchandise. We did debate going back to the centre, but the combination of our now being acclimatized and, well, pure laziness, meant that we didn't. What a pair of wallies! To be fair there were a couple of other, more defensible, reasons why we hadn't returned. In addition to assuming that we would regularly come across fresh streams, we also believed that we would be able to acquire water at many of the communities dotted along the shore. But herein lay the problem. If there were any streams they had eluded our scrutiny, and while the villages had come in quick succession during the first few hours after leaving Kisangani, it transpired that the further we travelled throughout the backend of yesterday, the less frequently they appeared – a pattern which had continued this day, to the extent that by the time our water supply had disappeared we hadn't seen anyone, not even a distant pirogue, for two hours. So we decided to do something drastic: we imbibed the river water.

Unlike a rivulet, which we presumed clearer, the stories about the toxicity of the Congo were rife, but then again we had by this time grasped that we could filter water by passing it through a shirt before adding our purifying tablets, which we decided we should double up on. Anyway, for all we knew the Congo's flavour might well have resembled that of bubblegum or chocolate (wake up, Sean – slap, slap – wake up). When it came to it, however, reality soon kicked in, as even the repugnant vomit flavour of our purifying tablets couldn't suppress what turned out to be the actual taste of the Congo – faeces.

"Argh!" I spat, my face reeling from the sensory blow.

"Ugh!" squirmed Shaggy. "Tell you what, I don't take shit from anyone, so I'll be damned if I'm going to drink the bloody stuff."

A minute later Shaggy's words rang true, for a large dollop of what genuinely looked like human excrement sailed by (if not human, then another similar-sized animal that ate peanuts). This stomach-turning spectacle was to be repeated often, along with the sighting of bladders and entrails of various breeds of half-eaten animal. Accordingly, we decided that we would never again drink from the river. Instead, we began looking out for lengthy foliage-free banks, as they would give us the best chance to catch sight of any fresh streams. Although few and far between, on such occasions we would scan the undergrowth while walking along the verge, towing the pirogue by the rope.

This time I was rather pleased when dusk arrived, as it brought immeasurable relief after paddling beneath the sun's intense glare for the best part of twelve hours, and especially since our thirst had now been curbed. Although the finding of riverbank hamlets and streams had become a lot less common (our river-water swig had taken place in the midst of a four-hour scarcity), we did in time happen upon the latter.

Becoming increasingly used to the Congo's dark surroundings, we pushed on for another five hours until we reached the bright lights of a community on the northern mainland, probably Yangambi. Feeling somewhat chuffed with our progress, we decided to moor here for the night — where there were lights, there were people, and where there were people there would certainly be fewer predators. The thing was, the man-eating kind weren't necessarily limited to four-legged beasts.

"Shall we go and introduce ourselves?" asked Shaggy.

"If they see us, yeah, but if not, why bother? We've still got some water left."

"What about food?"

"Surely you can hack not eating until we get to another settlement — when it's light."

"I guess so, particularly now that I'm thinking about cannibals."

"What the...? What brought that on? And what a time to do it!"

"You were on about food, and then I started thinking about that book of yours with the 'charred hands in the fire' bit."

"Ah, right. Yeah, but they said they only ate their own kind."

"Tell you what, then, you go and acquaint yourself. Let me know how it goes."

"Well, I would, but it wouldn't be right leaving you on your own. You know, bad manners and all that."

"Sure, sure."

As it was, we had presumed we would at some point come across cannibals, as, rightly or wrongly, we believed they might be found anywhere along the Congo. Naturally we feared them, but then again we feared everything and everybody. The difference with cannibals was that our concerns had been assuaged by stories such as the one above, where explorers spotted human remains in the fire of a tribe of man-eaters. Noting their guests' unease, the tribesmen doubled over with laughter and said that they would never eat *muzungus*. Consequently, our only real fear in this department was the Ngombe killers, but then again Eugene had insisted their territory lay beyond our destination.

After another fleeting debate, we resolved to stick to the cautious policy. Even though finding villages had become gradually harder, we nonetheless believed that we would stumble upon at least one from which we could procure sustenance the following day. Cementing the decision, while the folk of this community may well have invited us into their midst with open arms, we remembered only too well Larry X's "at night — beware" warning, and our subsequent incident with the motorbike gang. As such, we felt that the smart option was to play it safe by seeking out company only during daylight hours, and then only if it was truly warranted. In many ways this would mean our loss, but we were here to 'take on' the Congo, not make lots of friends. At least that's what we told ourselves, so we secured the pirogue against a clearing that was close to the village but not so near that we would be noticed. Then we lay down to rest, presupposing our crack-of-dawn departure would be sufficiently early to guarantee we were gone long before any life stirred.

Unable to sleep properly the entire night, I woke from a light doze to find a motorised pirogue zigzagging in front of us (so much for our strategy of not being seen), which was ironic, since I had fallen asleep dreaming we had one. Although rare, we had seen a couple en route, and combining our limited progress and pain of back, how I longed for my dream to turn real. Had we possessed a propelled dugout, I believe we would have loved every minute of our cruise. Okay, almost every minute.

Unidentified, our vessel had evidently been spotted, and the locals who owned the powered pirogue had been too curious to let sleeping dogs lie. Struggling to see its contents properly, our inquisitors drew closer and closer, until they ventured so close that they awakened the previously peaceful Shaggy — not by the sound of their engine, but by the swell of their wake, soaking him to the bone. Once we had shown our faces, however, they off quicker than a Death Machine nosedive.

Albeit only 5am, we reckoned it would be futile trying to eek out another half-hour's kip, so we returned to our long haul in search of Bumba. Or, as we renamed it, The Jewel of the Congo.

Our nickname for Bumba was coined during one of our isolation/pain/hunger-relieving conversations. Together with sports and rain-forest journeys, one of our shared passions was the Silver Screen, and Shaggy and I often debated the virtues of films we both enjoyed, more often than not the 1930s/40s 'Golden Years'. Of course every decade has its gems, and in the 1980s one of these was the wonderful jungle adventure *Romancing the Stone*. Considering our present location, and its being the only film we had seen at the cinema during our Bournemouth days, it was only a question of time before we got around to discussing it. Since its sequel was called *The Jewel of the Nile*, it doesn't take a genius to work out from where Shaggy plucked: The Jewel of the Congo.

By noon I began to feel that the long shifts had advanced us a fair distance, so was now sure we could reach The Jewel before the riverboat — as long as we gave it our all. And by that let me emphasise the word 'we', for the key to any Bumba success lay in not just my determination to beat the boat, but also Shaggy's. He needed to assume a 'race-mode' too. The good news on that score was that my lone haste was about to change.

"Let's try picking up the pace," he said, imparting an attitude that until now had belonged only to me.

"Sound's like your '*if* we get to Bumba before the boat' has turned into '*let's* get to Bumba before the boat'."

"It has now that I'm thinking about its schedule."

"Schedule? What do you mean?"

"I mean it's just crossed my mind that the riverboat might well get to Kinshasa before our visas expire. If we're on it, we won't have to renew them, and boat tickets are cheaper so it will save us a few quid."

Silly me. When touting for a boost in effort on Day One, I hadn't thought to go for my buddy's Achilles heel — being a tightwad.

"Come on then, Shaggy, let's beat that bloody boat."

"Too right."

The race was on.

With the uplift in spirits we urged each other to paddle faster and faster, even though, like the day before, the sun beat down relentlessly, not exactly a good sign given that we had yet to come across a village, and doubly so since it wasn't long before we were again out of water. Food and a few strong painkillers for our backs wouldn't have gone amiss either. Luckily, an enormous island with a good stretch of sand was soon at hand — its forested apron set back for once, by roughly five yards — and we decided would be much better off towing the pirogue while we walked along the bank. Although the principal reason for this was that it enabled us to keep moving forwards as we searched for water and fruits, it also gave our tortured backs a well-earned rest — not least Shaggy's. Because the pirogue was designed to be paddled standing upright, to get any sort of propulsion we had had to elevate ourselves and were using our rucksacks as seats. The drawback for Shaggy was that the floor curved upwards to my rear, which meant that my 'seat' was higher than his, and the higher one sat in the hull, the less the pressure on the back. We did on one occasion try swapping positions, but by this time we were so used to our initial arrangement that we soon changed over, which I deemed a mercy. Lord knows how sore my back was, but whenever I saw Shaggy stretch or feel for his, I just thanked my lucky stars I wasn't at the bow.

Seeking sustenance and resting our backs notwithstanding, walking on the islands also helped us collect more memories. Beating the boat was one thing, but our aim had been to enjoy a Congo adventure, not just to race past everything willy nilly; there was no point in rushing to the riverboat if it meant missing out on any good stuff along the way, a thought that was exemplified perfectly by this island stroll. Aside from being our longest 'hike' since Kisangani, the pleasure of our two-hundred-yard amble was amplified by an unforeseen guest — a kingfisher which hopped from tree to tree the entire way, watching our every move.

This was why the islands were so perfect. After all, an El Dorado, a Holy Grail, some Scooby Snacks, who was to know what treasures we might have fallen upon? And yet...

Nightmare! Without warning, the sky turned from its customary dazzling blue to the shadowy grey connected with the dreaded rain cloud. Soon the heavens opened, and when it rained in Zaire, it really rained. With the downpour came vicious gales that transformed the sedate river into a tumult of *muzungu*-drowning waves. So we quickly tied the pirogue to the sturdiest-looking tree and took refuge beneath the ensuing mass of jungle — a daunting experience in itself, as who knew what fanged or clawed creatures lurked within?

The storm raged on, so fiercely that at one stage I fully believed it wasn't going to quit and would render us stuck on the island all night (standing in the dark with the predators and creepy crawlies). In a way the deluge was a blessing, as at least we managed to collect a degree of water, although this was far from enough to cover the rest of the day.

Ninety minutes passed and still the skies thundered. Quite where it was all coming from was anyone's guess; it was certainly a surprise to us, as to date we had faced only those momentary, but almighty, cloudbursts at Kisangani. Just as we were losing faith, however, the clouds dispersed and our once unwelcome friend the sun shone down again. Cold and wet, but at least unbitten, we leapt into the pirogue and strove on.

*'we quickly tied the pirogue to the sturdiest-looking tree
and took refuge beneath the ensuing mass of jungle'.*

We managed an hour of paddling before being caught by another torrent. As before, we were about half a mile from the nearest mainland, so again sought refuge on an island. Unfortunately this was only an islet, and the ferocious waves that crashed against its clay bank caused it to crack, crumble, and slide into the murky mire. A highly unsavoury tight spot for us, but beyond trying to stay clear of the edge there was nothing we could do. So we shivered and waited, hoping the gales would relent before they had time to annihilate our little retreat. But there was no stopping the power of nature, and the island began to slowly disintegrate around us.

"Bloody typical," was predictable from Shaggy.

"Tell me about it. We spend ninety minutes freezing our balls off on the last island, and now this."

"Since when have you had any balls?"

"Says the eunuch."

"Says the soprano."

"I think you'll find eunuch tops soprano."

"You're the expert."

Although we had employed our usual banter to make light of a bad situation, the reality was that "this", as I succinctly put it, was rapidly turning into our most overwhelming hurdle yet. One might even say our inescapable end, as we sat defenceless whilst wave after formidable wave smashed into the diminutive isle. Ruthless breakers that, if they didn't engulf the island first, would surely overturn the besieged pirogue, or have it escape its anchor and whip away. And as these terrible consequences drew ever nearer, so stronger grew our feelings of helplessness. Strong enough for me – Mr 'I'll Be Okay' – to seriously wonder whether we were going to get out of this fine mess in one piece. Surviving iffy planes, suicidal taxi drivers, hulking baboons and motorbike gangs was one thing, but now came the prospect of having to tackle what, inside, we always knew would be our greatest trial – the wrath of the Congo.

* * *

Tick tock. Tick tock. Tick tock. Tick tock. Ninety inches, eighty inches, seventy inches, sixty inches – little by little the eroding bank continued to edge towards us, as against it the explosive waters beat out an unremitting war cry, the gales whipping the river into such a furore that any attempt to reach the mainland remained suicidal folly. Caught between the devil and the deep blue sea, into the mix the beleaguered pirogue rocked ever more ominously, its aggressive jerks threatening to uproot the already storm-weakened tree to which we had tethered it. Yet, with the rains still drenching us to the bone, through every nail-biting sway and pounding wave all we could do was watch silently, as living off borrowed time we figuratively crossed our fingers, hoping against hope that the island would outlast the blitz. But as the seconds and minutes ticked agonisingly by, tragedy seemed to spiral unavoidably closer, and slowly but surely I began to understand what it was like to await the hangman's noose, as the knot in my stomach tightened progressively, the moment of doom looming ever larger. And through it all there was absolutely nothing we could do except pray for a miracle, while every now and then a glint of sunlight poked teasingly through the blackened sky. It gave us hope, but unfortunately it was false, for just as suddenly the light was gone, and once more a calamitous end came calling. Tick tock. Tick tock. Tick tock. Tick tock.

Mercifully, there was a let-up in the storm – a bona fide one this time. Whether this meant it was dying out altogether or merely tempting us to presume so, we didn't know. What we did know was that, although it was some distance away, this was our chance to make the mainland. Any doubt as to whether we should attempt it was quelled by the thought that the island might literally soon be gone. So we pressed on, and as Shaggy went to untie us I hoisted myself into the pirogue and readied my paddle. In an act of defiance I then turned to look at the calmer but still menacing swirls of the ocean-like obstacle we were about to face, and with my most spirited glare beckoned the river to 'bring it on'. If I was going to exit this world, it wasn't without putting up one hell of a fight. A second later I felt the pirogue angle as Shaggy embarked behind me, a movement that corresponded with something else: a disquieting noise that forced me to swiftly revolve. It was then that I saw a most astonishing sight – half of the island had vanished.

"Whoa!"

Hesitation reigned. It was like that moment when, in his mind's eye, a cricket umpire plays again what may or may not have been an LBW. That instant when all around ceases to exist whilst the brain puts things into perspective. Was it my imagination, or had half an island just been wiped out? If so, what a brilliant piece of timing on our part. Especially since the now-defunct half was that on which we had sat. All the same, minds can play tricks. I did a quick assessment: There was a raging torrent? Check. The island was subsiding? Check. There were previously more trees and bushes? Check. Half the island is now missing? Yes! Check! Bloody hell, and how lucky that Shaggy, who only a second earlier had stood in the exact same spot that now held nothing but water, had managed to get into the piro... managed to get into... into the... the... Shaggy? Where the hell was Shaggy? Surely not overboard. As choppy as the waters were, the storm's lull had ensured they weren't *that* turbulent. 'Hang on a minute, Sean – think,' I told myself. 'Did he even get into the pirogue? The tilting you assumed was Shaggy's weight had happened at the same time the island had collapsed. Holy shit, it was the island that had caused the lift, not Shaggy! So that means...'

I replayed the scene in which I had last seen him. Yes, he had been standing on this side of the island. But had he been captured by the abyss? Yet it was only too obvious: Lee Walker, son, brother, nephew, grandson, was now a victim of the Congo.

Never one for accepting defeat before the fat lady sings (although unfortunately for Shaggy, I'd heard her belt out quite a few tunes over the years), as pointless as it seemed I scanned the area for any signs of life, but there was nothing. Not a jot. *Nada*. Even so, I was about to shout for my lost friend ...when a certain someone appeared beaming from behind the remaining bushes.

"You idiot! I thought you'd gone into the drink!"

"With that Bollock-Muncher thing lying in wait down there? You must be nuts!"

We both laughed — a mixture of Shaggy's witticism and nervous relief, because at least one of us had all but bought the deeds to Davy Jones' Locker. Hurriedly, Shaggy explained that he'd been forced to dive behind the bushes in order to avoid going down with the island, which only served to remind us that the other half was likely to follow suit. So, with the fat lady still ready and waiting in the wings, we terminated our chatter and started out towards the mainland.

We got lucky setting off when we did. Not only did we time it to perfection with regards to the storm dying out, but minutes after our departure we also looked back to see that the entire island had completely disappeared, swallowed by the rage of the all-consuming river.

Don't screw around with the Congo.

We weren't remotely about to do so.

Or were we?

After surviving two storms we figured we'd had a pretty rough day. We certainly hadn't counted on that old maxim we had been so quick to dismiss: bad luck comes in threes, the third instalment often being the worst.

Between our position and our objective lay another little island, the protection of which we had just passed when ...bang! Like a bear rounding on two bees, the mother of all storms struck.

What to do? Withdrawing to the island would have been the level-headed solution, but after seeing what happened to the last one, no thanks. So now the question was this: Could the bear catch the bees? Yet caught we were. Out in the open. This frenzied, rampant storm that appeared to come from Hades' very depths now threatened to destroy both the pirogue and all its contents, as nature's unbending fury turned on us. The heavens, the waves, the winds — all conspired against us, especially the pelting rain, which robbed us of our sight. But we refused to submit, and despite the savage winds and torrential downpour we struck out into the volley of waves. Huge swirling waves that — boom! — rocked the pirogue against the mouth of the storm. Nevertheless we soldiered on; aching limbs and mounting pains now pushed aside, we fought on and on, struggling towards a mainland that edged oh-so-slowly nearer. And although our strength had been sapped by a lack of food and water, and by too much sun, our arms, unrelenting metronomes, continued to tear at the paddles, while at the same time I hollered at Shaggy, trying to motivate a heart I hoped had not yet resigned itself to death. For surely, had the pirogue over-turned, that would have sealed our fate, as time and time again our embattled vessel swayed, tilted and threatened to go under. Yet time and time again, instead of sinking it soared and gave us hope to fight on. And fight on we did.

Boom! Another wave.

Boom! And another.

By this time we were tired. Very tired. But we knew something that Hades didn't — we had been here before. As athletes we had been at the door of exhaustion, been to that brink we call the pain barrier. The early morning runs; the sprint drills; the track repetitions; driving ourselves through the mud of a cross-country race; endless forays up a quarter-mile sand-hill while lactic acid coursed through the body, and fit-to-burst lungs screamed: 'No more! No more!' As competitors we trained ourselves to push right to the limit of fatigue. As winners we had learned to go that one step further — to embrace it. Today we drove ourselves back to that threshold, but this time there wasn't a thumbs-up from our coach, no personal best time to gain, no ribboned medal at its conclusion. This time it was different. This time it was for our lives.

Boom! Another wave, and we were nearly upended.

Despite my optimism, throughout our ordeal I was planning what I would do in such an instance. 'Should I try to cling to the pirogue?' I asked myself. 'Yes, grab it and attempt to ride out the storm. But, hold on, what if it gets washed away? Swim, Sean, swim. At least try to float. Leave the rucksack, it's unimportant. Worry about its contents later, just save yourself. What about Shaggy, should I help him? No, he's healthy, he can take care of himself. Focus on you. Hang on, here comes another wave. Hold your breath. Shit, I can't see. The spray, the rain, I can't see anything. So what? Keep paddling. Metronome, think metronome. You haven't overturned yet. You can still make the mainland. Just keep going. Come on, Sean ...Come on ...Come on! ...Come on!!! ...Come oooooooooooooooon!!!'

BOOM!!! The biggest of all waves hit us at an unforgiving angle, and in truth that should have been it, curtains. Only there are certain things in life that remain unexplained outside the basic fact that there are some people who simply refuse to lie down and die. Fortunately for me, the person sitting in front of me that thundery day was one of those individuals. One of those die hard characters who point-blank decline to succumb. And whilst, okay, I had yelled encouragement in an effort to motivate Shaggy, I hadn't really needed to. Whoever had been in the pirogue with me, that's how I would have played it — it was just my way. In situations like this, when your back's against the wall, the last person you want to be sharing such an adventure with is one who needs motivating. That's why I was more than happy to have

Shaggy on my side, as no way would he resign himself to death. Sure, there were times in Bournemouth when he would idle on the sofa, dead to the world, and the rest of us would be compelled to tell him, "Come on, let's go." And yes, Shaggy's slothfulness in Zaire had often presented itself in the form of wanting to hang around waiting for lifts rather than keep walking. But these were times when our survival hadn't depended upon it. Had it done so, believe you me that man would have 'been there'. Like a Formula One supercar with the engine switched off, Shaggy's inactive side may well have registered nothing, but depress the button and you had a turbo-charged, never-say-die mega-machine who didn't know the meaning of defeat, even in the face of impending doom. So don't kid yourself one iota; you'd need more than the ferocity of nature to kill off tough-as-old-boots Lee 'Shaggy' Walker. Frankly, that went for me also — so fuck you, Hades.

Eventually, and not before time, we came through the worst of the storm and reached the left-hand bank and the sanctuary of a village, which could only mean one thing: we had done it. We had weathered the tempest. We had beaten nature. We had survived. We were alive.

We had four lives left.

Chapter 12

THE INNER JOURNEY

At the village we were able to obtain some water and what turned out to be our only meal for the day, a bunch of bananas. We were also offered some smoked fish, but my typically thrifty and immovable pal wasn't pleased with their prices and, in spite of our dearth, since they refused to barter, he refused the fish. We declined something else as well — their advice. The villagers were adamant that the storm would come again, insisting it would be insane to carry on. However, fuelled by our craving to make Bumba (and Shaggy asserting their advice was more a ploy to keep us there to fleece), we ignored the warnings and forged onwards, this time remaining as close to the bank as possible. In doing so, we managed to push through the last of the winds and, despite our quandary, began to make headway.

Although we had recovered some since the storm, by now we were fairly beat and any additional strife would undoubtedly be met with great disapproval. And yet, if there's one lesson I had learned in my twenty-three years, it was that one doesn't always get what one wants — and I most definitely did not want to be bothered by a group of hysterical children howling at me from the bank. But there they were, around thirty cherubim running adjacent to the pirogue, all of them shrieking, "Tourists! Tourists! Tourists!" Each and every one of them set on outdoing those other angelic tots who had tried to pierce our eardrums way back in Rwanda.

It wasn't just the infuriatingly repetitive high-pitched 'fingernails down a blackboard' chant that grated, for over time I truly didn't like being referred to as a "tourist". I know it seems snobbish, but when you have stayed with and journeyed with the locals, when you have eaten in and crapped in the bush, you don't want to be called a 'mere' holidaymaker. After all, "I've spent time in Africa" may be a sincere declaration, but it's a different statement when coming from a person who has endured a year of backpacking through jungles and deserts, as opposed to the person who uses it after a one-week all-inclusive luxury break in the Seychelles. Of course I'm not knocking holidays or holidaymakers, and I also understood that these children had only the one non-African word for all foreigners, but this didn't prevent it from rankling me. Especially since I had already heard the same ear-splitting chant numerous times during our first day on the Congo, a grievance I shared with other *travellers*.

"Tourists! Tourists! Tourists!"

The cherubs followed us for several minutes: "Tourists! Tourists! Tourists! Tourists! Tourists! Tourists! Tourists!" they cried. Now and again I shouted for them to quit, but the "Tourists! Tourists!" persisted.

One boy, deciding to be different, then continuously requested we buy his dog! But every time we refused, he looked baffled, as though he couldn't twig why two 'tourists', travelling down the Congo in a pirogue, wouldn't want to purchase a dog. So he carried on asking.

As much as I like children, had I been capable of it I might have dunked my head in the Congo and endeavoured to smash the world breath-holding record until we had passed by (The Muncher would have loved that), as again I yelled at them to shut up and again they paid no heed... "Tourists! Tourists! Tourists!"

"Talk about Sod's Law!" I eventually barked above the din. "We've spent the best part of three days trying to find banks with a decent clearing, and now I can't wait for this one to end!"

Equally frustrated, Shaggy hit upon what seemed a good idea.

"Tell you what, Sean — universal language! One...two...three..."

"FUCK OFF!!!" we both blasted.

Our synchronized chorus froze the wee angels dead in their tracks. Superb.

Shaggy and I began laughing, the act of swearing at a party of small children appealing to some innately juvenile sense of humour, even though the little darlings probably had no idea of what we had said. Then, within seconds... "Tourists! Tourists! Tourists!"

At the outset, we had decided on the sensible approach of sticking to the same bank from which we had departed, the right-hand (north) bank, until we had arrived at Bumba, also on the right. Thanks to our early days' paddling 'technique', however, which had us involuntarily criss-crossing the river regardless, that tactic had quickly evaporated. Accordingly, once our proficiency improved, we decided we might as well chop time off our voyage by cutting corners whenever the Congo meandered (hence our ending up on islands at the centre). Taking our present status into consideration, we were justly ecstatic to notice the next bend meant we would have to cross over to the right and, once the waters became calm enough, a feeling of liberation seeped over us as the cries of "Tourists! Tourists! Tourists!" faded into the distance.

Although the cherubim and their shrilling mantra had gone, a small part of that encounter had stayed with me, namely the boy who had tried to sell his dog — it was a reminder that I hadn't seen my own mutt for four weeks now. Luckily for Shaggy he didn't at that time have a pet, but for soft sod here the guilt trip about leaving my English bull-terrier, albeit with my parents, and also theirs (although I classified him as mine), made the inner journey every bit as tough as the outer. A dog might not be a child or partner, but they're still your little piece of emotional attachment. Moreover, while it's never easy to leave behind your family and friends, for peace of mind at least you can say to them, "Do not worry, I will be coming back." You can also attempt to let them know that you are fine via one or two forms of communication. Crucially, though, they *know*. They know why you have gone. They know where you have gone. They know you are supposed to be returning. Your dog doesn't. Your dog has no idea. The only thing it knows is that for all of their life you've been there, and then in a heartbeat you don't exist. They scent the air, and you're not there. They walk around your home, but you are nowhere. You can't give them comfort by saying, "Look, I'm coming back." All they can do is wonder if you ever will. Yet when each day you don't, no doubt they grieve in their own small way. And didn't I know it.

Everything comes at a price.

In time night fell, and with it the sun's heat, denying us the opportunity of drying our damp clothes and sodden footwear. It wouldn't have mattered anyway, for the rains struck again, but this time they weren't nearly as harsh. Since we were also spared the tempestuous winds, we figured it best to struggle on, believing that if we moored for the night we would freeze half to death. Cold and wet, our plan now was to bite the bullet and revise past policy. We would somehow find a native camp and hope they'd have a fire to warm ourselves. In the event, however, any light we saw came from the opposite bank, a squillion miles to our left. A sad fact, but had we thought back we would have realised that we hadn't seen another pirogue since 'teatime', some five hours ago. Indeed, from here on we would see little sign of human life for quite some time.

Trying to keep warm by paddling, we stuck with it until midnight before finally admitting defeat — a total of seventeen hours for the day, which equalled our best. While we failed to find a village, all was not lost, for another 'bright' Sean and Shaggy idea had long since hatched. Still super determined to beat the riverboat, now that we had become familiar with the surroundings, we resolved to do something utterly outrageous. Perhaps the long paddling shifts had made us a little too self-assured, but between us we decided to take a chance and try to float the entire night, even while asleep. Barmy? Absolutely! Do note, though, that our original plan had been to take turns sleeping. However, after such a gruelling day we realised that not only was there very little chance of staying awake half the night each, but in all sincerity we were also too jaded to be arsed to even try. So we agreed to literally go with the flow. Besides, storms apart, everything had passed mainly without any hassles, so why not? Of course a storm may well rear its ugly head, but, applying the law of averages, we figured that we were good for at least two days of calm. Idiots! Anyway, if we had managed to elude disaster thus far, who was to say we couldn't keep on doing it? After much initial concern, we slowly drifted off into the land of nod.

The night went without mishap.

Day Four on the river, I woke a good twenty minutes before the sun rose and cursed my luck for it, as my clothes were still freezing and wet. Seconds later and Shaggy awoke to the same complaint, so without delay we began paddling, trying to reheat our damp bodies. While we hadn't managed to get much sleep the previous night (catnapping for fear of upending in the dark), it was obvious that we had never been in any sort of difficulty. So, after a short discussion, we decided that from this moment on we would try to float the entire night every night. Just as zany, we also decided to expose ourselves to the sun for longer periods. Not too much of course, but with more 'cooking' we reckoned we would definitely be warm the next night, rain or no rain.

It was the first and only overcast day of our whole voyage.

Sigh.

In spite of the clouds, by mid-morning both of us had completely dried off and were stripped to our shorts. Alas, our tops were not the only things that had been stripped that morning, for Hercules Shaggy managed to break his paddle — stripping the odds of our making The Jewel before the riverboat from an even-money flutter to a mammoth odds-against.

Whenever we needed to moor to a bank (usually in a hectic race to shit somewhere less messy than in our grits), we found it simpler to manoeuvre the pirogue by sticking our paddles into the riverbed, which was normally shallow around a clearing, and levering it to the side. On this particular morning, however, the riverbed Shaggy hastily jammed his paddle into decided it wasn't going to give it back, and when he yanked at it a touch too keenly — as you would, if bursting for a crap — the bloody thing snapped in half. Too desperate to stand and weep, we had leapt behind opposing bushes and after a relieving clear-out returned to inspect the damage.

"Did you keep the receipt?" I asked.

"Think I chucked it with the flask and chocolates."

"Fair enough."

By freaky coincidence, the first people we came upon for eighteen hours, a company of women, breezed by in their pirogue and, having noticed our predicament, gifted us a spare paddle.

Despite the charitable deed, for which we of course felt indebted, there was a catch: it was no bigger than a table-tennis bat. The upshot being that we were still faced with the same one-paddle dilemma.

Using brain cells we thought had long since migrated, we decided on an alternative scheme. Having bumped into a bunch of women, we concluded that some form of habitation couldn't be too far away, so banked on procuring not only much needed sustenance, but also a more sizeable paddle.

We were right, for their village was around the next bend. The snag was, we became caught in a current that was taking us away from the settlement, but with the help of some passing fishermen we managed to find the right channel in which to steer the pirogue, and very soon Shaggy was disappearing into the jungle with one of the villagers.

Word of our arrival ran wild, and presently I was subjected to the rest of the tribe's inquisitiveness. This meant that I was confronted by a wall of about a hundred villagers, something I was not entirely over the moon about, although not because I didn't like attention — being in the spotlight I could take or leave, depending upon its nature, of course. Had I been in receipt of an Academy Award or Olympic gold, then sure, no worries; bring it on. But being the centre of attention because I was Sean McCarthy 'the thing' was different. I didn't know why I felt like an object — I had been faced with a similar situation when buying the pirogue from Woody Strode and had experienced no such awkward feelings. The difference, maybe, was that Woody's village was close to Kisangani, so their people would have regularly encountered muzungus; plus Shaggy hadn't vanished from sight. On the other hand, there was something else, something more basic. At Woody's village, or indeed any of the places we had hitherto come across, I had interacted. And this, in retrospect, was the key difference. At this new village, there was no interaction. No one spoke to me. No one gestured. No one moved a muscle. They just stood and stared. To the point that I became so overtly conscious of the two hundred eyes now fixed on my every move, and the eerie silence that went with it, that I couldn't help but mutter for the speedy return of Shaggy. Overhearing my deliberation, my audience just looked at each other as if to say, 'Did you hear it mumble?'

To be fair, my sensation of awkwardness was probably as much my fault as theirs. Had I gone amongst them, shook hands, intermingled, there's every chance that I would have been made to feel comfortable. Even so, a wave of relief washed over me when I spied a returning Shaggy, particularly as he was carrying a brand new paddle, which was thankfully far superior to the table-tennis bat we had so generously been handed – although still not as substantial as the original. It made sense that Shaggy also try to get as much food and water as possible, but he returned only with our waterbottles refilled, the paddle, and one pineapple. Apparently the paddle was "a steal", but the man he'd departed with had, amid the usual welter of "Give me"s, demanded prices for food and water that were somewhat outlandish (or at least Shaggy's idea of outlandish), and refused to drop them. As with the smoked fish the day before, my buddy had therefore purchased the bare necessities only, even though over the past three days we had eaten a combined total of: a bit of corned beef, a dash of margarine, three pineapples, and a handful of bananas. During the forthcoming days we would eat only the new pineapple and a bunch of bananas we had yet to buy, end of story. And that's despite day-long paddling shifts that, when coupled with the heat and humidity, had us burning calories like Grand Tour cyclists.

Good job I was on a diet.

With a new paddle in hand we pushed on, stoked by our desire to make Bumba, again ignoring the listless flow, the immutable scenery, the concealed wildlife, the dehydration, the runs, and the continual nagging pain about our backs, forging onward, always moving, forever trying.

It wasn't too long after leaving the fishing village that Shaggy and I reached a critical milestone: Basoko, which was the biggest settlement between Kisangani and Bumba. The significance to us, however, lay not in its dimensions (nor in the fact that it would have been at this point that we would have emerged, had we been able to paddle from Epulu), but more notably because Basoko was the first concrete sign that we had passed the halfway stage. As such, we were greatly fuelled by the assumption that we were now on course to arrive at The Jewel sometime during the weekend, and therefore didn't want to stop for anything unless we categorically had to, so decided to press on. This may seem like a strange decision, but it wasn't made without further cause, as our primary thoughts had been to drop anchor and acquire extra provisions here — although our sojourn at the last village was still relatively recent, it made sense to obtain whatever nourishment we could. However, upon drawing closer to the bank, all we ran into was a gathering of finger-pointers, each of whom seemed to expect a handout upon their "Give me" command. While this was irritating, it wasn't the main problem — we were used to it by now, after all. No, the trouble arose when we tried to negotiate an exchange of goods for groceries, yet received replies tantamount to: "Get stuffed, arseholes." Add this to our belief that there would soon be another village from which to gain supplies, and we rejected going ashore — a decision that turned out to be one of those "don't fret yourself about that iceberg" clangers. As far as gaining rations at the next village went, it certainly wasn't to be this day.

Looking back, it could be argued that our negativity towards the Congo's Give-Me men was influenced by our memory of the lovely, benevolent people we had met whilst hitchhiking in eastern Zaire. That's why, despite our misgivings, Shaggy and I could never in reality make a fail-safe assessment of them. Had we taken time to familiarise ourselves, who knows, like the young Give-Me fisherman who had later redeemed himself by helping us paddle, perhaps our grievances might have been mitigated. Besides, our *muzungu* forefathers surely had to take a dose of the blame. Britain, France, Portugal, Germany, Russia, Italy, Holland, Spain — in the 'Scramble for Africa' they all had blood on their hands, and none more so than the former ruler of where we were, King Leopold II of Belgium. Having spent over two decades robbing their land and mutilating and butchering millions of Congolese in the process, his ousting in 1908 didn't stop more rich foreigners from coming over and 'buying' whatever they wanted. So how could I possibly complain when they asked for a morsel back? All the same, after countless random groups of people have insisted you give them your every possession, whilst their offspring are in unison shrieking at full pelt down your poor lugholes, it's hard not to have some reservations.

Although the Give-Me men and their kids' screeches remained a thorny pain in the rump whenever we came across them, rather than shout obscenities back as I had with the wee mites the previous day, I decided to adopt a course of action that had worked well for us from time to time: humour. A perfect example of which was here at Basoko, where I learnt that mimicry could be used to calming effect.

I didn't know how but, though I hadn't practised at all, I found I could somewhat competently imitate the resident language. Of course I never knew what on earth I was saying, and without doubt my words never meant anything, but to another foreigner I appeared able to speak the native tongue. So, once we had sussed we were going to get little from the Basokians beyond a shower of "Give me"s, when next the fishermen called to us, motioning with their arms for us to hand over our stuff, I just shrugged and, making sure I used the correct inflections, answered accordingly: "Unaka jouibanawi umbuska lana wombungi", or whatever. Then the villagers and I would strike up a dialogue of sorts, in which I would simply respond to their gestures. At first Shaggy was astounded by my 'knowledge' of (presumably at this location) Lingala, but when I professed not to have a clue as to what I was babbling, he burst out laughing, thereafter joining in the 'conversation' with much aplomb himself.

The Give-Me men aside, luckily we hadn't yet run into any large critter problems on or around the Congo — Shaggy spied one water snake, and that was it. Of course that's not to say that a diarrhoea-inducing beast wouldn't crop up, and on the river our animal worries included the two highlighted so memorably by the "one of them's bound to eat you" Kiwis — crocodiles and hippopotamuses (the latter is, surprisingly, the most prolific mammalian killer of man in Africa). From what I had read, neither of them needed to be a worry to us, as supposedly they inhabited only lakes and small rivers. The obvious problem with this is that crocodiles and hippos don't read! Besides, who was to say that they didn't populate one of the Congo's narrow, reed-filled channels? And if they did, and we ended up in the self-same strait, and then in our complacency we saw a fresh water rivulet and made an ignorant beeline for it... Well, it might prove to be a case of 'Goodbye world — hello afterlife'. Of course this was all conjecture, but until that moment, we tried to remain as cautious as possible.

While anything big had thus far been too afraid to cross our all-powerful rampaging path, there was one species that definitely fancied its chances: bloody flies, the worst of which, throughout the day, were the dreaded and ever-voracious horseflies.

Illustrative of the entire voyage, there was always at least one fly of some type kicking around, although I rarely bothered swatting them, choosing to get on with my paddling and ignore them as best I could. Whenever one of those sabre-toothed horseflies decided to drop in on me for its afternoon snack, however, a good old-fashioned swat was undoubtedly the order of the day; those buggers really could bite. Ordinarily a few swipes and they'd tuck tail and flee, and yet on this occasion, no matter how often I lashed out, I could not deter the two 'adversaries' I now found buzzing behind my seemingly yummy bare back. Through sheer boredom I eventually quit trying. Besides, they hadn't actually tried to bite me, it was just the thought that they might that had propelled me to swat at them.

"Did you kill those horseflies?" asked Shaggy, his back to me of course.

"Nope."

"Did they go away?"

"Nope."

"Why don't you kill them, then?"

"Not fast enough. Mind you, there's some other kind of fly, a little one, perched about two feet away from me."

"Kill that, then."

"Nah, it's okay. It's just sat there peaceable-like, minding its own business."

Minutes ticked by, and although the horseflies continued to buzz annoyingly behind me, I somehow managed to keep my cool and disregarded the potential danger. More fool me...

'Chomp!'

Reeling in agony I leapt to my feet, as the last few ounces of sanity eroded with that one, painful bite.

"That's it! That—is—it!" I bellowed, turning on my antagonists. "I'm going to kill them, I'll bloody well kill them I will! They—are—dead—meat!"

Shaggy began laughing. "Did one bite you?"

"*Bite* me? The little shit's taken a huge lump out of my back! I'm going to damned well kill it! ...When I get hold of it."

Luck went my way, as one of the horseflies then foolishly decided to perch on my rucksack.

"A-ha! There's one of them now. Ha! Ha! Ha!"

I was half-wild with vengeance now and, laughing like a deranged idiot, roared triumphantly as I trapped the fly under my mum's once-clean towel.

Deciding on a really evil execution, I figured a slower death was far more appropriate than the usual crushing approach, and I gently felt beneath the towel until I had enclosed the horsefly in my hand. Still maniacally snorting, I then pushed it into the river.

"What's happening?"

"I'm going to drown it," I gloated.

Despite my anger, after only a moment I removed the fly from the water. As much as I had told Shaggy I was intending to top it, and as much as I had at the time meant it, once my hand was immersed my true self kicked in — drowning anything, even a fly, wasn't and isn't part of my natural make-up. Instead I changed strategy, deciding a quick dunking would soon smarten it up a bit, and have it scurrying off and leave me alone, which was my objective in the first instance. Of course there was another reason I changed my mind mid-dunk: a rather vivid image of The Bollock-Muncher biting my hand off. So sod that! The thing is, one should learn to do things the easy way, not least when on the Congo. The little shit scurried off alright, only to go fetch its crony and come back for another bare back banquet.

Groan.

Later, as the two horseflies returned again and again (and again and again I tried, and failed, to swat them), my line of vision caught the small fly I had let live earlier, still perched in the same position two feet away.

"Hey, Shaggy."

"What?"

"You know that little fly you said I should kill but I let it off."

"Yes."

"It's still here."

"So?"

"I reckon," I said, looking for some kind of retribution, "the little swine is the radio man for the two horseflies, and every time I try to corner one of the shits, it signals to them."

"Could be."

"Hmm."

Moments later...

'Splat!'

Funnily enough, once the little fly had been disposed of, I had few problems eradicating the two horseflies.

Contrary to the evidence presented I wasn't a completely heartless fly executioner, and even saved a few which had landed on the water. At a glance you would be forgiven for assuming these little creatures were dead, with their wings stretched out flat. But this day my curiosity got the better of me and I fished out an attractively marked butterfly. To my great surprise it wasn't dead at all. So, as it was still too damp to fly off, I decided to place it in the pirogue, giving it the chance to dry and regain its strength.

No doubt these actions will have some people thinking: "Weirdo." However, in this 'other world', far removed from what your average Johnny Foreigner would consider the norm, at the time it just seemed to be the right thing to do, not to mention giving myself something to think about beyond pain of back and dryness of throat, etc. Besides, after reading innumerable superhero comics as a child, I had and still have a compulsion to be heroic, even towards creepy-crawlies. Soon I had repeated this procedure enough times to start my very own insect football team, and although it wasn't often, whenever we moored to the bank I would replace them back on land.

Weirdo indeed.

After another few hours' paddling, twilight was practically upon us and we were happy to take a short break for the one part of the day that subsequently became a daily fix of utopia. The reason for this was simple: the sunsets on the Congo were extraordinarily stunning, and sure enough, at its usual time, the sun began to gradually disappear and for a few glorious minutes cast a sunset as opulent and beautiful as any sight I had ever witnessed – the descending rays of amber light advanced across the treetops in such a speckled fashion that it was impossible to do anything other than fall spellbound. The rainforest's once diversely coloured orchids, brown creepers and mixed greenery eventually faded to grey, while bias heat waves distorted the Congo's glistening wake, adding to its magnificence and entrancing us with its beauty. Unbelievably breathtaking, and with our outlines diminishing against the encroaching night, I quickly snapped out of my trance and reeled off a hatful of photos to ensure our memories of the incredible view would never be forgotten.

What a crying shame, then, that these particular photos went awol.

Having floated successfully right through the preceding night, we had already agreed to continue with this policy, so pushed on until 9:30pm before abandoning our paddles and lying back in the pirogue. Unlike the 'wintry' evening we had spent searching for a village the previous day, during our subsequent nights on the Congo Shaggy and I would always spend a half hour or so just reclining and gazing out across the moonlit rainforest before settling down to sleep. Although this was immeasurably relaxing, we would nonetheless tell jokes, offer opinions, revisit past tales, work out riddles, anything. Anything that might, although surrounded by the ever-enchanting splendour of the jungle, help us to forget that we felt like we were two of the loneliest people on earth.

"This is an easy one," I said. "If at gunpoint you were made to pick between spending twenty-four hours in one of three rooms, which would you go for? One that is full of murderers with knives? One that is full of lions that haven't eaten for two years? Or one that is full of venomous snakes?"

What seemed an age passed by before my cogitating friend replied.

"Can't think. Bet it's one of those bloody obvious ones an' all."

"You want the answer?"

"Hold on, give me a minute."

A minute came and went.

"Well?"

"I'm still thinking."

"Come on, Shaggy, it's easy."

"Hang on, hang on."

Yet another age.

"You give in?"

"No, no, leave it with me."

"Strewth, how long do you need?"

"Tell you what, if I don't get it by the time we get to Bumba, give it me then."

"You mean, The Jewel of the Congo."

"Naturally."

With Shaggy still chewing over the riddle, we continued our chit-chat, this time regurgitating our African experiences to date, although in due course there was a pause in the conversation. Staying with the subject, my mind drifted back to the events we had mulled over. Back to one episode specifically, a time that encompassed a couple of days in Rwanda and a brief but rather innocent addition to the adventures of Sean McCarthy. In fact, the tale began in Nairobi, on the Kigali-bound plane I had just boarded, with the voice of a straggler saying, "Is this the plane to Rwanda?"

The question had been posed by a well-tanned twenty-six year-old whom I shall name Cal, since she was from California. Travelling alone and vacationing for one week only, Cal had spent stopover time in London and Nairobi en route to her eventual destination, Kigali. Here, like most if not all of the holidaymakers we had noted, she had pre-booked a short tour to see the mountain gorillas. With this being a whistle-stop visit, on the plane she had advised me that Thursday sundown and Friday morning would be her only free time. After that she would be flying back to Nairobi. If I wanted to come to her hotel and say hello during this brief time, then fine.

So there I was.

Paradoxically, regardless of what, if I'm candid, was something of a 'Don Juan' reputation when I was in my early twenties, pre-departure I was fully prepared to accept my African escapade as a dating-free expedition. The challenge to this guideline came on the plane from Nairobi, when Ali, noting Cal's solitude, defied me to obtain a date with her. For my part, in agreeing to the dare I figured that I would at least be able to kill time should we be forced to hang around waiting for our visas — which certainly proved to be the case — although her pretty face and slim, but curvy in all the right places, frame helped sway things too!

With a boyfriend back in the States, Cal hadn't come to Africa for romance, so that evening it wasn't I alone who dined with her at the Meridian but also Shaggy. Not until my return the following morning did I get to spend any one-on-one time with her, even if that period remained platonic, in spite of her admitting she found me "dashing" (aw, shucks). Then again I was in a romantic mood, so put it to Cal that she should come with us down the Congo. I did a passable job too, making the "once in a lifetime" trip sound nothing more than a light-hearted but wonderful jaunt. The sun would beat down, and as Shaggy and I joyfully paddled, ardent sunbather Cal could lie in the middle of the delicately swaying pirogue, tanning herself and eating various tropical fruits. Of course, whilst I had never been down the Congo, I might have painted a somewhat more idyllic picture than the probable reality. But it was hard not to be gripped by the blend of Cal's allure and, even more overwhelming, the desire for amour when seduced by the enchantment that was Africa. As such, even with Cal appearing too set in her ways to go for it, I hoped I could induce her otherwise. Hoped that my 'dashingness' would win the day. Hoped that once Cal was involved with the adventure, she would soon come around to it. What I hadn't realised was just how off-the-scale I had been on all counts: that Cal would require a little more than my per-suasions, and that rather than the joyride I had been depicting, our ensuing Congo journey would be filled with all the hardships to date — plus a few as yet to be recounted. Be that as it may, it all sounded terrifically appealing to her. So much so that perhaps Cal might even have gone with us if she hadn't had a conference to return to. What-ever the reason, it just wasn't to be, and come noon she had her guide drop me off at the compound, allowed me to kiss her on the cheek, then left.

Forever.

Although that was the last time I ever saw Cal, after she returned home she sent a letter and photographs to the English address I had given her. In her letter she remarked how she would love to be back in the tropics, amongst the magic and the romance of Africa. She also disclosed something else — she had left her boyfriend.

'I guess he just wasn't dashing enough,' she confessed.

After I had recalled the tale of Cal, I gave a short sigh then looked across the pirogue's walls and listened to the beat of the waves. I was still on the Congo.

"Hey, you awake, Shaggy?"

"Barely."

"What are you thinking about?"

"That bloody riddle!"

"Ha, that figures."

"You?"

"Oh, nothing."

"Anyway, I'm off to sleep now."

"Same here."

"Night."

"Night."

With that I pulled my mum's once-clean towel and my thinner-than-thin sheet and mosquito netting over me, then snuggled back further into the dugout. With the thoughts and dreams of a romance lost, I gradually fell asleep, whilst the pirogue zigzagged its way down the Congo, past the jungles, past the tribes, and past the many other slumbering denizens of the rainforest.

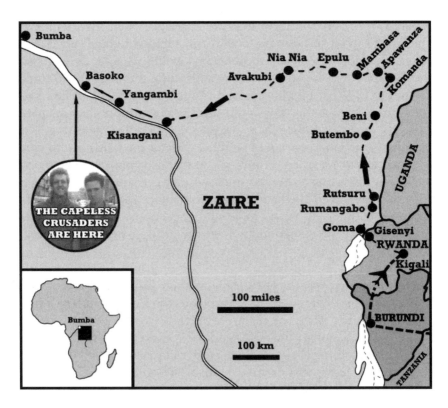

Chapter 13

GODS OF THE RIVER

Friday, 7th July. Day Five in the pirogue was a complete reverse of Day Three. The wet, cold, predominately grey day that had soaked us from top to toe, was replaced by the cloudless, dry, blisteringly sunny day we had been wishing for yesterday. A day late and much too hot. Running out of drinking water the preceding night only exacerbated the situation, particularly when combining the extreme heat and our high calorie-burn. And with the sun dehydrating us as never before, we began to wilt and crack under its escalating glare. So much so that, whilst we had promised ourselves to never again savour the Congo, desperate times called for desperate measures.

"Argh!"

"Ugh!"

That second mouthful each was the last time we sampled the river.

With the necessity of obtaining liquid more pressing than ever, we had hoped to find another riverbank village, but in this remote locale there were none. We did spy a couple of natives among the bush, but our shouts to them were met only by silence. Just as frustrating, the equally scarce sighting of a pirogue would be that of a speck on the other side of the Congo. To address our dilemma we instead focused on spotting a fresh water rivulet, which meant directing our eyes inland and sticking as close to land as physically possible. In itself this wasn't too tricky, as we were travelling down the right-hand side of the river and, as I've said before, the pirogue always strayed towards the right. By now, though, we had become fairly adept at paddling and had little problem maintaining a set distance from the verge — although this policy had its own drawback, for every now and again the adjacent mass of jungle poked out a bit more than our established gap. Ordinarily this wouldn't have posed much of a task, as it wasn't too difficult to alter course and circumnavigate any wayward objects. However, now that our attention had been diverted landward, only too often we would find ourselves suddenly confronted by oncoming branches. Without much time to change direction, this would cause us to paddle like madmen in an effort to avoid the obstacle, a feat made all the more fiddly by the current, which drew us like a magnet whenever the pirogue neared an impediment. The outcome was that every so often we would graze a tree, or catch the edge of overgrown shrubs, but we were never in any real danger, nor were harmed in any way — until this morning. As we approached what back home would be lunchtime, we again found ourselves looking inland for a rivulet, when ...pow! Our senses went to red alert.

That it had gone unnoticed was testament to how anxious we were to find water, and with but seconds in which to adjust, we certainly didn't have time to round the colossal branch now blocking our way, its heavy tangle of leafy stems defended by an assemblage of needle-sharp thorns.

Calculating that we could squeeze under it, Shaggy instinctively lay flat, expecting the pirogue's walls would offer protection against the more concerning offshoots. Normally I would have followed suit, but I'm afraid I had digested too many superhero comics to risk my pal being snared, so continued paddling an extra nanosecond. The theory was that if I pushed Shaggy's end of the pirogue out of harm's way, he would be saved. And guess what? It worked. For although my actions had ensured that I would head straight towards the perilous centre, my partner in crime succeeded in passing safe and sound through the branch's outer edges. To achieve this I was forced to keep paddling right to the wire — but I got my nanosecond wrong. By concentrating on rescuing Shaggy (I know, I know — hero), I hadn't allowed myself enough time to drop below the sides of the pirogue, and as I hastily lay down I left my hands too high and my paddle somehow got trapped in the stems. 'No chance,' I told myself, 'we're not losing another paddle,' and, in spite of the might of the current and the weight of the pirogue acting against me, I clung on, leaving my hands and arms exposed.

Bad move.

The thorns were merciless. I writhed in agony as they ripped easily into my flesh, my do-or-die effort seemingly for nought as the paddle was dragged from my fading grip. To add to my woes, my hands were now hooked by the barbs, and the pirogue slowed to a standstill. But the Congo's power was not to be denied, and there was an almighty jerk, which wrenched me free and spewed the pirogue out the other side.

Instantly in even more pain, I hoisted myself into a sitting position and glimpsed at my now swollen and bloody palms — my blisters had been joined by deeply embedded thorns. So I used the back of my hands to feel for the enormous scratch marks etched in my forehead, unaware until this moment of the army of angry ants that had spilled on to me from the branches above. But all I could think about was getting back the errant paddle and, having seized the table-tennis bat, as the ants crawled over my body and the thorns speared further into my hands, I brushed aside all and sundry, and together with Shaggy frantically struck out back towards the half-decent paddle, now hanging in the bush.

For what seemed a generation we wrestled against the unrelenting current, the pirogue neither travelling forwards nor backwards, as muscle-memory kicked in, our bodies and minds taking us back to the storm. Back to metronoming. Back to single-minded focus. Back to being athletes. Back to the training sessions. Back to those reps, those sand-hills, those damned sand-hills. Only this time the prize was neither life nor Olympic dream – this time the winner's medal was that solitary paddle. A piece of wood that at once became chalice both golden and poisoned, as desire met need met frustration met fatigue, met the one thing we didn't want – failure. But through it all we realised that we just did not have the tools, nor the strength, and moments later we gave in. The Congo's current may have been slow, but it was frighteningly powerful. Moreover, I had still to rid myself of the many ants now swarming over my body, and while I dunked my arms and legs into the water, Shaggy rushed over to help swat at my intruders – although his suggestion that I should leap headfirst into the Congo didn't seem the least bit tempting. Not with The Bollock-Muncher lurking beneath the waves! With that thought now in mind, I believe I set a speed record when retracting my limbs from the river. I then tweaked the majority of the thorns painfully from my hands, bandaged the lacerations, and shrugged at the deeper ones that would remain embedded for some time yet. I had so many pains by now that they melded into one dull ache anyway.

The half-decent paddle now lost and no kindly ladies or on-hand villages to provide another, I decided to have a go at repairing the damaged one, which we had frugally kept hold of. Quite surprisingly I managed to accomplish this, with the aid of a vine, a lot of patience, a bit of hidden strength, and Shaggy's green sticky-tape, which, to stop it from becoming overly sunburnt, I also stuck on my nose.

Everything now seemed to be on the road to recovery, although the usual suspects still plagued us: the heat, the slow pace, the lack of food, our physical pains, and recently a fear not only of things such as storms and predators, but also of something else that can kill most effectively – complacency. Above all of them came a need for liquid that outstripped even that of our first day's hitchhiking, when we had scavenged from a murky puddle. Back then, the dehydration was as much due to our not yet being used to expending energy in such ruthless conditions. Today, our dryness was due more to the sun's fierce intensity, by far the severest we had encountered.

Unable to find water but refusing to waste more time by sheltering under the trees, as we had done now and again on this exasperatingly hot day, we continued frying under the cruel rays of the African sun. Soon we had very little energy, but even the decision to down paddles and drift provided no real respite, as various cooling methods, such as dunking our towels into the Congo then draping them about ourselves, brought only temporary relief in a world far removed from the English climate we knew.

Mid-afternoon, and we had been under the sun's glare for some eight hours. Still no sign of a cloud. No village. No food. No water. Any of these would have done, but it has to be said that as much as we had been craving the lot, the detection of fresh running water was undeniably paramount — yet there was nothing. Horribly dehydrated, it almost reached the stage where I might have contemplated not only imbibing the Congo again, but also praying to God, the lost Ark, the burning bush, the sun, the moon, even Elvis, when luck finally caught up with us.

Water.

Having secured the pirogue, we jubilantly made a beeline for the rivulet we had uncovered — a sliver of a stream that emerged from the rainforest's apron and cut a small groove across five yards of muddy banking — and eagerly filled our bottles. As a rule, after we'd strained water and added our anti-bacterial tablets, we followed a 'just in case' policy of waiting a minute longer than necessary before drinking, but we were so keen to replenish ourselves that we thought 'sod it', and gulped the lot down. Whatever the rights and wrongs, it didn't make a jot of difference, as we had both caught dysentery anyway.

My encyclopaedia tells me that dysentery is an 'infectious disease caused by a bacterium, often found in contaminated water'. Also, that the symptoms are 'profuse watery bowel motions that may contain blood and mucus, accompanied by fever and sickness'. What it does not say is that, despite my preferring to make merriment of our own profuse watery bowel motions, the truth of the matter was that having dysentery meant that we were also consumed with episodes of acute pain. In my case, the most dreadful gut cramps you could conceivably imagine were compounded by what felt like a cannon-ball lodged up my arse.

The water was good. Very good. In fact, it was too good, for so engrossed were we with drinking that we didn't pay enough heed to the sinking-sand-type mud that had started to envelope us. Naturally we tested it, seeing how far down each foot would go before placing all of our weight forward. Yet those precious seconds we had spent drinking without thinking, those extra inches that Shaggy had taken, now caused him to submerge past his knees, and suddenly our priorities changed.

Humorous to him at first, Shaggy realised he wasn't just stuck, he was still heading south. Luckily — with my vastly superior, Samson-like strength — I managed to break free and jumped into the trees to look for a broken branch, which fortunately the ground was littered with.

"Grab this," I said, thrusting one end of a dead bough at Shaggy, whilst making sure I didn't get too close to him — no sense in us both perishing.

Shaggy caught hold of the branch, which disintegrated before we'd even had time to pull on it.

"Sorry about that, I'll get a better one."

"Take your time," joshed Shaggy.

I snatched up another dead branch and tried it against my knee.

Snap.

Then another.

Crackle.

And another.

Pop.

"Any chance of you lending me a hand?"

"Don't you worry, one of these branches has to be okay."

"Speaking from an entirely selfish point of view, I'd like to think so."

Shaggy's witticism was cool, yet a hint of vocal restraint told me he was becoming more concerned.

"You just hang on, mate."

"Well, I had planned to nip to the shops, but okay."

I tried more branches.

Rip.

Break.

"You found anything yet?"

Crunch.

Split.

"Not yet."

Shatter.

Tear.

"Bet if I owed you money, I'd be out by now."

Bust.

Sever.

"Too bloody right."

Erupt.

Fracture.

Splinter.

Crumble.

EXPLODE!

Eventually I picked out a workable branch, and with the aid of our returning strength Shaggy managed to make good his escape and we survived one more day.

Three lives left.

While rehydrating had given our ever-waning vigour a much needed lift — and the ability to speak more coherently, now that our mouths and throats weren't frazzled to a cinder — as soon as that problem was out of the way (for now), our myriad other troubles came hurtling to the fore. And so back to square one with the mind games, especially now, on this most vicious of days.

To alleviate things, I followed the same procedure that had helped assuage our Congo problems on prior occasions — I burst into song, trilling out a few favourites, such as the ever-inspiring 'Jerusalem'. To compensate for my tone deafness, Shaggy chipped in with his own brand of strangled vocal, which might have been good for the soul, but not for anything with ears.

In time we retired from our warbling, and with it so returned our sombre mood. At first we talked of how we had been so sure that we would discover at least one village, or one fruit-bearing tree, or one clear stream, each day. When that tête-à-tête dried up we got round to another favourite tear-jerker — reflecting on the things we had been missing from back home. Trust me when I say there's nothing like a bit of suffering to help you value the things you take for granted and now miss — family, friends, pets, sports, books, music; in fact, virtually everything. And definitely, without question, food. By this I mean: good food, bad food, nutritious food, shite food; any kind of food, just as long as it was emphatically and unequivocally FOOD.

"Hey, Sean, what about this then — mashed potatoes, carrots, peas, a nice steak, lashings of gravy, and perhaps a few Yorkshire puddings thrown in on top?"

"Oh yes. And what about a big pizza?"

"I'd settle for a small one."

"Aye. Then there's a plate of chips, a few sausages, mushrooms, a couple of fried eggs..."

"With toast?"

"Sure. Anything like that."

We both sucked in some air. Food, lovely, lovely food.

Interestingly, the foodstuff I hankered after the most (alongside ice cream) was something I hadn't eaten since being a teen, which was a certain pie my mother used to bake. I was unsure of the exact recipe, but nevertheless tried explaining it to my fellow paddler.

"My mum used to make this walloping meat and potato pie every teatime. Okay, it probably wasn't *every* teatime, but it seemed that way. Anyway, she'd bung the lot into a big Pyrex glass bowl — stewing beef, potatoes, gravy — and then she'd do the pastry. Obviously I'd pester her to let me knead the dough, that way you could nick a bit and eat it. We would roll it really thick, then place it on top of the stew and fire everything into the oven. When it came out, the pastry would be all crispy and dead chunky, and you could mix it with the gravy to moisten it. Believe me, that was good stuff." I didn't have to sense him doing it, I knew Shaggy would be picturing it, scenting it, tasting it. I certainly was. "I've not had that for years, but when I get back the first thing I'll do is ask my mum to run the recipe by me. I'm definitely making that when I get home."

"Yeah, me too," said Shaggy, tittering.

There followed a few seconds of silence, then...

"We sometimes had sponge pudding for afters."

"Oh stop it, Sean. I can't take it anymore."

More chuckling preceded another spell of silence.

Shaggy was the first to break.

"We used to have sponge pudding an' all."

"I'd love one now."

"That's two of us. I'm not bothered what flavour. Syrup, raspberry, lemon, anything."

"What about Spotted Dick?"

"Now there's a blast from the past."

"Or treacle."

"Toffees."

"Chocolate."

"I could murder a Curlywurly."

"I could murder a Curlywurly — and a Twix, Picnic, Flake, Topic."

"Dairy Milk, Wispa, Toffo, Yorkie, Marathon, Dairy Milk."

"You said Dairy Milk twice."

"I like Dairy Milk."

"What about Mars? If I buy a Mars I put it in the freezer, and then slice bits off it."

"Freezer? Fridge for me."

"Bloody hell, Shaggy, that takes way too long. Ten minutes in the freezer is like an hour in the fridge. Why wait longer?"

"Suppose so."

"Then again, sometimes I bite the chocolate off the sides and then split half of it into the Milky Way bit and the toffee bit."

"Biting the chocolate off the sides wouldn't make a difference."

"You're joking! Course it does. Just try it."

"Oh sure, here's one now. Two secs whilst I just get it out of the fridge. Sorry, freezer."

More sniggering.

Another lengthy pause.

Shaggy broke again.

"I could murder some cereal an' all."

"Weetabix is my favourite."

"Yeah, mine too."

"Alpen and Ready Brek are good."

"Alpen, Ready Brek, Cornflakes, Rice Crispies."

"Porridge."

"Frosties."

"And wash everything down with a freezing cold drink."

"Oh no, why did you mention that! Tell you what, Sean, I'd give anything for some pop right now."

"Remember all those refrigerated Pepsis we had in Epulu?"

"Oh, don't."

"Imagine one of them trickling down your throat right now."

"Noooo."

"Just imagine the icy coldness of that Pepsi as it comes out of the fridge."

"Stop it."

"Or lemonade, orangeade, cream soda, Dandylion and Burdock."

"Stop!"

"Irn Bru."

"Made in Scotland."

"From girders."

We sucked in more air, and then both retired to our own private thoughts, each of us fantasizing about what we would devour once we returned to a more populated setting.

Even though we hadn't eaten for twenty-four hours, the lack of food was far from our only concern, what with the sun still blazing down and our water supply dwindling again. The reality, however, was that our problems would dissolve — if we could just get to Bumba. But with the heat foiling any kind of decent paddle projection, and the complete absence of wind marring any speed that might be mustered by the current, the actual distance we were covering was laughable. So, from here on in, it would be some form of momentum I'd be praying for.

Another hour passed. Travelling by the north-bank again, it was late in the afternoon and nearly time for tea: a swig of water. The heat was still electrifying and there were more tired strokes. Then, feeling something alien on my back — a faint breeze — I turned to look over my shoulder.

"Look at that, Shaggy!"

A mile back upriver and heading straight at us was an inky set of clouds. We knew they were coming our way, as we could feel the gust picking up directly behind. Then the winds blew heavier and heavier and our speed radically increased. It was at that point that we realised this wasn't merely a breeze homing in on us but, more worryingly, a battalion of storm clouds, not entirely unlike to those that had almost upended us two days earlier — we could gauge how far away they were because the once-calm 'flat' river had now kicked up into a crushing mob of waves. Waves that with every second bore down on us.

In view of the circumstances, we momentarily ceased paddling and watched in awe, as the formidable tempest drew closer and closer. Regardless of the imminent jeopardy, I have to say that a huge block of rollers tumbling towards you is quite a marvellous sight, although any shocked silence was soon pierced by Shaggy's, "We're going to get pissed wet through again!" He'd had to shout because the winds had picked up so much that it was getting difficult to be heard. Yet he was wrong, for, as the rising waves drew nearer still, it dawned on me that there was no rain at all — just a force-nine gale.

"I don't think so!" I hollered back, the waves looming ridiculously close. "It's only a wind storm!"

"Oh well, thank the heavens for that, were not going to get rained on at all ...just drowned! Shouldn't we moor the pirogue to the bank?! Fast!"

The waves were as good as on us now and Shaggy had to shout at the top of his voice to be heard above the gusting wind and crashing breakers. And yet, perhaps a little too full of myself after our great victory in the last 'island-swallowing' battle with the elements, all at once I was a swashbuckling captain onboard an Elizabethan galleon, and I promptly denounced my colleague's defeatist suggestion. After all, the lengthy island running parallel about 150 yards to our left had produced a long channel, which funnelled everything forward. This meant that, unlike on the preceding day, these waves were heading in the direction we wished to travel, and at speed, so why not make use of them?

"Let's ride with it!" I bellowed.

"Are you off your rocker?!"

"Maybe, but I came here for a spot of excitement and by gad I'll have it! Are you with me?!"

I'd definitely watched too many pirate films.

Despite his having little choice in the matter, the waves now upon us, Shaggy sensed not only a thrill in my madness but also a belief that we could truly ride these whitecaps without capsizing.

"Alright then, you mad bastard! But I do hope you've insured this thing!"

Now travelling at a pace we could only have dreamed of before, Long John Shaggy and Blackbeard Sean enthusiastically thrashed at each wave, as the once-cumbersome pirogue fairly zoomed past the veiled denizens, jockeying on powerful swells that, despite there being no rain, not only had us drenched to the bone, but also made sure we found it hard to keep the pirogue from smashing into the bank. So Shaggy decided to rectify the problem ...Congo-style.

"Let's go out to the middle!" he roared.

Evidently I wasn't the only one off his rocker.

On any other day we might not have risked such a crazy stunt — although sure, I would do it again — as nutcases both, we discarded the safer route and headed out towards the ominous core, each gripped by both 'the moment' and a deep-seated instinct to step outside our comfort zone.

By the gods of the river it was the right option. Once at the centre, the dugout moved with such dolphin-like finesse that Shaggy and I practically danced on the Congo like surfers. Into the bargain, now driven by a force of nature, the pirogue became a veritable missile. As though launched from a slingshot we rocketed forward, speeding as never before, riding the waves onwards and onwards, as five, ten, fifteen minutes elapsed and still we whizzed past the spooling forest, its previously sedate greenery at once a backdrop blur of whirling pastels — shades and shadows that morphed into a living symphony of wild 'Faster! Faster!' encouragement. And with its hypnotic 'chant' inducing us to embrace an ever-increasing tempo, we hammered incessantly at the waters, metronoming our arms and forgetting not only how shattered we were but also the magnitude of the waves. Yet whenever the pirogue threatened to go under, up we bobbed, giggling and grinning and barking orders at each other, as though we really were the crew of an Elizabethan galleon. White water rafting, eat your heart out! We continued to 'live the dream', as we surfed, smiled, jockeyed and laughed, near enough flying down the Congo for a good twenty minutes. Twenty minutes of fun. Twenty minutes of madness. Twenty minutes of defiance. Twenty minutes of all-out, coming-of-age, action-packed, no-stopping-us-now, death-defying ecstasy. Oh yes, THIS was the Indiana Jones stuff!

Eventually the storm outran us and headed off further downriver, leaving us once again in tranquil waters. This time, however, we had joyous smiles on our faces, as we knew we had just enriched our quest by having as much of an exhilarating ride and as much enjoyment as we could ever have imagined.

Then we were back in the slow current, paddling tediously, without any more clouds, under the hot, blazing sun.

As if the cruel heat, lack of food, dreary pace, bodily pain, and fear of any number of things, weren't bad enough, it wasn't long before we had again finished our water. But all was not lost, because once more Lady Luck was just around the corner — this time, literally. After twenty-four hours of nothingness, we at long last came across a small village. Here, we were able to purchase sustenance in the shape of a bunch of tiny bananas and some water, albeit only enough to last the night. Still, it gave our verve another shot in the arm, and with it the ability to ride out the rest of the day — by far the most remorseless to date — without any additional distress.

Although our earlier surfing escapade had left us soaked to the skin, while the sun's rays had proved to be an absolute nightmare all day, they at least did a tremendous job of drying us completely before nightfall. Happy in the knowledge that we would be warm, once again we hoped to make up for any lost time by opting to float the night.

Oddly, while I had an inherent fear of things that go bump during the hours of darkness (in this case, our overturning in a flash storm, or plunging into a bank crammed with awaiting predators), there was a flipside. Remaining in the pirogue at night while still afloat was not only a quicker way of reaching Bumba, but as it turned out was also a very relaxing way of sleeping, maybe as relaxing as I had ever known. And not just because, after a typical dawn-til-dusk, and beyond, paddling stint, we could rest our aching backs and drained limbs. There were two other factors. The first was the amount of warmth the river managed to retain after enduring a full day's sunshine. This would then heat up the underside of the pirogue, which, providing it didn't rain, helped to keep things nice and snug. The second reason was one that did away with the machismo and took you back to childhood — the peaceful way in which the current gently rocked the pirogue, like a cradle.

Posing for the camera gave Shaggy's back a well-earned rest.

Despite the snugness and cradle-like rocking, it was never possible to get a full night's sleep on the Congo, each evening holding some kind of alarm once we had downed paddles, such as when a chugging noise and bright lights woke us at approximately two o'clock the previous night. Rousing ourselves, an immediate panic set in, as all indications confirmed that the riverboat was about to come crashing down on us, even though the channel we had floated down seemed far too small for what we understood to be a gigantic craft. Once focused, however, our qualms were soon dispelled, for attached to the impending bend was a wooden jetty, on the other side of which lay a clearing that, judging from the several piles of stacked logs, appeared to be some form of wood yard – its functioning generator unveiling the source of the chugging. At first glance the place seemed deserted, and whereas my race-mode mindset told me to keep going and pass by, curiosity had got the better of me, so I endorsed Shaggy's proposition that we should moor and investigate. Besides, given that there was a generator and lighting, we had assumed that there would be at least one guard on hand, and therefore a likelihood of obtaining, if not food, certainly water. When it came to it, though, irrespective of combing the entire hockey-pitch-sized clearing, we found nothing beyond the generator, not even a pathway out – and definitely no people, water, or food, nor anything else of any use or significance – so headed back to our pirogue and Congo snooze.

While being woken by things such as the wood yard was acceptable (its exploration may not have concluded with something noteworthy, or particularly adventurous, but it was still a change from the norm, still interesting, still a positive), being woken or kept awake by more problematic, negative stuff did bother us. For a start, purely getting to sleep was always a struggle for me, care of the unceasing presence of the ever-spiteful African flies.

For some reason, whenever I nuzzled under my mum's once-clean towel and my thinner-than-thin sheet and mosquito netting, I always seemed to take a fly with me, unknowingly perched in my ear (not a horsefly, or I would have had no ear left). Only having bedded down would I hear a predictable "buzz, buzz", right smack in my lughole — whereupon I would attempt to rid myself of it by poking and then punching ten bells out of my ear. Then, once the buzzing had gone, I'd resettle myself, and yet as soon as I was nigh-on asleep the blasted thing would start up again. Eventually, after much readjusting and umpteen more pokes and punches, I would yell in frustration, throw the netting off, shake it vigorously, and then quickly re-cover myself before the fly had time to return. Peace at last. Or so I had presumed, for as with all unhappy endings, no sooner would I get back to my almost-asleep mode than I'd hear that seemingly obligatory "buzz, buzz" noise again, right bang in my ear.

Having weighed up whether or not these phantom flies were all in my mind, and not finding a solution, in due course I bedded down knowing the buzzing would soon begin and trained myself to deal it regardless. Mind you, if you think about what flies usually squat on, and imagine how 'clean' I was considering I hadn't adequately washed for days, using wet-wipes only, it's hardly surprising.

The other wake-inducing things were a little more troublesome, like the occasions when we would be stirred by the sensation and sound of rushing water, as the pirogue was forced through a small gap between two islands. Upon realising this, we would immediately come round, sit straight up, paddle for a bit, then, once all felt calm, lie back down and drift off to sleep. Then there were the moments when one of us would feel the pirogue thump into something and wake to find ourselves caught against the bank, again enmeshed in a shrouded mass of overhanging black forest. As usual, this caused more panic than the rushing water, and whichever unfortunate one of us had become jungle fodder would shout for his ally to rouse and get him the hell out of there. Worse even than this were the times we would wake to find the sky so dark that we couldn't even see each other, let alone land. A somewhat terrifying predicament when you're encircled by God knows what, in the middle of an immense forest and, more daunting, a river so titanic we might have been at sea. Amplifying my trepidation was the memory of the storms. Who's to say they wouldn't strike again? And if they did and we were caught out at the centre of the Congo, at night, in the dark?

Gulp.

The possibility of flies, rushing water, dense jungle, darkness, and storms notwithstanding — not to mention the ever-present Bollock-Muncher — we downed paddles as usual. It was time to sleep.

Normally the more laidback, Shaggy slept soundly that night, but not I. Just before the point of shutting my eyes, I had become fascinated by a multi-coloured flashing arc of light that I had noticed in the distance downriver. Fascinated and apprehensive, that is, for like any animal I am always hesitant about something I don't understand, and for the life of me I couldn't work out what on earth I was looking at.

At this juncture the Congo was punctuated by a host of lengthy islands, some miles in length, and we had floated down a slender channel between two of these, the banks of which were so laden with tall 'barnyard' grasses that in places it left only thirty yards of breadth. Quite whether it was this that had caused our already listless speed to decrease, who knows, but I couldn't help wondering if we had coasted into an eventual dead-end tributary (which subsequently, and luckily, we hadn't). Even so, the curious glow I'd spied up ahead had become far too engaging to fret about anything else. Utterly mystified, I even woke Shaggy, who muttered something about the Northern Lights and went back to sleep.

I couldn't tell precisely where the strange light was coming from, as the channel in which we were floating meandered so much I could never see further than a hundred yards in front — and that was rare, since it was typically less than half that distance — but when the arc did flash, about every two minutes, I could make out, above the tree-tops, that we were heading in its direction.

The closer the object of my curiosity got, the more it struck me as being a huge lightning bolt (and I had seen one of those up close, when it tragically killed a pupil at my school nine years earlier), which appeared to stem from one side of the channel and blaze across to the other. Whatever it was, the only explanation I could think of was that someone had built a large power station on each bank, and they were erratically transferring a giant electrical charge from one to the other. At least that's what it looked like, but whatever the facts were, I had no answer, and repeatedly my psyche warned "turn back, turn back". But I simply lay there, glued to the sight of this omnipotent lightning flash criss-crossing our path ...and coming nearer and nearer.

* * *

Closer drew the vast bolt. A mishmash of creams, yellows and pinks, a dominant hue wasn't easy to decipher, despite being pitched against the backdrop of the rainforest, itself a web of dark and smouldering evergreens, with splashes of brown bark jutting out from behind moss-covered trunks, branches and vines. Colours and shapes that would otherwise melt into shadows were now lit by rays of moonlight that punctured the canopy and shimmered on the Congo, reflecting shafts of light back into the woods and enabling me to see all before me without too much nocturnal hindrance.

Nearer still came the charge, as the pirogue snaked its way through the reed-filled waterway and past the sleepy jungle, and whilst my unease should have made me halt our progress, I was too awestruck and befuddled by the exceptionally picturesque, mesmerising show of energized brightness. So on we carried, the bolt so heart-stoppingly close that around one of the next few corners I knew it would be over us.

The first corner came and went. Then the second ...the third ...the fourth. At the fifth I braced myself, but instead of stark apprehension I felt an unusual sensation, my fear entwined with a fusion of both discovery and beauty, which only increased as the fifth bend turned into the sixth, and then the seventh, the eighth. And yet, because of the nature of the islands, the narrowing river zigzagged so much and the corners now followed so frequently together that not only did it become wholly impossible to calculate where the arc was (which made it even more of a thrill, never knowing when it would out of the blue materialise), but at any given point the pirogue almost seemed like it was heading back on itself.

Wait! I briefly held my breath. 'This is it. It's here. It's around this next bend,' I told myself, the suspense intensified by the lethargy of the pirogue, which crept around the turn so slowly that I had time to steal glimpses of a jungle so beguiling it was a shame that my attention was otherwise preoccupied, its entombing foliage creating such alluring imagery, I might well have been in a fairytale. Yet what I had assumed to be the last turn came — and then went, as the closer we drew to where I supposed the spectacle would be, the more I realised we would be bypassing the strange flash, as at last I caught sight of it, now appearing further away to my right, back down the Congo. And with it the hope of unearthing the source of my intrigue.

Although the bizarre light continued to glow periodically, and even though it would eventually vanish into the night, right up until that last sighting its flashes were still beautiful, still enchanting, still perplexing, and still a phenomenon whose origin, even to this day, I wish I knew.

Day Six on the river. Again we were up and ready to go before 6am, the thought of yesterday's thorns encounter surfacing momentarily, as my improved but still throbbing hands took their first painful heave on the paddle. But it wasn't to last. With the ache in my back every bit as prevalent — as were the other pangs and twinges that went along with what had been, in this most pitiless of arenas, five days of blood, sweat and fears — everything again fused into one. Besides, another recollection prevented me from succumbing to any physical discomfort — the memory of something that had happened to us only four hours earlier. It was a stern reminder that, although floating during the hours of darkness helped us gain ground, the latent dangers were indubitably far greater. For when one's main sensory defence — vision — has been severely hampered, then the prospect of being injured, or worse, when faced with such things as storms or wild animal attacks increases accordingly. Particularly if one becomes too complacent and familiar with one's surroundings — or too busy being fast asleep. And so to the panic-inducing incident in question. For the second night in a row, we had been awoken by what sounded like the chugging of the riverboat, though on inspection was fortunately just a tug. So why was this dangerous? While our riverboat assumptions had brought an inevitable welter of despair — under no circumstances did we want to miss that boat — the more worrisome aspect of the tug's presence was that the wretched thing nearly smashed into us! And because having one's head caved in wasn't going to be the best way to beat the boat to Bumba, I just thanked my lucky stars we had woken in time.

Two lives left.

Now that we were back paddling we had something else to cheer about. Unlike the last couple of days, there were one or two more pirogues about — although mostly, and typically, on the other side of the Congo — and these and the tug combined to give us much heart from the belief that we must be nearing a large settlement, hopefully The Jewel. If all went to plan we would be there ahead of midnight. Arriving any later would doubtless equate to floating straight past while asleep (hello, Ngombe). In an attempt to discover how close we were, on the occasions that we were in vocal range of any fishermen, we asked them the correct distance to our finish line. Normally we would be greeted by a nonplussed look, while the few who did offer a reply proffered nothing logical. Answers of 800km, 500km, 250km, and 2,000km, in that order, were clearly way off the mark, although I did have a theory.

"In all fairness, these people probably don't understand our dodgy French."

"How else do you say Buum-baa?"

"Maybe we should ask for The Jewel of the Congo."

"Or, Le Jewel du Congo," said Shaggy (in his dodgy French).

"Ha, good one. Anyway, forget kilometres. I just wanted someone to say 'It's around the next two bends' or 'It's half a day's pirouging', or something."

"I just want to hear 'My place is around the next corner, come and have a break and some coffee'."

"And ice cream."

"Chocolate."

"Cream cakes."

"Your mum's meat and potato pie."

More giggling was followed by a lengthy pause, then...

"Say, did you ever work out the answer to that riddle?"

"Might have."

"That means you didn't! Sheesh. Come on, Shaggy, it so simple a kid would get it."

"I'm sure they would, but I'm afraid I'm going to have to pass."

"You want the answer?"

"Yeah, go on."

"You really want to know?"

"I do."

"Thought you wanted to wait until Bumba."

"Bugger Bumba, what's the answer?"

"You really, really want to know?"

"Get on with it!"

"Oh no, I can't remember. Damn."

"Very funny."

"Okay — it's the lions."

"The lions...? Go on."

"Because if they haven't eaten for that they'll all be dead. Duh."

"Eh? I think I'm missing something here."

"It's called a brain."

"Yeah, yeah. Anyhow, let me get this right. I have to pick between three rooms to spend twenty-four hours in. One has some psychos in it..."

"Murderers."

"Murderers, psychos. So the *murderers* have all got knives, yeah?"

"Yep."

"And one of the other rooms has venomous snakes in, and I'm assuming you meant snakes like black mambas and king cobras, that kind of thing?"

"Yep."

"And the last room has some lions that haven't eaten for two days. So where's the dead bit come from? If we can do two days without any food, I'm sure some lions could hack it an' all."

"What are you on about, two *days*? It's two *years*."

"Years? You said two days."

"No, I said years."

"You definitely said days."

"I did not."

"You did."

"No, I didn't."

"I'm telling you, you did."

"Why would I say days?"

"I give in, why did you say days?"

"I didn't. You just misheard me."

"Well take that paddle out of your gob. Bloody hell, all this time, racking my brains."

"Ha, you dipstick."

While we still oblivious as to how far away Bumba was, we were as hapless when trying to find food and water – to a degree because the fishermen who'd given us the unlikely distances were as ineffectual when it came to revealing the whereabouts of their villages. And when we did eventually pinpoint what totalled three hamlets, any attempt to converse with the occupants brought only the wrong conclusions. At the first village we received bewildered expressions. At the second, a plethora of "Give me"s. At the third, its gathering of ladies actually seized their children and with a petrified look sprinted off into the bush!

"What have I told you about wearing that aftershave?" I quipped.

"What have I told you about letting them see your face?" Shaggy retorted.

As much as our jests helped make light of the terribly frustrating situation, they were nonetheless exchanged in the midst of paddling away rapidly – for all we knew, the retreaters had rushed off to get reinforcements with an accompanying, "Quick, bring some weapons and save us from these two ghastly creatures!" – although with our luck it was probably more like, "Quick, these gentleman are in need of provisions. Bring the cakes and lemonade, and ...oh, where have they gone?"

Success came in the afternoon, when we located another rivulet, and fortunately no sinking sand. Recognising that this might be the only water we would come across all day, which turned out to be the case, we again drank until our bellies ached, before refilling our water-bottles and striving on, in search of The Jewel.

The rest of the day proved to be much the same as the previous one – our personal gripes, the fierce heat, the pursuit of sustenance, the tired eyes and arms, little sleep, our multitude of fears. It was at times tediously monotonous, but we still felt as though we were achieving something. Even if circumstances had prevented us from paddling to Kinshasa, 230 miles of piroguing down the mythologised Congo was certainly a story worth telling – for two lowly no-marks, anyway. Plus we had the cosy riverboat to wind down on. If only we could make it to Bumba on time, that is.

If only.

It's peculiar how, although you are so very close to something you have yearned for that you can almost taste it, you can still back off, you don't try as hard, you think you've made it. Well, this happened to us. Like a fatigued athlete way ahead of the field and closing in on the finishing line, we found ourselves beginning to slow, as though we knew we were home and dry, even though we had absolutely no idea whether we were. Of course the brutal heat didn't help our dilemma, but the biggest stumbling block, as ever, lay within ourselves. Yet no matter how much we told ourselves to paddle harder – on the off chance that the riverboat might pass us down a different channel – we didn't seem to have the willpower, or the energy, and our strokes became markedly slower. Half the time we quit paddling altogether and let the current, though still very slow, do all the work, while we basked in the greater glory of the magnificent scenery.

As evening arrived and began to settle in, again the sunset was too exquisite to ever imagine, and yet there we were, floating in what had in earlier years been but a dream.

Because of our many rests, now that the night was upon us, we decided to press on for as long as humanly possible, but there was still no sign of The Jewel. Torch in one hand and map in the other, I tried figuring out where we were, ultimately deciding we should be joined before long by another river, to our right. This would indicate the last few kilometres to our cherished end goal, which with any luck would instil some faith, since ours appeared to sag with every stroke. Then ...bam!

Out of nowhere something frighteningly powerful grasped us.

It was a fast-flowing current, one that kept us towards the right-hand bank of a Y-shaped junction, but led us in a direction away from the course we had been taking. We decided this must have been the other river, but to us it looked as if we were heading *up* it, as the fork we had been pulled on to seemed to be angled back the way we had come. In a state of panic, we desperately tried to paddle against the current. Yet it was just too strong for us. We were trapped.

Although it looked as if we were travelling the wrong way, at some point my rationality resumed and I assured a less convinced Shaggy that it was impossible to float upriver. But he refused to consider basic logic, and cited the small "disguised mini-submarine" island that we had spotted heading the other way on Day One of our voyage. An argument broke out, as neither of us was sure of either notion, which inevitably ended in furious exchanges of no-holds-barred language.

"If you would care to remember, Sean, you fucking dickhead, you yourself said anything was possible in Africa!"

"Not floating upriver, *you* fucking dickhead. I suppose Lord fucking Lucan is going to come riding past on fucking Shergar!"

The slanging match continued until we both decided that in all likelihood we were simply going around a large island (meaning, I was right – ha), but that whatever direction we might be heading in, it didn't matter. With our lack of vigour and the too-powerful current, we couldn't do a thing about it anyway, and if by some freak chance we were heading the wrong way, then, like the possibility of floating past Bumba whilst asleep, it was merely our destiny. So we dropped both the squabble and paddles, stretched our backs, and took in the moonlit view, as the pirogue drifted past the enchanting jungle and veiled wildlife on its way to wherever it may roam.

Soon we fell asleep, each of us dreaming about waking up to what would be a wondrous sight – that of Bumba, Le Joyau du Congo.

The following morning we were woken abruptly by a group of fishermen. Deciding to take a closer look, they had paddled out to where our pirogue was now floating, and were in the process of peering over the top of me when I opened my eyes, at which they shot off. It was a good job they had woken us because moments later I asked other passing fishermen the location of Bumba and was courteously informed it was only minutes away, along the right-hand bank.

Damnation, for the speedy current we had unsuspectingly become caught in was now dragging us to the left-hand side of an extremely long island. According to the fishermen, if we remained in this wrong channel we would finish up going straight *past* Bumba ...and towards the Ngombe's waters.

FUCK THAT.

Determined to avoid a long haul back upriver, we again feverishly paddled against the direction of the flow, our last ounce of energy being squeezed into those exhausted strokes. But even if we had been at our healthiest we could not have altered course, and we ended up, albeit in calm waters, precisely where we hadn't wanted to be, on the left-hand side of the island.

Dejected but committed to try again, we decided that this time we would stick as close to the bank as humanly possible and, if need be, tow ourselves around using the reeds.

Though energy-sapped we truly did give it all we had. However, as with any other time we had ventured to wrestle the too-hefty pirogue against the Congo's elemental movement, we only manged to get so far before the flow overwhelmed us, and after spending what seemed an age in the exact same place, we were forced to yield. Dispirited but not yet out of it, we were on the verge of taking the reed-clutching option when a couple of watching fishermen decided to lend a hand. Given the all-clear, the man with a withered leg — the other a mass of knotted Ulysses-like muscles — moved into the centre of our pirogue and, between the three of us and his expertise, we at last managed to get out of the left-hand current and rounded the island, ending up what transpired to be less than a kilometre away from one of the most welcome sights we had ever seen...

The Jewel of the Congo.

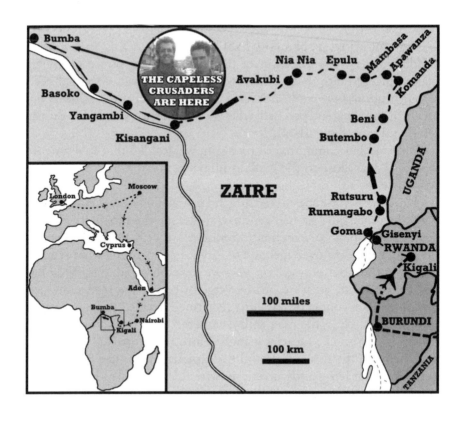

Chapter 14

THE JEWEL OF THE CONGO

My first impression of The Jewel was that it was, yet wasn't, like Goma. While similar dusty roads reminded me that a Spaghetti Western set designer had at one point come calling, luckily Bumba didn't exude any bad vibes. More notably, though, like Goma it also had electricity. Creature comforts, however limited, appealed greatly after our taxing journey.

Having thanked the fisherman who had aided us – another shining example of the contrast between the river's generous people and its Give-Me folks – we landed the pirogue upriver of the centre, where-upon we were soon reminded of our true location. Instead of Clint Eastwood and Lee Van Cleef, we were confronted by a sea of locals, who instantly began bartering with us over anything they or we had. We waved the all-pervasive Give-Mes away.

Still unsure whether we had missed the boat, before any haggling was allowed we first asked the essential, "Le grand bateau – arrivé?"

But the citizens insisted that no large craft had yet appeared. It would be here later today, maybe tomorrow.

We were over the moon.

"We've done it," said Shaggy, shaking my offered hand in triumph – mercifully not too hard, since some of the thorns hadn't yet worked their way out.

"Yeah. Well done, mate."

Given our long slog and tenacious effort, one might be forgiven for wondering why we hadn't danced around and bellowed "We've done it!" and "Yeah!", but the truth of the matter was that we were too tired and weather-beaten to muster energetic celebration, despite having only recently awoken from a full night's sleep, which was never especially deep, given our subconscious awareness of the possibility of careering into the jungle – or upending, only to be faced with The Muncher. Besides, we had been given erroneous information many times over the past few weeks, so who was to say whether the handful of non-English speakers with whom we were now communicating had got their facts right, or had fully understood our request? Until we were on that boat, this adventure was still ongoing.

Understandably sceptical, I continued my enquiries. We needed riverboat details and tickets, so where was the office? We also wanted to know where we might obtain water, since we had again run out of it the previous night. The answers came thick and fast. The office was in town, a half-mile walk. The water we could no doubt get from a house now being pointed at, a prefab-like cottage set in its own small complex, which the villagers said belonged to an ecclesiastical mission -ary. The place under discussion may not have been far off but it was up a steep incline, so it was with an inward groan that I left Shaggy in his element, bartering, and made my way to the front door.

No missionary.

Apparently he was still in transit, returning from a vacation in his homeland of America. Fortunately for me, his caretaker was on hand and following a touch of good old-fashioned grovelling I was shortly handed a red plastic mug, which I was then allowed to dip into an outdoor storage bin full of rainwater. The mug wasn't big, and I made damned sure I filled it to the very brim before letting the liquid slide down my eager throat. Despite its being warm, when considering my week of severely restricted liquid intake, together with the sun now streaming down even this early, believe me that water was as welcome as a giant-sized Knickerbocker Glory. So cheeky bugger here availed himself of a second helping. A third and fourth would have been much appreciated, but I decided not to push it and asked if my pal could also get a share. Judging by the keeper's expression, this new request created an inner turmoil between doing the right thing and a worry that there was a horde of us, all of whom he was inviting into a place he didn't actually own. Thankfully the debate turned my way, and in no time my compatriot was groaning his own way up the steep incline – which caused him to miss my much-lauded impersonation of a passing bossy-boots old man, but with a thirst to be quenched I guess he wasn't too grief-stricken. Presently we reverted back to our conventional roles. Shaggy delved back into his treasured wrangling, whilst I headed into town. My purpose was clear: acquire sustenance and find that ticket office.

Although my preliminary take on Bumba was that of another Wild West settlement, the more I wandered alongside the powerful spread of the Congo, the more The Jewel lent itself to a somewhat different portrayal. Despite its Belgian history, I couldn't help but picture a colonial town evoked by many a movie exhibiting Britain's imperial past, although as it might appear many years after its resources were too depleted for the khaki-sporting trespassers to hang around any longer. Gabled dwellings that had seen far better days sat opposite weathered concrete landings and brick embankments, while a rickety dockyard with commandingly tall, but idle, loading cranes competed against sporadic greenery and hinted at an active commercial past. In amongst everything came several dilapidated buildings. And whether official-looking blocks with crumbled plaster, or ancient clapboard metal structures, it all added up to a place that looked as though it might have once been a plucky adversary of the illustrious river and put up a brave fight, but unsurprisingly lost.

Sticking to the directions I had been given, I eventually located the ticket office, but couldn't identify the correct entrance by which to make a purchase – not that it mattered, since every door was locked. Concerned that our transport home would arrive at any moment (and with no tickets we would be left standing – if not crying – on the bank, waving as the riverboat disappeared towards Kinshasa) I began asking anyone passing for directions to where it would dock. Maybe I would find some answers there.

Providence dealt me a splendid card. The second person I stopped, apparently a student of English at Kinshasa University, back visiting his family during the holiday season, was also scheduled to take the riverboat. By his estimation, it had been due to land at least two days earlier, but with delays being the norm, he claimed it would now be arriving some time later that evening.

"This is the office," said 'Scholar', pointing to the nearest locked door. "Because it's Sunday they won't be open until tomorrow, but don't worry if the boat comes today. People need to buy tickets and load goods. It will not sail until late tomorrow."

Until now I had not dared to fully accept that the riverboat had yet to land. However, now that I was conversing with someone who not only spoke excellent English but also had a vested interest in its arrival, I finally assented to believe we had truly made it on time, so afforded myself a surreptitious clenched-fist victory gesture. That it was due imminently provided the cherry on the cake. What timing!

Despite my optimism, I reminded myself that the adventure would be over only when I was sat, feet up, on the riverboat (for all I knew the tickets may have sold out), so I politely asked Scholar to escort me to where it would be docking. The student obliged my request, but when I asked the whereabouts of any place that sold food and drink, the only assistance he could offer was, "The shops are also closed."

"Bloody typical!" would have been Shaggy's predestined response, but fortunately Scholar hadn't yet finished.

"But the bars will all be open."

Phew, a reprieve.

Scholar then walked me part-way along one of the manifold tree-lined streets to the centre, but just as we were in the throes of saying goodbye, two smartly dressed locals unexpectedly challenged me.

"We must talk to you. We are from Immigration. You must show us your passport."

I couldn't believe it. One minute I was looking forward to a restful period of being calmly sailed away from my achieved Congo ambition, and the next I'm fronting a pair of jobsworths, no doubt looking to justify their status by finding any possible reason to detain Shaggy and me – and prevent us from getting on that boat. Moreover, whilst their suits and command of English cried out 'bureaucrats', for all I knew they might well have been con artists, hoping to fleece me out of anything they could. Intuitively distrusting of them, warranted or not, my cynicism ran deep. As such, I wasn't keen to show them a single thing, above all my precious passport, regardless of their motives.

"Let me see some identification of yours first!" I demanded.

While I had every right to be dubious, at the same time ticking off African authority figures wasn't remotely wise, so when the image of Cheesy flipping his lid when riled popped into my mind, I inwardly slapped myself for reacting as I had. Especially when my confronters whipped out what could only be described as very authentic-looking official papers.

Whoops.

To augment my clanger, Scholar's goodbye handshake included a verbal reassurance of their legitimacy, so I gingerly handed over my passport, ready to snatch it back should my suspicions be realised and they tried to run with it.

Once again my luck was in. Not only did they turn out to be the real deal, but seeing my visa had another ten days before expiry they also freely returned my ID, and not just with gratitude. Seemingly our meeting had not been by accident. The story of the pirogue journey, they confessed, had spread like wildfire. Everyone had heard of it. We were stars. And there was I thinking they were here to scupper me.

"You are brave to try this," said one of them.

"Yes, we are very impressed," added the other, their niceness flying in the face of my perception of immigration officers.

Though jaded, with all this flattery I was suddenly able to stand a little taller, not that the goodwill was unlimited. Scholar now gone, despite my declaring that Shaggy's visa read exactly the same as mine, they insisted that I take them straight to him, which did grate, bearing in mind I had yet to obtain nourishment.

To make the most of the situation, en route to Shaggy and trusting the officials would be more clued-up than Scholar, I decided to pick their brains about the riverboat. I also asked how we might go about securing visa extensions, if it came to light that more time was needed.

"The boat will not be here tonight. Probably tomorrow, departing Tuesday," I was told, which put a new downer on me, since Scholar's 'Monday' prediction was more compatible with my haste to complete our Congo quest and head off home. Nevertheless, their next piece of information was far more heartening.

"You won't need to add to your permits. It will take only a week to get to Kinshasa. The current is faster from here. Your ten days will be more than enough."

This news was excellent, despite my pessimism about the current (which might well have been quicker but never 'fast'), and meant we'd be able to get to Kinshasa, then out of Zaire, before the existing visas ran out, saving us time, aggravation, and another small fortune. Then again, second-guessing the riverboat's actual arrival was a lottery — apparently a couple of days behind schedule, who was to say that those days might not turn into a week or more, fast current or not? In view of that, I took note of where they said their headquarters were and readied my dwindling cash reserve to take a big hit.

Back at the pirogue, haggling Shaggy had exchanged a sweatshirt for some bread and a cache of various fruits, and as soon as the officials had checked his visa and left, conveying heartfelt goodbyes and good luck as they went, we voraciously wolfed the lot. Telling him the news about saving cash on the visas — his basis for putting in extra legwork — made his feast even sweeter. But there was a bigger fish that had to be fried: the pirogue. Whilst I had become rather attached to it after all we had been through, at the end of the day it was now redundant, and we were surrounded by potential customers. Pre-Bumba we had talked about this moment, and although selling it hadn't been at the top of our agenda, there was no sense in doing without what might prove to be much-needed money. So we started the auction.

The bidding was up to Z 5,000 when I left an absorbed Shaggy wheeling and dealing and headed back in to town. Now that we had eaten, our priorities centred on obtaining more fluids; the taste of the missionary's rainwater and the juices of the fruits served to remind us how dehydrated we were.

While my general intentions were to find any form of drinkable fluid, something else was preying on my mind. Something that now obsessed and drove me the way the idea of reaching The Jewel before the riverboat had done. Something that I hoped I might find in one of Bumba's many bars, and if you want a clue or two: it was cold, wet and bubbly, but it wasn't alcoholic. It was also another reason why I had only part-rehydrated myself with rainwater at the missionary's cottage — a little like being hungry but refusing to snack, if it means spoiling a forthcoming banquet. This may seem a trifle excessive, but when you have a hankering, you have a hankering. And oh boy, did I have a hankering.

Family, friends, pets, your favourite foods — it's understandable to miss anything you are accustomed to once it is no longer there, and especially so when one places oneself in such an unforgiving setting as central Africa. Of the things I pined for, one that was impossible to forget was obviously liquid, and in my case this meant fizzy pop. In particular, and above the many I would have paid a king's ransom for, was my then-favourite, straight from the fridge of course. A few years earlier this would have been cream soda (the green one); a few years later, cherryade, for my favourite occasionally changed in this area. However, like the actor Sir John Mills in the movie *Ice Cold In Alex*, where his character is forced to cross a barren desert with a group of people and ends up in a bar ogling an eponymous ice-cold tumbler of beer, over and over I pictured myself gazing at my then-favourite — a glass of chilled raspberryade.

Minutes later I was in the process of scouring the centre for a bar that was open, when I noticed someone paying me special attention. Naturally on my guard, I returned a once-over and took stock of my findings: local; trim; roughly my age. Hmm? While the smart trousers and shoes indicated that my observer had something about him, I assumed the man too young to warrant being in a position of concern to me, meaning an immigration officer or policeman. Besides, the last two officials had worn formal shirts, not a polo. None the wiser, out of politeness I gave the watcher a nod, upon which he signalled to ask if it was okay to approach. 'Here we go,' I thought, my cynicism kicking in again, 'another Limpet.' But I decided to cut him some slack and beckoned the man over.

Happily all went well. Echoing the immigration officers' "spreading like wildfire" opinion, upon hearing what he described as the "famous pirogue trip of two crazy foreigners" (I loved his "crazy" description), he had decided to track us down in the hope that we would converse with him; he wanted to keep up to the mark with his English. No less obsessed with the thought of ice-cold raspberryade, I agreed to chat to the man, but only on the condition that he direct me to every bar he knew — as much as I doubted I would find my pop Holy Grail in this neck of the woods, let alone in a bar, I was tenacious enough to give it my best shot. If you don't try you don't get, and all that. And anyway, even if none of the bars sold raspberryade, as long as it was freezing, any other drink would suffice, for I also craved *cold*.

"No bars are yet open," I was told.

The look on my face must have given a new meaning to Joseph Conrad's 'The horror, the horror'.

Attempting to compensate, my latest associate proposed to guide me to some nearby cafés, an offer I quickly accepted.

During the walk over, I discovered that the mature twenty-one year-old was another undergraduate of Kinshasa University, this time studying engineering, back home on summer leave. I was to find out far more about Mathew Lisamba-Gioma throughout our brief time together, the most notable detail being that his continent of birth was where any resemblance to Limpet started and thankfully ended. This meant there was no sneaking in bags, no grabbing our food, no hanging around just to see what he could get out of us — and no attempts to hold Shaggy's hand either. Other than that, the things that stuck in my mind about Mathew were threefold. First of all, he liked dancing. Secondly, like many Zairians at the time, a photograph of President Mobutu took pride of place on his bedroom wall (whether this was due to admiration or fear, in Mathew's case it was hard to tell. Whenever questioned he denounced any criticism of Mobutu, although he had blatantly stuck by his Christian first name, despite the president having banned them. Perhaps he believed the rarer spelling with one 't' made it less Western). Thirdly, as often as possible, he liked to use the word 'fuck'.

Unsurprisingly, the first café we arrived at didn't sell raspberryade, although they did have one of the colas, which, without a fridge, they kept on view in the scorching sun, by now at its most searingly hot, so I declined that purchase.

The second café mirrored the first — except this one had a fridge. However, anticlimax of all anticlimaxes, it hadn't worked for yonks.

And so to what appeared to be the final café. Although basic, the third stood out from the others for one awfully good reason. Behind the counter was something that looked especially interesting to me — another refrigerator, but this one actually worked.

Fully aware of my requirements by now, Mathew insisted that he negotiate with the proprietor for me.

"What are you selling from your fucking fridge?"

"Lager."

"Don't you have fucking raspberryade?"

"I've never even heard of it."

"Fuck me. Do you have anything that isn't fucking alcoholic?"

"No, we don't."

"Fucking hell."

Although the conversation had taken place in Lingala, I got the gist of it and certainly understood all the "fucks" Mathew had thrown in for my 'benefit'. On the off chance that the owner had understood also, and taken offence, I piped in and motioned to the man to show me the contents of the fridge. In an effort to salvage a sale, he swiftly granted my request, and sure enough there in front of me stood a nice array of lagers, looking very sumptuous due to their arctic-cold, frosted appearance. Oh my.

What to do? While lager usually left me feeling dehydrated, and that was the last thing I wanted, the self-evident coldness forced me to consider buying one — until I spied something different. Different yet incredibly appealing. Tucked away and half-hidden, I again risked Mathew speaking for me. I wanted to know if the large jug I was now pointing at contained what I suspected.

"Yes, it does," confirmed the proprietor.

"Thank fuck," said Mathew.

"Does your friend want a glassful?"

"Fuck, yes."

Again I jumped in.

"Combien?"

The man gave me his price, which I quickly paid.

Naturally it took the proprietor an age to get his backside in gear, faffing about with nothing important before oh...so...slowly pouring the drink, my mouth endeavouring but failing to salivate at the mere look and sound of the liquid splashing into the tumbler, let alone the idea of how it would feel against my shrivelled tongue. The 'chink' of glass against glass as he eased the jug, even.......more.........slowly, back amongst the fridge's other vessels teased me further, goddammit.

When finally the glass was in my hand, like the renowned titular scene in *Ice cold In Alex* I took a long look at the beverage I'd been handed (okay, it wasn't that long, but the length of time it took the Mr Tease to transport it to my impatient grasp deserves the prose) before allowing my fingers to greedily close around the snowy outer layer. But there was no John Mills pause from me, its prized kernel of nectar lifted instantly to my willing mouth.

At this moment I could have gulped it down, but took my time, savouring every nuance of the liquid's texture — the delicacy of its touch; the wetness; the chill against my throat. However, unlike the murky and warm rainwater I had sampled at the missionary's house, it was the combination of clarity and coldness of this drink that did it for me. Oh yes, despite my desire for raspberryade, or anything fizzy, anything pop, I have to say that of all the drinks I've ever had, it was that lone glass of liquid that stands out as my most memorable.

So hats off to iced water.

After the delights of my finest-ever drink, I decided to introduce Mathew to Shaggy, who had failed to secure an acceptable bid for the pirogue. As you would, I ribbed my pal that when it came to bartering he was clearly not as talented as the great Sean, furthering the banter by explaining (in nauseating detail — twice) the astonishing healing qualities of, "a thirst-quencher that is so gorgeously cold and out of this world that it blows the temptation of Pooh Bear's honey off the planet." Goodness knows why this led the still-dehydrated Shaggy to refer to me as someone with no known father, after which he asked me to stay with the pirogue so that he too could sample the "Wonder Drink". But Mathew had a far better idea. Promising that the chances of the unsold pirogue being stolen were next to nothing, he suggested we would probably be able to leave our belongings "in fucking town" at the Catholic mission — where, apparently, he had learned to speak English! Being tied to neither bags nor pirogue sounded an admirable plan to us, and before long we had reached the place in question. Yes, we could leave our bags.

"That priest was a nice person," I said, as we departed the mission. "Surely he didn't teach you to swear?"

"Fuck, no. I picked that up later."

It felt good not having the weight or worry of our rucksacks as we ambled about The Jewel. A sense of well-being that increased further when Mathew started singing our praises once again, this time telling anyone he knew words to the effect of: "These are the two celebrities currently hitting the fucking headlines." Since both our new friend and the story appeared to be somewhat popular, in next to no time we were receiving a fair amount of back-slapping homage, to the point that we finished up strutting like a couple of prize peacocks. All we needed now was the Bee Gees' 'Stayin' Alive' as a backdrop and we were sorted.

"See those fuckers over there staring at you," continued Mathew, "fuck, man, they know of you. You are fucking famous."

"Yeah," said Shaggy, "bet they're saying — 'That tall blond bloke, wow, that's the real Indiana Jones'."

"Nah," I countered, "they're saying — 'That dark-haired guy, he's the real James Bond. The blond fella is Chewbacca from Star Wars'."

"You mean Han Solo."

"Princess Leia, actually."

"Says Yoda."

After Shaggy's sampling of "Definitely the coldest, most beautiful thirst-quencher", we visited Mathew's family home, which was typical of most of the smaller abodes around Bumba — a single-storey, but roomy, clay shack that stood back from a tree-lined, dusty, potholed and pavementless road.

We stayed only briefly at Mathew's, just long enough to kill time before the bars' opening hour, then headed straight to them.

No raspberryade.

To moderate this earth-shattering catastrophe, we instead stopped off at an allegedly cheap restaurant. Despite receiving our colas right away, as expected we had to wait an age for the meal, and after a full hour's conversation on myriad subjects, Shaggy decided to lighten the discussion.

"Do you know the answer to this, Mathew? If you were forced to choose between spending twenty-four hours in one of three rooms, which would you pick? One that is full of lions that haven't eaten for two years, one that is full of venomous snakes, or one that is full of murderers with knives?"

Mathew hardly blinked: "The fucking lions. If they haven't eaten for two years, they will be fucking dead."

"Bit quicker than you, Shaggy," I joshed.

"You definitely said two *days*."

"Sure, sure."

More joking helped fill the next twenty minutes, but come another twenty — and still no meal — we were all talked out, although I eventually broke the silence.

"Listen to this, I've been doing some maths. We spent a total of six days on the Congo. That's six times twenty-four hours, which is one-hundred-and-forty-four. Now then, we floated each night except for the first two, where we moored for an average of seven hours each, so that's take fourteen. If we also subtract time for stopping — so we've got the storms, buying foodstuff, finding water, getting some shade, and exploring that wood yard, etcetera, I reckon that totals about five hours — so that's minus five and fourteen, so nineteen. Anyway, take that from one-hundred-and-forty-four..."

"Wake me when you've finished," said Shaggy.

"Isn't that what your last girlfriend used to say?"

"No, she used to ask why your nickname is Inchworm."

"I hope you told her that that was the distance from the floor."

"I did, but then she asked if you were a leg amputee from birth."

"I am, but don't these six-feet-long false legs look good."

Mathew's polite chuckle told me that whilst he was enjoying the repartee, our very British humour had undoubtedly become lost on him. Since Shaggy's asphyxiated expression also told me he had been checkmated, I gladly returned to the subject under debate.

"As I was saying, the total hours travelled is one-hundred-and-forty-four take nineteen, that's one-hundred-and-twenty-five. The number of miles is two-hundred-and-thirty. From that we can work out our average speed."

"Which is?" asked Shaggy.

"Work it out."

Shaggy groaned but had a bash anyway. "To get miles per hour it would be two-hundred-and-thirty divided by one-hundred-and-twenty-five, right?"

"Correct."

"Okay, so that's about..."

"One-point-fucking-eight," cut in engineer Mathew.

"Ooh, close enough. One-point-eight-four to be exact."

"Miles per hour?" asked a shocked Shaggy. "Bloody hell, I knew it was slow but I hadn't realised it was that slow."

"*Fuck*," said Mathew.

The pirogue voyage wasn't the only thing lacking progress. Despite the restaurant being quiet, we had to hang around for another twenty minutes before getting our meal. Then we were overcharged, and all three of us indulged in a few harsh words with the manager, Mathew effing for all he was worth.

Believing that the riverboat wouldn't be arriving until tomorrow, our next objective was to book into a doss-house. We subsequently obtained a decrepit 'prison cell' room, situated in a row of five or six, with a battered chair and desk, and a pair of battered beds, with no bathroom or toilet. All the same, it was somewhere to sleep, and for the equivalent of only fifty pence each per night, even Shaggy couldn't protest. We retrieved our paraphernalia from the mission and moved in.

In general, when you retain a room you have to leave by a pre-established time the following morning. This constitutes "one day", irrespective of whether you have checked in the previous afternoon, evening, or even in the early hours of the morning. However, since we were now pretty adept at the African way (haggle over everything), we had managed to talk this owner into letting us pay for one night only, on the proviso that we left no later than twenty-four hours after our teatime arrival. Had we not wangled this, we would have had to move our stuff out before 10am, or pay for two days.

At this juncture I was more than happy. Even if we'd had to pay a pound each for two days, it was still a very reasonable figure, despite the bleakness of the room. So no way was I going to complain at fifty pence. Nor indeed was Shaggy, until he later discovered the locals had to pay only half as much, which induced a predictable, "Is he taking the piss?"

Just as when we had a couple of times been required to pay more for hitches here in Zaire, personally I didn't mind coughing up a little extra. As long as that's all it was, a little bit. Of course, had the surplus fare been expected of me in a wealthier setting I might not have been so lenient, but these people were in comparison with our standard of living very poor. Rather than being an excessive payment for me, the twenty-five pence difference seemed a revenue for them that was hard to begrudge. But Shaggy wasn't so understanding.

"It's not the money, it's the principle," he contended. "What does it matter where you come from, everyone should pay the same." But in time he relented. "Alright, let's just leave it. Tell you what, though, I'll bet that toe-rag tries to renege on our deal."

That evening Mathew led us back to Bumba's centre, passing a scattering of little stalls that sold various edibles — we plumped for goat meat, sweets and gum — on the way to the most significant event of the evening: The Jewel's very own open-air disco. This consisted of a wooden dance-floor and bar, surrounded by lots of benches. What we understood to be French as well as African music was played via a tape-recorder and loudspeaker, and the people of Bumba, Mathew in particular, danced with much style, while anyone not boogieing drank copious amounts of booze. Not us two Brits, mind you. Even though we were each handed a lager by a reverential contact of Mathew, to be blunt we only accepted them out of courtesy and, try as we might, neither of us could finish them — the memories of Primus and waking in the morning with dehydration had completely put us off alcohol.

Lager aside, the night looked like it was going to be a pleasant one when Mathew started bringing over more acquaintances to meet the piroguing celebrities, who again paid us much reverence, patting our backs and toadying around us. If only they had played 'Stayin' Alive'! Apparently, nobody had ever before paddled a pirogue from Kisangani, foreigner or local. While I greatly doubted the latter, our being the first *muzungus* was a belief I'd always held, though couldn't verify or refute. The articles I knew of involved only Western crafts, not native dugouts, but being no expert on the subject I kept my views to myself. Why put a dampener on our bout of stardom? Besides, who's to say we weren't the first? When researching Congo pirogue descents in the 1990s, journalist Jeffrey Tayler found nothing that didn't sound like ours. And to date, I have never come across an earlier report either. I certainly wouldn't wager against our being the only blockheads in the history of the Congo, indigenous or not, who ever chose to float in a pirogue night after night whilst its entire crew slept. So that's not bad, is it?

In later years the tale of two foreign canoeists eaten by cannibals became something of a Congolese legend. "This story is now repeated to any Westerner who shows up in that part of the world," *Outside* magazine's executive editor Grayson Schaffer told me in 2013. Of the versions I've read, most describe the duo as being Belgian (renowned white water rafter Hendrik Coetzee cited this account as his motive for avoiding the Ngombe waters prior to his untimely death by Congo crocodile in 2010), although one narrative tells of two Englishmen who capsized after being struck by a barge. Another has the ill-fated twosome being devoured by cannibals but without any mention of a pirogue. All known chronicles cite 1989 or the late 1980s, and also the Ngombe area beyond Bumba. Piecing these facts together, I firmly believe the story is ours. For a start, two sets of two Europeans in the same period is surely too much of a coincidence. Secondly, it would make sense that any locals who saw a pair of *muzungus* paddling past might presume them to be Belgians, considering that Zaire had been colonised by Belgium. Thirdly, before Eugene's intervention, we had told many people that we were intending to paddle from Kisangani all the way to Kinshasa. The fact that we were spotted here, there and everywhere en route to, but never after, Bumba would doubtless lead some to think that we had therefore come a cropper. Fourthly, I later learned that the Ngombe weren't 'just' alleged thieves and murderers, but also cannibals, hence the belief that we had been consumed. Fifthly, I contacted the Belgian authorities to ask if any such deaths had been documented. Whilst they admitted to knowing very well the misfortune dugout tale, they insisted that no fatalities of any kind had ever been reported.

Whatever the truth concerning our journey's status, the whole day seemed to be rounding off nicely — with the exception of one thing. The illustrious piroguers were just too dog-tired to participate in anything remotely energetic, which was something of a shame. Not only did we want to continue soaking up the adulation, but since this was in effect the last night of our pioneering dugout adventure, naturally we also wanted to enjoy it, be with the people, paint the town red. Yet despite its being relatively early, with much regret we were forced to bid both Mathew and our 'fans' goodnight, and we withdrew to the confines of our doss-house jail.

Above: *Mathew, with accompanying picture of President Mobutu.*
Below: *Shaggy in the doss–house 'prison cell'.*

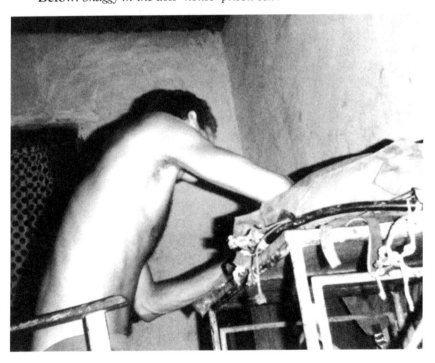

The lighting in our cell was connected in series to the lights in the others and, whether you wanted them to or not, at 10:30pm they all went out simultaneously, prison-style. Fortunately, come this hour we had long since arrived back and completed all relevant activities — primarily, filling in our diaries and 'washing' (the scent of those *Wet Ones* wet-wipes still takes me back to Africa). Now we were ready to sleep the entire night, if at all possible. Needless to say, in the event it wasn't. Not when you have profuse watery bowel movements.

I was about three hours into a half-decent sleep when I awakened, again feeling those now familiar strains pulling and pushing on my worn-out guts. Fully conscious of all encroaching dangers, I urgently leapt to my feet and hurriedly made for the awaiting lavatory roll, strategically placed at the very top of my rucksack. Smart move, yes? In general it would be, but there was a teeny weeny glitch. You see, when organising my 'escape plan' I hadn't thought of something rather important — there wasn't a light switch. And it was pitch-black. The upshot being that I couldn't see where on earth my sodding rucksack was, or Shaggy's torch. So by the time I had groped around the floor, finally recovering my bag, felt for the toilet roll, then spent I don't know how long feeling the walls of the room in an effort to find, as Mathew would put it, the fucking door, I had shit myself good and proper. That said, having become used to such unpleasant incidents I automatically shifted into the now customary 'Operation Clean Up'... Locate a big bush. Remove your one remaining pair of grits and sling the shit behind said bush. Give one's backside and grits a rinsing in a convenient puddle. Shower both with talc. Put grits back on. Go back to bed.

Repeat tomorrow.

The following day Mathew arrived mid-morning and straightaway informed us that the riverboat would land "at fucking seven" tonight. At least that was the general consensus on the street. In truth nobody actually knew, which was seemingly the case throughout our travels; timing didn't appear to matter to most folk. Then again, we believed they would doubtless have a better idea at the booking office, which we were told would now be open — again, general consensus. So off we trundled to buy two tickets, my fingers firmly crossed, since I still had a suspicion something would go awry. Above all that the office would this day be shut, even though it was now Monday — just my luck it would turn out to be a bank holiday.

Thankfully my anxiety was unwarranted. The office was open, and five minutes later confirmation that the riverboat would indeed be here around 7pm was coupled with the clerk's offering of the usual ticket choices — first; second; economy. Deciding to discard the 'no cabin' economy option (for security reasons), we ended up paying £26 each for second-class tickets, which entitled us to a shared four-berth compartment. We could have paid double and luxuriated in our own room but, as you know, we were always looking to conserve money and figured that whichever two people we got lumped with, we would just make sure one of us was always there to protect our gear. That shouldn't be too hard to tolerate, we thought, not for what everybody was portraying as a fantastic journey. Particularly since the ticket clerk claimed that it would take even less than the "one week" quoted by the immigration officers — namely four days. What pleasure that news brought, and happy in the knowledge that our visas definitely didn't need to be extended, we headed back to the pirogue.

The curtain was coming down on our adventure.

A day earlier Shaggy had been presented with a range of amounts for the pirogue but had declined all, as the highest bid of Z 5,000 hadn't approached our pre-determined 'half its original price' minimum. However, now that reality had kicked in we were happy to take any-thing (even the second-best offer: Z 3,000 plus *their* dugout), and yet the prospective buyers who had swarmed around us yesterday had all disappeared. So we decided to paddle the pirogue upriver to a small fishing village Mathew had suggested to us, but even this stratagem brought little hope, for time after time we were refused by anyone we pitched to. Apparently the wood used to make our pirogue was 'old hat' and far too heavy for the purposes of these people. Whether they were saying that purely to barter us down to nothing, or whether our supplier Woody had indeed sold us a behind-the-times pirogue, the little tinker, who knows? The bottom line was that we were no closer to a sale, so we put our pitch on hold and sauntered over to a nearby market, where Shaggy and I each purchased a fork and a large cup. I also bought a T-shirt, imported from, of all places, England.

It was here that Mathew introduced us to his best friend, a gangly amateur boxer who looked far older than his nineteen years.

"John, these are the two men everyone is fucking talking about."

"Hello, John. I'm Sean."

"I'm Shaggy. Pleased to meet you."

"Hello, Mister Sean. Hello, Mister Shaggy. Pleased to fucking meet you too."

Evidently they were best friends.

For the rest of our time together, John — who always prefixed our names with 'Mister' — and Mathew meted out "fucks" as though their life depended upon it. As to the origin of this practice, seemingly an over-eager Johnny Foreigner had at some time instilled it in them as the in-phrase, by design or otherwise — although, for my sins, I must plead guilty to egging them on a little here and there. Whatever their motive, 'troopers' Shaggy and I were like saints in comparison.

By the afternoon we found ourselves on a sabbatical from Mathew and John and were back at our initial place of mooring, in the neighbourhood of the mission from where I had obtained my first taste of Bumba water. Albeit some distance from where the riverboat would be docking, we were needy enough to go back for another (free) sip — the seventeen-hour paddling shifts may have gone, but the sun still beat down with demonic intensity. Here, Shaggy chose to do the first stint of our hanging by the pirogue in case of any passing trade, whilst I groaned my way back up the 'vertical' incline. Once at the cottage I discovered that there had been a new development, for the missionary had returned. And what a congenial man he turned out to be. After accepting his request to enter, we briefly chatted and philosophised whilst I swigged his water, now sourced from a tap. His geniality was further endorsed when he told me of his wife's intention of making her own ice cream, which certainly made this Englishman's ears prick up, especially when he added, "It will be ready by five o'clock. Would you like to come back with your friends and try it?"

WOULD I?! Who do I fight? What a result! Moreover, although I would of course have preferred my indulgence-fix sooner rather than later — my tongue already waxing the floor at the mere thought of the ice cream — the timing was fine, as this would give us a full two hours to polish off the treat before the riverboat's consensual seven o'clock arrival.

At long last everything was going swimmingly, and with Lady Luck finally on my side I allowed myself another clenched-fist victory salute. Hallelujah! Halle—fucking—lujah!

Hold on. What was this? Noooooo! My euphoria had surfaced too soon. The words "ice cream" hadn't been in the air one minute when four hours ahead of its supposed appearance the riverboat came into sight — and my sweet-toothed dream met an instant demise.

"Bloody typical," moaned Shaggy, once I had told him about the misfortune as we exchanged duties. For my part, I was occupied by contrasting emotions. Absolute devastation, obviously, because I was going to miss out on ice cream (a big downfall for me — imagine how much I must have yearned for it after my Congo experience). On the other hand, there was the utter elation of genuine physical evidence that we had beaten the boat, not to mention the relief that our task was all but over. After everything we had been through, as much as we liked the people of Bumba we didn't want to stay put longer than necessary, especially since we had used up seven of our nine cat lives. Had our adventure lingered on, I doubted whether the remaining two would be enough to see us through. Besides, the sight of the riverboat signified not only the conclusion of our quest, but also the beginning of our journey home. Other things awaited, not least my next goal — if you're going to have ambitions, one should attempt to realise them. And didn't the Congo now know it.

With no takers, we decided to abandon any hope of flogging the pirogue, and to appease Shaggy (who resolved to "burn it rather than leave it to a sponger"), I later talked an unenthusiastic Mathew into selling it for his own gain. We then headed back to the prison cell to get our belongings. Whether we had sold the pirogue or not, the last thing we wanted to do was miss the boat.

There was an air of poignancy as I walked away from the pirogue for the last time. Despite its being the third member of our team for one week only, that dugout had unquestionably been our greatest ally. Storms, heat, jungle thicket: it had weathered all, and time and again had brought Shaggy and me back to shore safe and sound. Whilst our saviour was nothing more than a whittled log, being a sentimentalist I have to say I wish I could have kept it. Wish I could have transported it to England. Wish I could turn to gaze at it now as I compose these words. If you think of the wooden puppet Pinocchio, then you have that pirogue. It was more than just a piece of wood. So much more. No wonder I dissuaded Shaggy from inscribing 'The African Queen' on its side when we procured it. I wrote 'Mum' instead. It had surely looked after us like one.

Interestingly, with there being no logic in chopping up a perfectly floatable dugout, who's to say it doesn't still exist? Even more intriguing, with its distinctive welded metal circle, if it has survived these years it would certainly be identifiable. How fabulous it would be to find and reacquire it. How marvellous it would be, even just the one time, to lie in it at night again, under the stars, and simply float one's cares away.

Twenty-three hours after booking into the prison cell, we were checking out. Shaggy and Mathew took our bags outside, while John stayed on with me as I went to pay for the room. To be truthful, our splitting up hadn't come by chance, rather yours truly had engineered it in case the owner tried to break his promise and charge double – at this vital stage, Shaggy getting nicked for assault didn't best suit my plans for going home imminently.

Talk about prophetic. Having already lost out on the pirogue, the last thing we needed was Shaggy's "I'll bet that toe-rag tries to renege on our deal" premonition coming true, but when I tried to hand over the one-day fare, sure enough, the owner wanted paying for two. It was a good job I had left my pal outside! In quick retort, I reminded 'Toe-rag' of yesterday's "one day" arrangement. I also reasoned that, since we were leaving in less than twenty-four hours, if anything he owed us a rebate. This new philosophy caused him to suddenly come down with a bad case of 'I-don't-understand-you-itis', claiming that he couldn't debate the subject on the grounds that he comprehended neither my English nor my French. Do keep in mind he managed to tell me this in perfect English, the novelty of which continued as he pressed for double the cash: "Listen old bean, I'm afraid my English is a smidgen shy of the rudimentary, but how's about dispensing capital enough for two days, what?" Admittedly, in the scheme of things an additional pound was neither here nor there, but Shaggy wasn't the only person with principles. Toe-rag had made a deal, and once you have done that with me don't even think of changing it (unless, that is, you resemble The Hulk). Be that as it may, the owner stuck to his "Je ne comprend pas" crap, so I asked John to intervene and speak to him for me in Lingala. Seconds later Toe-rag had amazingly changed his mind, and I paid only the pre-agreed price.

The curtain was definitely coming down.

John and I exited the office and wandered over to where Mathew and Shaggy were waiting.

"Check this out, Shaggy. That doss-house owner had the gall to ask for two days after all."

"The slimy toe-rag! He can bugger off. No way I'm paying extra for that manky room."

"Yeah, fuck that," said Mathew.

"Please tell me you didn't give it to him, Sean?"

"Damned right I didn't. He kept pretending he couldn't under-stand me, so I had John talk to him and he caved in. Out of interest, what was it that you said to him, John?"

"I told him one fucking day only, Mister Sean, or else I would beat the *fuck* out him."

By the time we arrived at the harbour, the riverboat (the *Colonel Ebeya*, a colossal four-tier 'pusher' with six enormous barges attached) wasn't due to leave for another couple of hours, but as much as it was excruciatingly tempting to go back for the ice cream, we decided it would be wiser to get onboard as early as feasible in order to sort out a cabin. The thing was, the masses of people who had chosen the exact same approach, as well as those loading and unloading cargo, meant that we had a rather difficult job managing this without being pushed into the Congo. Indeed, once we had fully boarded, the tally for saving someone from slipping off the heavily populated deck stood at... Me: an old lady. Shaggy: two children. Mathew: two men. John: me! Still, at least we were onboard, which also meant that it was time to shake hands with and bid a fond farewell to our latest acquaintances.

"Thanks for rescuing me, John."

"No fucking problem, Mister Sean."

"Mathew, goodbye."

"Goodbye, Sean. Goodbye, Shaggy. Have a fucking safe trip."

Quite fittingly, that was the last we heard from Mathew and his friend John. We couldn't even make out their faces among the throng of friends and family waving the boat off, which was a pity. They were good people.

Although we had lost sight of our Bumban friends, it wasn't long before Shaggy espied some other familiar faces, on the next deck up, and called to them. It was the Kiwis, apparently making their way to the bar, so no surprises there.

"You're alive then, you mad bastards," said Goods.

"Is this a social visit or are you joining us?" asked Pricey.

"Definitely joining," Shaggy responded.

"Aye, sod hitchhiking to Kinshasa," I added, "thought we'd do the rest of the journey the easy way."

Monday, 10th July. Effectively the end of an adventure that started out over 4,000 miles, one continent and two seas from Africa's core, with a platform guard telling me to catch the wrong train, and taxi driver with only one testicle. Since then there had been many more characters who helped form this story, all of whom played a part in an escapade that in truth began far earlier than 1989, with an ambitious little boy who flicked through an atlas and found Africa, a place that seemed so far away and mysterious. One day he would go there. One day he would lead a life away from everyday drudgery and implement a childhood fantasy. One day he would visit that rich green area, that vivid blue line, that bastion that held both enchantment and menace. One day he would go to that ominous core they called Congo. One day he would also write of his adventure.

And here it is.

As I look back today on our exploits, I see not only how daring, carefree and at times completely raving bonkers Shaggy and I were, but also how rash, ignorant, dogmatic, and arrogant. But hey, full of beans, we were resilient young men trying to realise an audacious rite of passage. In paddling part of the Congo, I like to think we may have achieved it. Beyond that, it's almost impossible to make evaluations of our quest on any great scale. From Shaggy's viewpoint, he just wanted to spend time away from the cycle of normality. For me, the intention wasn't to discover another way of life or to 'find' or improve myself, although I like to think I accomplished the latter. I just wanted to be able to say... "I did it."

As we sailed away from Bumba, the fact that it had been precisely one month earlier that we had touched down in Nairobi was a little karmic. What better way to end my Congo chapter than that? Now to enjoy a peaceful trip home and tell tales of bravery and derring-do, of how we had sat on a 'live bomb' in England, of how we had 'nose-dived' on the way to Moscow, of residing with villagers, encountering motorbike bandits, drifting under the stars, escaping sinking sand and weathering storms. And to fulfil a book-writing ambition, of course. Well, that was the plan, only there was a slight snag. You see, when I told Pricey that we had jumped onboard the riverboat because Shaggy and I wanted to continue the rest of the journey "the easy way", his response was not what either of us expected.

"Easy way? I think you'd better have a rethink."

And do you know what? He was right. Although Shaggy and I were happy to step out of one adventure, we landed quite unwittingly into the lap of another. But that, of course, is a different story.

Sean and Shaggy return in *Escape from Congo*

POSTSCRIPT

For those whose appetite might have been whetted by my description of it, here's what my mum has to say about her meat and potato pie!

"A pie usually takes about two hours to make because the meat used isn't expensive frying steak but a cheaper cut of meat, which is first browned in a frying pan (to seal in the juices/flavour) and then covered in water and simmered for an hour or so. Add a stock cube twenty minutes before the meat is fully cooked, and put the vegetables in a pan and boil (vegetables being spuds, though I used to hide carrots in there). Preheat the oven to a medium heat, drain the vegetables and put them in a pie dish together with the cooked meat and some of the gravy. I use Atora Suet in place of lard — you don't find suet crust pastry on shop-bought pies. Make the pie crust pastry as directed on the suet packet, roll out to size and then cover the pie. Brush the top of the pastry with either milk or egg and then put in the oven for about half an hour until the crust is brown. I brown the meat in my pressure cooker, take it off the heat and then add a quarter pint of water. Cut the vegetables up small and place them into the metal pressure cooker baskets. Put these into the pressure cooker on top of the meat and steam under pressure for five minutes. Whilst it's steaming make the pastry crust and preheat the oven. Take the cooker off the heat, run under the cold water tap, take out the meat and vegetables, and put into a pie dish. Pour a small amount of the gravy over the contents. Cover the top of the pie dish with suet pastry and put into the oven for twenty minutes until the pie crust is golden. Put the rest of the gravy into the gravy boat and carry the pie and gravy on to the dining table."

www.seanofthecongo.co.uk